SWAN SONG

BY

JOHN GALSWORTHY

"We are such stuff
As dreams are made on; and our little life
Is rounded with a sleep."
—*The Tempest.*

NEW YORK
CHARLES SCRIBNER'S SONS
1928

TO

F. N. DOUBLEDAY

CONTENTS

PART I

CHAPTER   PAGE

   I. INITIATION OF THE CANTEEN . . . 3

  II. ON THE 'PHONE 12

 III. HOME-COMING 20

 IV. SOAMES GOES UP TO TOWN . . . 26

  V. JEOPARDY 36

 VI. SNUFFBOX 43

 VII. MICHAEL HAS QUALMS 54

VIII. SECRET 61

 IX. RENCOUNTER 69

  X. AFTER LUNCH 75

 XI. PERAMBULATION 81

 XII. PRIVATE FEELINGS 89

XIII. SOAMES IN WAITING 98

PART II

   I. SON OF SLEEPING DOVE 109

  II. SOAMES GOES RACING 117

 III. THE TWO-YEAR-OLDS 126

 IV. IN THE MEADS 136

  V. MEASLES 148

 VI. FORMING A COMMITTEE 155

 VII. TWO VISITS 170

Contents

PART II—*continued*

CHAPTER   PAGE

VIII.	THE JOLLY ACCIDENT	179
IX.	BUT—JON	187
X.	THAT THING AND THIS THING	193
XI.	CONVERTING THE SLUMS	201
XII.	DELICIOUS NIGHT	211
XIII.	"ALWAYS"	221

PART III

I.	SOAMES GIVES ADVICE	231
II.	OCCUPYING THE MIND	238
III.	POSSESSING THE SOUL	245
IV.	TALK IN A CAR	252
V.	MORE TALK IN A CAR	258
VI.	SOAMES HAS BRAIN WAVES	265
VII.	TO-MORROW	277
VIII.	FORBIDDEN FRUIT	285
IX.	AFTERMATH	289
X.	BITTER APPLE	296
XI.	"GREAT FORSYTE"	302
XII.	DRIVING ON	314
XIII.	FIRES	325
XIV.	HUSH	338
XV.	SOAMES TAKES THE FERRY	348
XVI.	FULL CLOSE	354

PART I

CHAPTER I

INITIATION OF THE CANTEEN

IN modern Society, one thing after another, this spice on that, ensures a kind of memoristic vacuum, and Fleur Mont's passage of arms with Marjorie Ferrar was, by the spring of 1926, well-nigh forgotten. Moreover, she gave Society's memory no encouragement, for, after her tour round the world, she was interested in the Empire—a bent so out of fashion as to have all the flavour and excitement of novelty with a sort of impersonality guaranteed.

Colonials, Americans, and Indian students, people whom nobody could suspect of being lions, now encountered each other in the ' bimetallic parlour,' and were found by Fleur 'very interesting,' especially the Indian students, so supple and enigmatic, that she could never tell whether she were 'using' them or they were 'using' her.

Perceiving the extraordinarily uphill nature of Foggartism, she had been looking for a second string to Michael's Parliamentary bow, and, with her knowledge of India, where she had spent six weeks of her tour, she believed that she had found it in the idea of free entrance for the Indians into Kenya. In her talks with these Indian students, she learned that it was impossible to walk in a direction unless you knew what it was. These young men might be complicated and unpractical, meditative and secret, but at least they appeared to be convinced that the molecules in an organism mattered less than the organism itself— that they, in fact, mattered less than India. Fleur, it seemed, had encountered faith—a new and " intriguing " experience. She mentioned the fact to Michael.

" It's all very well," he answered, " but our Indian

friends didn't live for four years in the trenches, or the fear thereof, for the sake of their faith. If they had, they couldn't possibly have the feeling that it matters as much as they think it does. They might want to, but their feelers would be blunted. That's what the war really did to all of us in Europe who were in the war."

"That doesn't make ' faith ' any less interesting," said Fleur, drily.

"Well, my dear, the prophets abuse us for being at loose ends, but can you have faith in a life force so darned extravagant that it makes mincemeat of you by the million? Take it from me, Victorian times fostered a lot of very cheap and easy faith, and our Indian friends are in the same case—their India has lain doggo since the Mutiny, and that was only a surface upheaval. So you needn't take 'em too seriously."

"I don't; but I like the way they believe they're serving India."

And at his smile she frowned, seeing that he thought she was only increasing her collection.

Her father-in-law, who had really made some study of orientalism, lifted his eyebrow over these new acquaintances.

"My oldest friend," he said, on the first of May, "is a judge in India. He's been there forty years. When he'd been there two, he wrote to me that he was beginning to know something about the Indians. When he'd been there ten, he wrote that he knew all about them. I had a letter from him yesterday, and he says that after forty years he knows nothing about them. And they know as little about us. East and West—the circulation of the blood is different."

"Hasn't forty years altered the circulation of your friend's blood ? "

"Not a jot," replied Sir Lawrence. "It takes forty

generations. Give me another cup of your nice Turkish coffee, my dear. What does Michael say about the general strike ? "

" That the Government won't budge unless the T.U.C. withdraw the notice unreservedly."

" Exactly ! And but for the circulation of English blood there'd be ' a pretty mess,' as old Forsyte would say."

" Michael's sympathies are with the miners."

" So are mine, young lady. Excellent fellow, the miner —but unfortunately cursed with leaders. The mine-owners are in the same case. Those precious leaders are going to grind the country's nose before they've done. Inconvenient product—coal ; it's blackened our faces, and now it's going to black our eyes. Not a merry old soul ! Well, good-bye ! My love to Kit, and tell Michael to keep his head."

This was precisely what Michael was trying to do. When ' the Great War ' broke out, though just old enough to fight, he had been too young to appreciate the fatalism which creeps over human nature with the approach of crisis. He was appreciating it now before ' the Great Strike,' together with the peculiar value which the human being attaches to saving face. He noticed that both sides had expressed the intention of meeting the other side in every way, without, of course, making any concessions whatever ; that the slogans, ' Longer hours, less wages,' ' Not a minute more, not a bob off,' curtsied, and got more and more distant as they neared each other. And now, with the ill-disguised impatience of his somewhat mercurial nature, Michael was watching the sober and tentative approaches of the typical Britons in whose hands any chance of mediation lay. When, on that memorable Monday, not merely the faces of the gentlemen with slogans, but the very faces of the typical Britons, were suddenly confronted with the need for being saved, he knew that all

was up ; and, returning from the House of Commons at
midnight, he looked at his sleeping wife. Should he wake
Fleur and tell her that the country was ' for it,' or should
he not ? Why spoil her beauty sleep ? She would know
soon enough. Besides, she wouldn't take it seriously. Passing into his dressing-room, he stood looking out of the
window at the dark square below. A general strike at
twelve hours' notice ! ' Some ' test of the British character ! The British character ? Suspicion had been dawn-
ing on Michael for years that its appearances were decep-
tive ; that members of Parliament, theatre-goers, trotty
little ladies with dresses tight blown about trotty little
figures, plethoric generals in armchairs, pettish and petted
poets, parsons in pulpits, posters in the street—above all, the
Press, were not representative of the national disposition.
If the papers were not to come out, one would at least
get a chance of feeling and seeing British character ;
owing to the papers, one never had seen or felt it clearly
during the war, at least not in England. In the trenches,
of course, one had—there, sentiment and hate, advertise-
ment and moonshine, had been ' taboo,' and with a grim
humour the Briton had just ' carried on,' unornamental
and sublime, in the mud and the blood, the stink and the
racket, and the endless nightmare of being pitchforked into
fire without rhyme or reason ! The Briton's defiant humour that grew better as things grew worse, would—he
felt—get its chance again now. And, turning from the
window, he undressed and went back into the bedroom.

Fleur was awake.

" Well, Michael ? "

" The strike's on."

" What a bore ! "

" Yes ; we shall have to exert ourselves."

" What did they appoint that Commission for, and pay
all that subsidy, if not to avoid this?"

" My dear girl, that's mere common-sense—no good at all."

" Why can't they come to an agreement ? "

" Because they've got to save face. Saving face is the strongest motive in the world."

" How do you mean ? "

" Well, it caused the war ; it's causing the strike now ; without ' saving face ' there'd probably be no life on the earth at all by this time."

" Don't be absurd ! "

Michael kissed her.

" I suppose you'll have to do something," she said, sleepily. " There won't be much to talk about in the House while this is on."

" No ; we shall sit and glower at each other, and use the word ' formula ' at stated intervals."

" I wish we had a Mussolini."

" I don't. You pay for him in the long run. Look at Diaz and Mexico ; or Lenin and Russia ; or Napoleon and France ; or Cromwell and England, for the matter of that."

" Charles the Second," murmured Fleur into her pillow, " was rather a dear."

Michael stayed awake a little, disturbed by the kiss, slept a little, woke again. To save face! No one would make a move because of their faces. For nearly an hour he lay trying to think out a way of saving them all, then fell asleep. He woke at seven with the feeling that he had wasted his time. Under the appearance of concern for the country, and professions of anxiety to find a ' formula,' too many personal feelings, motives, and prejudices were at work. As before the war, there was a profound longing for the humiliation and dejection of the adversary ; each wished his face saved at the expense of the other fellow's !

He went out directly after breakfast.

People and cars were streaming in over Westminster Bridge, no 'buses ran, no trams ; but motor lorries, full or empty, rumbled past. Some 'specials' were out already, and emaciated men were selling an emaciated print called 'The British Gazette.' Everybody wore an air of defiant jollity. Michael moved on towards Hyde Park. Over night had sprung up this amazing ordered mish-mash of lorries and cans and tents ! In the midst of all the mental and imaginative lethargy which had produced this national crisis—what a wonderful display of practical and departmental energy ! 'They say we can't organise ! ' thought Michael ; ' can't we just—*after the event* ! '

He went on to a big railway station. It was picketed, but they were running trains already, with volunteer labour. Poking round, he talked here and there among the volunteers. ' By George ! ' he thought, ' these fellows'll want feeding ! What about a canteen ? ' And he returned post haste to South Square.

Fleur was in.

"Will you help me run a railway canteen for volunteers ? " He saw the expression, ' Is that a good stunt ? ' rise on her face, and hurried on :

" It'll mean frightfully hard work ; and getting anybody we can to help. I daresay I could rope in Norah Curfew and her gang from Bethnal Green for a start. But it's your quick head that's wanted, and your way with men."

Fleur smiled. " All right," she said.

They took the car—a present from Soames on their return from round the world—and went about, picking people up and dropping them again. They recruited Norah Curfew and ' her gang ' in Bethnal Green ; and during this first meeting of Fleur with one whom she had been inclined to suspect as something of a rival, Michael noted how, within five minutes, she had accepted Norah Curfew as too 'good' to be dangerous. He left them at South Square in conference over culinary details, and set forth to sap the natural opposition of officialdom. It was like cutting barbed wire on a dark night before an 'operation.' He cut a good deal, and went down to the 'House.' Humming with unformulated 'formulas,' it was, on the whole, the least cheerful place he had been in that day. Everyone was talking of the 'menace to the Constitution.' The Government's long face was longer than ever, and nothing—they said—could be done until it had been saved. The expressions 'Freedom of the Press' and 'At the pistol's mouth,' were being used to the point of tautology! He ran across Mr. Blythe brooding in the Lobby on the temporary decease of his beloved Weekly, and took him over to South Square 'for a bite' at nine o'clock. Fleur had come in for the same purpose. According to Mr. Blythe, the solution was to 'form a group' of right-thinking opinion.

"Exactly, Blythe! But what is right-thinking, at 'the present time of speaking'?"

"It all comes back to Foggartism," said Mr. Blythe.

"Oh!" said Fleur, "I do wish you'd both drop that. Nobody will have anything to say to it. You might as well ask the people of to-day to live like St. Francis d'Assisi."

"My dear young lady, suppose St. Francis d'Assisi had said that, we shouldn't be hearing to-day of St. Francis."

"Well, what real effect has he had? He's just a curiosity. All those great spiritual figures are curiosities. Look at Tolstoi now, or Christ, for that matter!"

"Fleur's rather right, Blythe."

"Blasphemy!" said Mr. Blythe.

"I don't know, Blythe; I've been looking at the gutters lately, and I've come to the conclusion that they put a stopper on Foggartism. Watch the children there, and you'll see how attractive gutters are! So long as a child

can have a gutter, he'll never leave it. And, mind you,
gutters are a great civilising influence. We have more
gutters here than any other country and more children
brought up in them ; and we're the most civilised people
in the world. This strike's going to prove that. There'll
be less bloodshed and more good humour than there could
be anywhere else ; all due to the gutter."

"Renegade ! " said Mr. Blythe.

"Well," said Michael, "Foggartism, like all religions,
is the over-expression of a home truth. We've been too
wholesale, Blythe. What converts have we made ? "

"None," said Mr. Blythe. "But if we can't take children from the gutter, Foggartism is no more."

Michael wriggled ; and Fleur said promptly : "What
never was can't be no more. Are you coming with me
to see the kitchens, Michael—they've been left in a filthy
state. How does one deal with beetles on a large scale ? "

"Get a beetle-man—sort of pied piper, who lures them
to their fate."

Arrived on the premises of the canteen-to-be, they were
joined by Ruth La Fontaine, of Norah Curfew's ' gang,'
and descended to the dark and odorous kitchen. Michael
struck a match, and found the switch. Gosh ! In the
light, surprised, a brown-black scuttling swarm covered
the floor, the walls, the tables. Michael had just sufficient
control of his nerves to take in the faces of those three—
Fleur's shuddering frown, Mr. Blythe's open mouth, the
dark and pretty Ruth La Fontaine's nervous smile. He
felt Fleur clutch his arm.

"How *disgusting* ! "

The disturbed creatures were finding their holes or had
ceased to scuttle ; here and there, a large one, isolated,
seemed to watch them.

"Imagine ! " cried Fleur. "And food's been cooked
here all these years ! Ugh ! "

"After all," said Ruth La Fontaine, with a shivery giggle, "they're not so b-bad as b-bugs."

Mr. Blythe puffed hard at his cigar. Fleur muttered: "What's to be done, Michael?"

Her face was pale; she was drawing little shuddering breaths; and Michael was thinking: 'It's too bad; I must get her out of this!' when suddenly she seized a broom and rushed at a large beetle on the wall. In a minute they were all at it—swabbing and sweeping, and flinging open doors and windows.

CHAPTER II

ON THE 'PHONE

WINIFRED DARTIE had not received her ' Morning Post.' Now in her sixty-eighth year, she had not followed too closely the progress of events which led up to the general strike—they were always saying things in the papers, and you never knew what was true ; those Trades Union people, too, were so interfering, that really one had no patience. Besides, the Government always did something in the end. Acting, however, on the advice of her brother Soames, she had filled her cellars with coal and her cupboards with groceries, and by ten o'clock on the second morning of the strike, was seated comfortably at the telephone.

" Is that you, Imogen ? Are you and Jack coming for me this evening ? "

" No, Mother. Jack's sworn in, of course. He has to be on duty at five. Besides, they say the theatres will close. We'll go later. ' Dat Lubly Lady's ' sure to run."

" Very well, dear. But what a fuss it all is ! How are the boys ? "

" Awfully fit. They're both going to be little ' specials.' I've made them tiny badges. D'you think the child's department at Harridge's would have toy truncheons ? "

" Sure to, if it goes on. I shall be there to-day ; I'll suggest it. They'd look too sweet, wouldn't they ? Are you all right for coal ? "

" Oh, yes. Jack says we mustn't hoard. He's fearfully patriotic."

" Well, good-bye, dear ! My love to the boys ! "

She had just begun to consider whom she should call up next when the telephone bell rang.

"Yes?"

"Mr. Val Dartie living there?"

"No. Who is it speaking?"

"My name is Stainford. I'm an old college friend of his. Could you give me his address, please?"

Stainford? It conveyed nothing.

"I'm his mother. My son is not in town; but I daresay he will be before long. Can I give him any message?"

"Well, thanks! I want to see him. I'll ring up again; or take my chance later. Thanks!"

Winifred replaced the receiver.

Stainford! The voice was distinguished. She hoped it had nothing to do with money. Odd, how often distinction was connected with money! Or, rather, with the lack of it. In the old Park Lane days they had known so many fashionables who had ended in the bankruptcy or divorce courts. Emily—her mother—had never been able to resist distinction. That had been the beginning of Monty—he had worn such perfect waistcoats and gardenias, and had known so much about all that was fast—impossible not to be impressed by him. Ah, well! She did not regret him now. Without him she would never have had Val, or Imogen's two boys, or Benedict (almost a colonel), though she never saw him now, living, as he did, in Guernsey, to grow cucumbers, away from the income tax. They might say what they liked about the age, but could it really be more up-to-date than it was in the 'nineties and the early years of the century, when income tax was at a shilling, and that considered high! People now just ran about and talked, to disguise the fact that they were not so 'chic' and up-to-date as they used to be.

Again the telephone bell rang. "Will you take a trunk call from Wansdon?. . ."

"Hallo! That you, Mother?"

"Oh, Val, how nice! Isn't this strike absurd?"

"Silly asses ! I say : we're coming up."

"Really, dear. But why ? You'll be so much more comfortable in the country."

"Holly says we've got to do things. Who d'you think turned up last night ?—her brother—young Jon Forsyte. Left his wife and mother in Paris—said he'd missed the war and couldn't afford to miss this. Been travelling all the winter—Egypt, Italy, and that—chucked America, I gather. Says he wants to do something dirty—going to stoke an engine. We're driving up to the Bristol this afternoon."

"Oh, but why not come to me, dear, I've got plenty of everything ? "

"Well, there's young Jon—I don't think——"

"But he's a nice boy, isn't he ? "

"Uncle Soames isn't with you, is he ? "

"No, dear. He's at Mapledurham. Oh, and by the way, Val, someone has just rung up for you—a Mr. Stainford."

"Stainford ? What ! Aubrey Stainford— I haven't seen him since Oxford."

"He said he would ring up again or take his chance of finding you here."

"Oh, I'd love to see old Stainford again. Well, if you don't mind putting us up, Mother. Can't leave young Jon out, you know—he and Holly are very thick after six years ; but I expect he'll be out all the time."

"Oh, that'll be quite all right, dear ; and how is Holly ? "

"Topping."

"And the horses ? "

"All right. I've got a snorting two-year-old, rather backward. Shan't run him till Goodwood, but he ought to win then."

"That'll be delightful. Well, dear boy, I'll expect you. But you won't be doing anything rash, with your leg ? "

" No ; just drive a 'bus, perhaps. Won't last, you know.
The Government's all ready. Pretty hot stuff. We've *got*
'em this time."

" I'm so glad. It'll be such a good thing to have it
over ; it's dreadfully bad for the season. Your uncle
will be very upset."

An indistinguishable sound ; then Val's voice again :

" I say, Holly says *she'll* want a job—you might ask
young Mont. He's in with people. See you soon, then—
good-bye ! "

Replacing the receiver, Winifred had scarcely risen from
the satinwood chair on which she had been seated, when
the bell rang again.

" Mrs. Dartie ? . . . That you, Winifred ? Soames
speaking. What did I tell you ? "

" Yes ; it's very annoying, dear. But Val says it'll soon
be over."

" What's he know about it ? "

" He's very shrewd."

" Shrewd ? H'm ! I'm coming up to Fleur's."

" But, why, Soames ? I should have thought——"

" Must be on the spot, in case of—accidents. Besides,
the car'll be eating its head off down here—may as well
be useful. Do that fellow Riggs good to be sworn in.
This thing may lead to anything."

" Oh ! Do you think——"

" Think ? It's no joke. Comes of playing about with
subsidies."

" But you told me last summer——"

" They don't look ahead. They've got no more *nous*
than a tom-cat. Annette wants to go to her mother's in
France. I shan't stop her. She can't gad about while
this is on. I shall take her to Dover with the car to-day,
and come up to-morrow."

" Ought one to sell anything, Soames ? "

" Certainly not."

" People seem dreadfully busy about it all. Val's going
to drive a 'bus. Oh ! and, Soames—that young Jon
Forsyte is back. He's left his wife and mother in Paris,
and come over to be a stoker."

A deep sound, and then :

" What's he want to do that for ? Much better keep
out of England."

" Ye-es. I suppose Fleur——"

" Don't you go putting things into *her* head ! "

" Of course not, Soames. So I shall see you ? Good-
bye."

Dear Soames was always so fussy about Fleur ! Young
Jon Forsyte and she—of course—but that was ages ago !
Calf love ! And Winifred smiled, sitting very still. This
strike was really most ' intriguing.' So long as they didn't
break any windows—because, of course, the milk supply
would be all right, the Government always saw to that ;
and as to the newspapers—well, after all, they were a
luxury ! It would be very nice to have Val and Holly.
The strike was really something to talk about ; there had
been nothing so exciting since the war. And, obeying an
obscure instinct to do something about it, Winifred again
took up the receiver. " Give me Westminster 0000.
. . . Is that Mrs. Michael Mont's ? Fleur ? Aunt Winifred speaking. How are you, dear ? "

The voice which answered had that quick little way of
shaping words that was so amusing to Winifred, who in
her youth had perfected a drawl, which effectually dominated both speed and emotion. All the young women
in Society nowadays spoke like Fleur, as if they had found
the old way of speaking English slow and flat, and were
gingering it with little pinches.

" Perfectly all right, thanks. Anything I can do for
you, Auntie ? "

" Yes, my dear—your cousin Val and Holly are coming
up to me about this strike. And Holly—I think it's very
unnecessary, but she wants to *do* something. She thought
perhaps Michael would know——"

" Oh, well, of course there are lots of things. We've
started a canteen for railway workers ; perhaps she'd like
to help in that."

" My dear, that would be awfully nice."

" It won't, Aunt Winifred ; it's pretty strenuous."

" It can't last, dear, of course. Parliament are bound
to do something about it. It must be a great comfort to
you to have all the news at first hand. Then, may I send
Holly to you ? "

" But of course. She'll be very useful. At her age she'd
better do supplies, I think, instead of standing about, serving. I get on with her all right. The great thing is to
have people that get on together, and don't fuss. Have you
heard from Father ? "

" Yes ; he's coming up to you to-morrow."

" Oh ! But why ? "

" He says he must be on the spot, in case of——"

" That's so silly. Never mind. It'll make two cars."

" Holly will have hers, too. Val's going to drive a 'bus,
he says—and—er—young—well, dear, that's all ! My
love to Kit. There are a tremendous lot of milk-cans in
the Park already, Smither says. She went out this morning into Park Lane to have a look. It's all rather thrilling, don't you think ? "

" At the House they say it'll mean another shilling on
the income tax before it's over."

" Oh, dear ! "

At this moment a voice said: " Have they answered ? "
And, replacing the receiver, Winifred again sat, placid.
Park Lane ! From the old house there—home of her
youth—one would have had a splendid view of everything

—quite the headquarters ! But how dreadfully the poor old Pater would have felt it ! James ! She seemed to see him again with his plaid over his shoulders, and his nose glued to a window-pane, trying to cure with the evidence of his old grey eyes the fatal habit they all had of not telling him anything. She still had some of his wine. And Warmson, their old butler, still kept ' The Pouter Pigeon,' on the river at Moulsbridge. He always sent her a Stilton cheese at Christmas, with a memorandum of the exact amount of the old Park Lane port she was to pour into it. His last letter had ended thus :

" I often think of the master, and how fond he was of going down the cellar right up to the end. As regards wine, ma'am, I'm afraid the days are not what they were. My duty to Mr. Soames and all. Dear me, it seems a long time since I first came to Park Lane.

"Your obedient servant,

"GEORGE WARMSON.

" P.S.—I had a pound or two on that colt Mr. Val bred, please to tell him—and came in useful."

The old sort of servant ! And now she had Smither, from Timothy's, Cook having died—so mysteriously, or, as Smither put it : " Of hornwee, ma'am, I verily believe, missing Mr. Timothy as we did "—Smither as a sort of supercargo—didn't they call it, on ships ?—and really very capable, considering she was sixty, if a day, and the way her corsets creaked. After all, to be with the family again was a great comfort to the poor old soul—eight years younger than Winifred, who, like a true Forsyte, looked down on the age of others from the platform of perennial youth. And a comfort, too, to have about the house one who remembered Monty in his prime—Montague Dartie, so long dead now, that he had a halo as yellow as his gills had so often been. Poor, dear Monty ! Was it really forty-seven years since she married him, and came to live in Green Street ? How well those satinwood chairs with the floral green design on their top rails, had worn— furniture of times before this seven-hour day and all the rest of it ! People thought about their work then, and not about the cinema ! And Winifred, who had never had any work to think about, sighed. It had all been great fun —and, if they could only get this little fuss over, the coming season would be most enjoyable. She had seats already for almost everything. Her hand slipped down to what she was sitting on. Yes, she had only had those chairs recovered twice in all her forty-seven years in Green Street, and, really, they were quite respectable still. True ! no one ever sat on them now, because they were straight up without arms ; and in these days, of course, everybody sprawled, so restless, too, that no chair could stand it. She rose to judge the degree of respectability beneath her, tilting the satinwood chair forward. The year Monty died they had been recovered last—1913, just before the war. Really that had been a marvellous piece of grey-green silk !

CHAPTER III

HOME-COMING

JON FORSYTE'S sensations on landing at Newhaven, by the last possible boat, after five and a half years' absence, had been most peculiar. All the way by car to Wansdon under the Sussex Downs he was in a sort of excited dream. England ! What wonderful chalk, what wonderful green ! What an air of having been there for ever ! The sudden dips into villages, the old bridges, the sheep, the beech clumps ! And the cuckoo—not heard for six years ! A poet, somewhat dormant of late, stirred within this young man. Delicious old country ! Anne would be crazy about this countryside—it was so beautifully finished. When the general strike was over she could come along, and he would show her everything. In the meantime she would be all right with his mother in Paris, and he would be free for any job he could get. He remembered this bit, and Chanctonbury Ring up there, and his walk over from Worthing. He remembered very well. Fleur ! His brother-in-law, Francis Wilmot, had come back from England with much to say about Fleur ; she was very modern now, and attractive, and had a boy. How deeply one could be in love ; and how completely get over it ! Considering what his old feelings down here had been, it was strange but pleasant to be just simply eager to see Holly and ' old Val.'

Beyond a telegram from Dieppe he had made no announcement of his coming ; but they would surely be here because of the horses. He would like to have a look at Val's racing stable, and get a ride, perhaps, on the Downs before taking on a strike job. If only Anne were with

him, and they could have that ride together ! And Jon
thought of his first ride with Anne in the South Carolinian woods—that ride from which they had neither of them
recovered. There it was ! The jolly old house ! And
here at the door—Holly herself ! And at sight of his half-
sister, slim and dark-haired in a lilac dress, Jon was visited
by a stabbing memory of their father as he had looked
that dreadful afternoon, lying dead in the old armchair at
Robin Hill. Dad—always lovable—and so good to him !

"Jon ! How wonderful to see you ! "

Her kiss, he remembered, had always lighted on his eyebrow—she hadn't changed a bit. A half-sister was nicer
than a full-sister, after all. With full-sisters you were
almost bound to fight a little.

"What a pity you couldn't bring Anne and your
mother ! But perhaps it's just as well, till this is over. You
look quite English still, Jon ; and your mouth's as nice and
wide as ever. Why do Americans and naval men have
such small mouths ? "

"Sense of duty, I think. How's Val ? "

"Oh, Val's all right. You haven't lost your smile.
D'you remember your old room ? "

"Rather. And how are *you*, Holly ? "

"So-so. I've become a writer, Jon."

"Splendid ! "

"Not at all. Hard labour and no reward."

"Oh ! "

"The first book was born too still for anything. A sort
of 'African Farm,' without the spiritual frills—if you
remember it."

"Rather ! But I always left the frills out."

"Yes, we get our objection to frills from the Dad, Jon.
He said to me once, 'It'll end in our calling all matter
spirit or all spirit matter—I don't know which.' "

"It won't," said Jon ; "people love to divide things
up. I say, I remember every stick in this room. How are

the horses ? Can I have a look at them and a ride to-morrow ? "

" We'll go forth early and see them at exercise. We've only got three two-year-olds, but one of them's most promising."

" Fine ! After that I must go up and get a good, dirty job. I should like to stoke an engine. I've always wanted to know how stokers feel."

" We'll all go. We can stay with Val's mother. It *is* so lovely to see you, Jon. Dinner's in half an hour."

Jon lingered five minutes at his window. That orchard in full bloom—not mathematically planted, like his just-sold North Carolinian peach-trees—was as lovely as on that long-ago night when he chased Fleur therein. That was the beauty of England—nothing was planned ! How home-sick he had been over there ; yes, and his mother, too ! He would never go back ! How wonderful that sea of apple blossom ! Cuckoo again ! . . . That alone was worth coming home for. He would find a place and grow fruit, down in the West, Worcestershire or Somerset, or near here—they grew a lot of figs and things at Worth-ing, he remembered. Turning out his suit-case, he began to dress. Just where he was sitting now, pulling on his American socks, had he sat when Fleur was showing him her Goya dress. Who would have believed then that, six years later, he would want Anne, not Fleur, beside him on this bed ! The gong ! Dabbing at his hair, bright and stivery, he straightened his tie and ran down.

Val's views on the strike, Val's views on everything, shrewd and narrow as his horseman's face ! Those Labour johnnies were up against it this time with a vengeance ; they'd have to heel up before it was over. How had Jon liked the Yanks ? Had he seen ' Man of War ' ? No ? Good Lord ! The thing best worth seeing in America ! Was the grass in Kentucky really blue ? Only from the distance ? Oh ! What were they going to abolish over

there next ? Wasn't there a place down South where you
were only allowed to cohabit under the eyes of the town
watch ? Parliament here were going to put a tax on betting ; why not introduce the ' Tote ' and have done with
it ? Personally he didn't care, he'd given up betting ! And
he glanced at Holly. Jon, too, glanced at her lifted brows
and slightly parted lips—a charming face—ironical and
tolerant ! She drove Val with silken reins !

Val went on : Good job Jon had given up America ; if
he must farm out of England, why not South Africa,
under the poor old British flag ; though the Dutch weren't
done with yet ! A tough lot ! They had gone out there, of
course, so bright and early that they were real settlers—
none of your adventurers, failures-at-home, remittance-
men. He didn't like the beggars, but they were stout fellows, all the same. Going to stay in England ? Good !
What about coming in with them and breeding racing
stock ?

After an awkward little silence, Holly said slyly :

" Jon doesn't think that's quite a man's job, Val."

" Why not ? "

" Luxury trade."

" Blood stock—where would horses be without it ? "

" Very tempting," said Jon. " I'd like an interest in
it. But I'd want to grow fruit and things for a main line."

" All right, my son ; you can grow the apples they eat
on Sundays."

" You see, Jon," said Holly, " nobody believes in growing anything in England. We talk about it more and
more, and do it less and less. Do you see any change in
Jon, Val ? "

The cousins exchanged a stare.

" A bit more solid ; nothing American, anyway."

Holly murmured thoughtfully : " Why can one always
tell an American ? "

" Why can one always tell an Englishman ? " said Jon.

" Something guarded, my dear. But a national look's the most difficult thing in the world to define. Still, you can't mistake the American expression."

" I don't believe you'll take Anne for one."

" Describe her, Jon."

" No. Wait till you see her."

When, after dinner, Val was going his last round of the stables, Jon said :

" Do you ever see Fleur, Holly ? "

" I haven't for eighteen months, I should think. I like her husband ; he's an awfully good sort. You were well out of that, Jon. She isn't your kind—not that she isn't charming ; but she has to be plumb centre of the stage. I suppose you knew that, really."

Jon looked at her and did not answer.

" Of course," murmured Holly, " when one's in love, one doesn't know much."

Up in his room again, the house began to be haunted. Into it seemed to troop all his memories, of Fleur, of Robin Hill—old trees of his boyhood, his father's cigars, his mother's flowers and music ; the nursery of his games, Holly's nursery before him, with its window looking out over the clock tower above the stables, the room where latterly he had struggled with rhyme. In through his open bedroom window came the sweet-scented air—England's self—from the loom of the Downs in the moon-scattered dusk, this first night of home for more than two thousand nights. With Robin Hill sold, this was the nearest he had to home in England now. But they must make one of their own—he and Anne. Home! On the English liner he had wanted to embrace the stewards and stewardesses just because they spoke an English accent. It was, still, as music to his ears. Anne would pick it up faster now— she was very receptive ! He had liked the Americans, but he was glad Val had said there was nothing American about him. An owl hooted. What a shadow that barn cast—how soft and old its angle! He got into bed. Sleep—if he wanted to be up to see the horses exercised! Once before, here, he had got up early—for another purpose! And soon he slept; and a form—was it Anne's, was it Fleur's—wandered in the corridors of his dreams.

CHAPTER IV

SOAMES GOES UP TO TOWN

HAVING seen his wife off from Dover on the Wednesday, Soames Forsyte motored towards town. On the way he decided to make a considerable detour and enter London over Hammersmith, the furthest westerly bridge in reason. There was for him a fixed connection between unpleasantness and the East End, in times of industrial disturbance. And feeling that, if he encountered a threatening proletariat, he would insist on going through with it, he acted in accordance with the other side of a Forsyte's temperament, and looked ahead. Thus it was that he found his car held up in Hammersmith Broadway by the only threatening conduct of the afternoon. A number of persons had collected to interfere with a traffic of which they did not seem to approve. After sitting forward, to say to his chauffeur, "You'd better go round, Riggs," Soames did nothing but sit back. The afternoon was fine, and the car—a landaulette—open, so that he had a good view of the total impossibility of "going round." Just like that fellow Riggs to have run bang into this! A terrific pack of cars crammed with people trying to run out of town; a few cars like his own, half empty, trying to creep past them into town; a motor-omnibus, not overturned precisely, but with every window broken, standing half across the road; and a number of blank-looking people eddying and shifting before a handful of constables! Such were the phenomena which Soames felt the authorities ought to be handling better.

The words, "Look at the blighted plutocrat!" assailed his ears; and in attempting to see the plutocrat in question,

26

he became aware that it was himself. The epithets were unjust ! He was modestly attired in a brown overcoat and soft felt hat ; that fellow Riggs was plain enough in all conscience, and the car was an ordinary blue. True, he was alone in it, and all the other cars seemed full of people ; but he did not see how he was to get over that, short of carrying into London persons desirous of going in the opposite direction. To shut the car, at all events, would look too pointed—so there was nothing for it but to sit still and take no notice ! For this occupation no one could have been better framed by Nature than Soames, with his air of slightly despising creation. He sat, taking in little but his own nose, with the sun shining on his neck behind, and the crowd eddying round the police. Such violence as had been necessary to break the windows of the 'bus had ceased, and the block was rather what might have been caused by the Prince of Wales. With every appearance of not encouraging it by seeming to take notice, Soames was observing the crowd. And a vacant-looking lot they were, in his opinion ; neither their eyes nor their hands had any of that close attention to business which alone made revolutionary conduct formidable. Youths, for the most part, with cigarettes drooping from their lips— they might have been looking at a fallen horse.

People were born gaping nowadays. And a good thing, too ! Cinemas, fags, and football matches—there would be no real revolution while they were on hand ; and as there seemed to be more and more on hand every year, he was just feeling that the prospect was not too bleak, when a young woman put her head over the window of his car.

" Could you take me in to town ? "

Soames automatically consulted his watch. The hands pointing to seven o'clock gave him extraordinarily little help. Rather a smartly-dressed young woman, with a

slight cockney accent and powder on her nose ! That
fellow Riggs would never have done grinning. And yet
he had read in the ' British Gazette ' that everybody was
doing it. Rather gruffly he said :

" I suppose so. Where do you want to go ? "

" Oh, Leicester Square would do me all right."

Great Scott !

The young woman seemed to sense his emotion. " You
see," she said, " I got to get something to eat before my
show."

Moreover, she was getting in ! Soames nearly got out.
Restraining himself, he gave her a sidelong look ; actress
or something—young—round face, made up, naturally—
nose a little snub—eyes grey, rather goggly—mouth—h'm,
pretty mouth, slightly common ! Shingled—of course.

" It's awf'ly kind of you ! "

" Not at all ! " said Soames ; and the car moved.

"Think it's going to last, the strike ? "

Soames leaned forward.

" Go on, Riggs," he said ; "and put this young lady
down in—er—Coventry Street."

" It's frightf'ly awk for us, all this," said the young
lady. " I should never've got there in time. You seen
our show, ' Dat Lubly Lady ' ? "

" No."

" It's rather good."

" Oh ! "

" We shall have to close, though, if this lasts."

" Ah ! "

The young lady was silent, seeming to recognise that
she was not in the presence of a conversationalist.

Soames re-crossed his legs. It was so long since he had
spoken to a strange young woman, that he had almost
forgotten how it was done. He did not want to encourage
her, and yet was conscious that it was his car.

" Comfortable ? " he said, suddenly.

The young lady smiled.

"What d'you think ? " she said. " It's a lovely car."

" I don't like it," said Soames.

The young lady's mouth opened.

" Why ? "

Soames shrugged his shoulders ; he had only been carrying on the conversation.

" I think it's rather fun, don't you ? " said the young lady. " Carrying on—you know, like we're all doing."

The car was now going at speed, and Soames began to calculate the minutes necessary to put an end to this juxtaposition.

The Albert Memorial, already ; he felt almost an affection for it—so guiltless of the times !

" You *must* come and see our show," said the young lady.

Soames made an effort and looked into her face.

" What do you do in it ? " he asked.

" Sing and dance."

" I see."

" I've rather a good bit in the third act, where we're all in our nighties."

Soames smiled faintly.

" You've got no one like Kate Vaughan now," he said.

" Kate Vaughan ? Who was she ? "

" Who was Kate Vaughan ? " repeated Soames ; "greatest dancer that was ever in burlesque. Dancing was graceful in those days ; now it's all throwing your legs about. The faster you can move your legs, the more you think you're dancing." And, disconcerted by an outburst that was bound to lead to something, he averted his eyes.

" You don't like jazz ? " queried the young lady.

" I do not," said Soames.

" Well, I don't either—not reely ; it's getting old-fashioned, too."

Hyde Park Corner already ! And the car going a good twenty !

" My word ! Look at the lorries ; it's marvellous, isn't it ? "

Soames emitted a confirmatory grunt. The young lady was powdering her nose now, and touching up her lips, with an almost staggering frankness. 'Suppose anyone sees me ? ' thought Soames. And he would never know whether anyone had or not. Turning up the high collar of his overcoat, he said :

" Draughty things, these cars ! Shall I put you down at Scott's ? "

" Oh, no. Lyons, please ; I've only time f'r a snack ; got to be on the stage at eight. It's been awf'ly kind of you. I only hope somebody'll take me home ! " Her eyes rolled suddenly, and she added : "If you know what I mean."

" Quite ! " said Soames, with a certain delicacy of perception. "Here you are. Stop—Riggs ! "

The car stopped, and the young lady extended her hand to Soames.

" Good-bye, and thank you ! "

" Good-bye ! " said Soames. Nodding and smiling, she got out.

" Go on, Riggs, sharp ! South Square."

The car moved on. Soames did not look back ; in his mind the thought formed like a bubble on the surface of water : ' In the old days anyone who looked and talked like that would have left me her address.' And she hadn't ! He could not decide whether or no this marked an advance.

At South Square, on discovering that Michael and Fleur were out, he did not dress for dinner, but went to the nursery. His grandson, now nearly three years old, was still awake, and said : " Hallo ! "

" Hallo ! " replied Soames, producing a toy watchman's rattle. There followed five minutes of silent and complete absorption, broken fitfully by guttural sounds from the rattle. Then his grandson lay back in his cot, fixed his blue eyes on Soames, and said, " Hallo ! "

" Hallo ! " replied Soames.

" Ta, ta ! " said his grandson.

" Ta, ta ! " said Soames, backing to the door, and nearly falling over the silver dog. The interview then terminated, and Soames went downstairs. Fleur had telephoned to say he was not to wait dinner.

Opposite the Goya he sat down. No good saying he remembered the Chartist riots of '48, because he had been born in '55; but he knew his uncle Swithin had been a ' special ' at the time. This general strike was probably the most serious internal disturbance that had happened since; and, sitting over his soup, he bored further and further into its possibilities. Bolshevism round the corner —that was the trouble! That and the fixed nature of ideas in England. Because a thing like coal had once been profitable, they thought it must always be profitable. Political leaders, Trades Unionists, newspaper chaps—they never looked an inch before their noses ! They'd had since last August to do something about it, and what had they done? Drawn up a report that nobody would look at!

"White wine, sir, or claret?"

"Anything that's open." To have said that in the 'eighties, or even the 'nineties, would have given his father a fit! The idea of drinking claret already opened was then almost equivalent to atheism. Another sign of the slump in ideals.

"What do *you* think about this strike, Coaker?"

The almost hairless man lowered the Sauterne.

"Got no body in it, sir, if you ask me."

"What makes you say that?"

"If it had any body in it, sir, they'd have had the railings of Hyde Park up by now."

Soames poised a bit of his sole. "Shouldn't be surprised if you were right," he said, with a certain approval.

"They make a lot of fuss, but no—there's nothing to it. The dole—that was a clever dodge, sir. Pannus et circesses, as Mr. Mont says, sir."

"Ha! Have you seen this canteen they're running?"

"No, sir; I believe they've got the beetle man in this evening. I'm told there's a proper lot of beetles."

"Ugh!"

"Yes, sir; it's a nahsty insect."

Having finished dinner, Soames lighted the second of his two daily cigars, and took up the earpieces of the wireless. He had resisted this invention as long as he could—but in times like these! "London calling!" Yes, and the British Isles listening! Trouble in Glasgow? There would be—lot of Irish there! More 'specials' wanted? There'd soon be plenty of those. He must tell that fellow Riggs to enlist. This butler chap, too, could well be spared. Trains! They seemed to be running a lot of trains already. After listening with some attention to the Home Secretary, Soames put the earpieces down and took up ' The British Gazette.' It was his first sustained look at this tenuous production, and he hoped it would be his last. The paper and printing were deplorable. Still, he supposed it was something to have got it out at all. Tampering with the freedom of the Press! Those fellows were not finding it so easy as they thought. They had tampered, and the result was a Press much more definitely against them than the Press they had suppressed. Burned their fingers there! And quite unnecessary—old-fashioned notion now—influence of the Press. The war had killed it. Without confidence in truth there was no influence. Politicians or the Press—if you couldn't believe them, they didn't count! Perhaps they would re-discover that some day. In the meantime the papers were like cocktails—titivators mostly of the appetite and the nerves. How sleepy he was! He hoped Fleur wouldn't be very late coming in. Mad thing, this strike, making everybody do things they weren't accustomed to, just as Industry, too, was beginning—or at least pretending—to recover. But that was it! With every year, in these times, it was more difficult to do what you said you would. Always something or other turning up! The world seemed to live from hand to mouth, and at such a pace, too! Sitting back in the Spanish chair, Soames covered his eyes from the light, and the surge of sleep mounted to his brain; strike or no strike, the soft, inexorable tide washed over him.

A tickling, and over his hand, thin and rather brown, the fringe of a shawl came dangling. Why! With an effort he climbed out of an abyss of dreams. Fleur was standing beside him. Pretty, bright, her eyes shining, speaking quickly, excitedly, it seemed to him.

"Here you are, then, Dad!" Her lips felt hot and soft on his forehead, and her eyes—— What was the matter with her? She looked so young—she looked so—how express it?

"So you're in!" he said. "Kit's getting talkative. Had anything to eat?"

"Heaps!"

"This canteen——"

She flung off her shawl.

"I'm enjoying it frightfully."

Soames noted with surprise the rise and fall of her breast, as if she had been running. Her cheeks, too, were very pink.

"You haven't caught anything, have you—in that place?"

Fleur laughed. A sound—delicious and unwarranted.

"How funny you are, Dad! I hope the strike lasts!"

"Don't be foolish!" said Soames. "Where's Michael?"

"Gone up. He called for me, after the House. Nothing doing there, he says."

"What's the time?"

"Past twelve, dear. You must have had a real good sleep."

"Just nodding."

"We saw a tank pass, on the Embankment—going East. It looked awfully queer. Didn't you hear it?"

"No," said Soames.

"Well, don't be alarmed if you hear another. They're on their way to the docks, Michael says."

"Glad to hear it—shows the Government means business. But you must go up. You're overtired."

She gazed at him over the Spanish shawl on her arm—whistling some tune.

"Good-night!" he said. "I shall be coming up in a minute."

She blew him a kiss, twirled round, and went.

"I don't like it," murmured Soames to himself; "I don't know why, but I don't like it."

She had looked too young. Had the strike gone to her head? He rose to squirt some soda-water into a glass—that nap had left a taste in his mouth.

Um — dum — bom—um—dum—bom—um—dum—bom! A grunching noise! Another of those tanks? He would like to see one of those great things! For the idea that they were going down to the docks gave him a feeling almost of exhilaration. With them on the spot the country was safe enough. Putting on his motoring coat and hat, he went out, crossed the empty Square, and stood in the street, whence he could see the Embankment. There it came! Like a great primeval monster in the lamplit darkness, growling and gruntling along, a huge, fantastic tortoise—like an embodiment of inexorable power. 'That'll astonish their weak nerves!' thought Soames, as the tank crawled, grunching, out of sight. He could hear another coming; but with a sudden feeling that it would be too much of a good thing, he turned on his heel. A sort of extravagance about them, when he remembered the blank-looking crowd around his car that afternoon, not a weapon among the lot, nor even a revolutionary look in their eyes!

"No *body* in the strike!" These great crawling monsters! Were the Government trying to pretend that there was? Playing the strong man! Something in Soames revolted slightly. Hang it! This was England, not Russia, or Italy! They might be right, but he didn't like it! Too —too military! He put his latchkey into the keyhole. Um —dum—bom—um—dum—bom! Well, not many people would see or hear them—this time of night! He supposed they had got here from the country somewhere—he wouldn't care to meet them wandering about in the old lanes and places. Father and mother and baby tanks—like —like a family of mastodons, m—m? No sense of proportion in things like that! And no sense of humour! He stood on the stairs listening. It was to be hoped they wouldn't wake the baby!

CHAPTER V

JEOPARDY

WHEN, looking down the row of faces at her canteen table, Fleur saw Jon Forsyte's, it was within her heart as if, in winter, she had met with honeysuckle. Recovering from that faint intoxication, she noted his appearance from further off. He was sitting seemingly indifferent to food; and on his face, which was smudged with coal-dust and sweat, was such a smile as men wear after going up a mountain or at the end of a long run—tired, charming, and as if they have been through something worth while. His lashes—long and dark as in her memory—concealed his eyes, and quarrelled with his brighter hair, touzled to the limit of its shortness.

Continuing to issue her instructions to Ruth La Fontaine, Fleur thought rapidly. Jon! Dropped from the skies into her canteen, stronger-looking, better knit; with more jaw, and deeper set eyes, but frightfully like Jon! What was to be done about it? If only she could turn out the lights, steal up behind, lean over and kiss him on that smudge above his left eye! Yes! And then—what? Silly! And now, suppose he came out of his far-away smile and saw her! As likely as not he would never come into her canteen again. She remembered his conscience! And she took a swift decision. Not to-night! Holly would know where he was staying. At her chosen time, on her chosen ground, if—on second thoughts, she wanted to play with fire. And, giving a mandate to Ruth La Fontaine concerning buns, she looked back over her shoulder at Jon's absorbed and smiling face, and passed out into her little office.

And second thoughts began. Michael, Kit, her father;

the solid security of virtue and possessions; the peace of
mind into which she had passed of late! All jeopardised
for the sake of a smile, and a scent of honeysuckle! No!
That account was closed. To reopen it was to tempt
Providence. And if to tempt Providence was the practice
of Modernity, she wasn't sure whether she was modern.
Besides, who knew whether she *could* reopen that account?
And she was seized by a gust of curiosity to see that wife
of his—that substitute for herself. Was she in England?
Was she dark, like her brother Francis? Fleur took up her
list of purchases for the morrow. With so much to do, it
was idiotic even to think about such things! The telephone!
All day its bell had been ringing; since nine o'clock that
morning she had been dancing to its pipe.

"Yes. . . .? Mrs. Mont speaking. What? But I've ordered them. . . . Oh! But really I *must* give them bacon
and eggs in the morning. They can't start on cocoa only.
. . . How? The Company can't afford? . . . Well! Do
you want an effective service or not? . . . Come round to
see you about it? I really haven't time. . . . Yes, yes . . .
now please do be nice to me and tell the manager that they
simply must be properly fed. They look so tired. He'll
understand. . . . Yes. . . . Thank you ever so!" She hung
up the receiver. "Damn!"

Someone laughed. "Oh! It's you, Holly! Cheese-par-
ing and red tape as usual! This is the fourth time to-day.
Well, I don't care—I'm going ahead. Look! Here's Harridge's list for to-morrow. It's terrific, but it's got to be.
Buy it all; I'll take the risk, if I have to go round and
slobber on him." And beyond the ironic sympathy on Holly's face she seemed to see Jon's smile. He should be properly fed—all of them should! And, without looking at her
cousin, she said:

"I saw Jon in there. Where has he dropped from?"

"Paris. He's putting up with us in Green Street."

Fleur stuck her chin forward, and gave a little laugh.

"Quaint to see him again, all smudgy like that! His wife with him?"

"Not yet," said Holly; "she's in Paris still, with his mother."

"Oh! It'd be fun to see him some time!"

"He's stoking an engine on the local service—goes out at six, and doesn't get in till about midnight."

"Of course; I meant after, if the strike ever ends."

Holly nodded. "His wife wants to come over and help; would you like her in the canteen?"

"If she's the right sort."

"Jon says: Very much so."

"I don't see why an American should worry herself. Are they going to live in England?"

"Yes."

"Oh! Well, we're both over the measles."

"If you get them again grown-up, Fleur, they're pretty bad."

Fleur laughed. "No fear!" And her eyes, hazel, clear, glancing, met her cousin's eyes, deep, steady, grey.

"Michael's waiting for you with the car," said Holly.

"All right! Can you carry on till they've finished? Norah Curfew's on duty at five to-morrow morning. I shall be round at nine, before you start for Harridge's. If you think of anything else, stick it on the list—I'll make them stump up somehow. Good-night, Holly."

"Good-night, my dear."

Was there a gleam of pity in those grey eyes? Pity, indeed!

"Give Jon my love. I do wonder how he likes stoking! We must get some more wash-basins in."

Sitting beside Michael, who was driving their car, she saw again, as it were, Jon's smile in the glass of the windscreen, and in the dark her lips pouted as if reaching for it. Measles—they spotted you, and raised your temperature

How empty the streets were, now that the taxis were on strike! Michael looked round at her.

"Well, how's it going?"

"The beetle man was a caution, Michael. He had a face like a ravaged wedge, a wave of black hair, and the eyes of a lost soul; but he was frightfully efficient."

"Look! There's a tank; I was told of them. They're going down to the docks. Rather provocative! Just as well there are no papers for them to get into."

Fleur laughed.

"Father'll be at home. He's come up to protect me. If there really was shooting, I wonder what he'd do—take his umbrella?"

"Instinct. How about you and Kit? It's the same thing."

Fleur did not answer. And when, after seeing her father, she went upstairs, she stood at the nursery door. The tune that had excited Soames' surprise made a whiffling sound in the empty passage. "*L'amour est enfant de Bohême; il n'a jamais jamais connu de loi; si tu ne m'aimes pas, je t'aime, et si je t'aime, prends garde à toi!*" Spain, and the heartache of her honeymoon! "Voice in the night crying!" Close the shutters, muffle the ears—keep it out! She entered her bedroom and turned up the lights. It had never seemed to her so pretty, with its many mirrors, its lilac and green, its shining silver. She stood looking at her face, into which had come two patches of red, one in each cheek. Why wasn't she Norah Curfew—dutiful, uncomplicated, selfless, who would give Jon eggs and bacon at half-past five to-morrow morning—Jon with a clean face! Quickly she undressed. Was that wife of his her equal undressed? To which would he award the golden apple if she stood side by side with Anne? And the red spots deepened in her cheeks. Overtired—she knew that feeling! She would not sleep! But the sheets were cool. Yes, she preferred the old smooth Irish linen to that new rough French grass-bleached stuff.

Ah! Here was Michael coming in, coming up to her! Well! No use to be unkind to him—poor old Michael! And in his arms, she saw—Jon's smile.

* * * * *

That first day spent in stoking an engine had been enough to make anyone smile. An engine-driver almost as youthful, but in private life partner in his own engineering works, had put Jon 'wise' to the mystery of getting level combustion. "A tricky job, and very tiring!" Their passengers had behaved well. One had even come up and thanked them. The engine-driver had winked at Jon. There had been some hectic moments. Supping pea soup, Jon thought of them with pleasure. It had been great sport, but his hands and arms felt wrenched. "Oil them tonight," the engine-driver had said.

A young woman was handing him 'jacket' potatoes. She had marvellously clear, brown eyes, something like Anne's —only Anne's were like a water nymph's. He took a potato, thanked her, and returned to a stoker's dreams. Extraordinary pleasure in being up against it—being in England again, doing something for England! One had to leave one's country to become conscious of it. Anne had telegraphed that she wanted to come over and join him. If he wired back "No," she would come all the same. He knew that much after nearly two years of marriage. Well, she would see England at its best. Americans didn't really know what England was. Her brother had seen nothing but London; he had spoken bitterly—a girl, Jon supposed, though nothing had been said of her. In Francis Wilmot's history of England the gap accounted for the rest. But everybody ran down England, because she didn't slop over, or blow her own trumpet.

"Butter?"

"Thanks, awfully. These potatoes are frightfully good."

"So glad."

"Who runs this canteen?"

"Mr. and Mrs. Michael Mont mostly; he's a member of Parliament."

Jon dropped his potato.

"Mrs. Mont? Gracious! She's a cousin of mine. Is she here?"

"Was. Just gone, I think."

Jon's far-sighted eyes travelled round the large and dingy room. Fleur! How amazing!

"Treacle pudding?"

"No, thanks. Nothing more."

"There'll be coffee, tea, or cocoa, and eggs and bacon, to-morrow at 5.45."

"Splendid! I think it's wonderful."

"It is, rather, in the time."

"Thank you awfully. Good-night!"

Jon sought his coat. Outside were Val and Holly in their car.

"Hallo, young Jon! You're a nice object."

"What job have *you* caught, Val?"

"Motor lorry—begin to-morrow."

"Fine!"

"This'll knock out racing for a bit."

"But not England."

"England? Lord—no! What did you think?"

"Abroad they were saying so."

"Abroad!" growled Val. "They would!"

And there was silence at thirty miles an hour.

From his bedroom door Jon said to his sister:

"They say Fleur runs that canteen. Is she really so old now?"

"Fleur has a very clear head, my dear. She saw you there. No second go of measles, Jon."

Jon laughed.

"Aunt Winifred," said Holly, "will be delighted to have Anne here on Friday, she told me to tell you."

"Splendid! That's awfully good of her."

"Well, good-night; bless you. There's still hot water in the bathroom."

In his bath Jon lay luxuriously still. Sixty hours away from his young wife, he was already looking forward with impatience to her appearance on Friday. And so Fleur ran that canteen! A fashionable young woman with a clear and, no doubt, shingled head—he felt a great curiosity to see her again, but nothing more. Second go of measles! Not much! He had suffered too severely from the first. Besides, he was too glad to be back—result of long, half-acknowledged home-sickness. His mother had been home-sick for Europe; but *he* had felt no assuagement in Italy and France. It was England he had wanted. Something in the way people walked and talked; in the smell and the look of everything; some good-humoured, slow, ironic essence in the air, after the tension of America, the shrillness of Italy, the clarity of Paris. For the first time in five years his nerves felt coated. Even those features of his native land which offended the æsthetic soul, were comforting. The approaches to London, the countless awful little houses of brick and slate which his own great-grandfather, 'Superior Dosset' Forsyte, had helped, so his father had once told him, to build; the many little new houses, rather better, but still bent on compromise; the total absence of symmetry or plan; the ugly railway stations; the cockney voices, the lack of colour, taste, or pride in people's dress—all seemed comfortable, a guarantee that England would always be England.

And so Fleur was running that canteen! He would be seeing her! He would like to see her! Oh, yes!

CHAPTER VI

SNUFFBOX

IN the next room Val was saying to Holly:
"Had a chap I knew at college to see me to-day. Wanted me to lend him money. I once did, when I was jolly hard up myself, and never got it back. He used to impress me frightfully—such an awfully good-looking, languid beggar. I thought him top notch as a 'blood.' You should see him now!"

"I did. I was coming in as he was going out; I wondered who he was. I never saw a more bitterly contemptuous expression on a face. Did you lend him money?"

"Only a fiver."

"Well, don't lend him any more."

"Hardly. D'you know what he's done? Gone off with that Louis Quinze snuffbox of Mother's that's worth about two hundred. There's been nobody else in that room."

"Good heavens!"

"Yes, it's pretty thick. He had the reputation of being the fastest man up at the 'Varsity in my time—in with the gambling set. Since I went out to the Boer war I've never heard of him."

"Isn't your mother very annoyed, Val?"

"She wants to prosecute—it belonged to my granddad. But how can we—a college pal! . . . Besides, we shouldn't get the box back."

Holly ceased to brush her hair.

"It's rather a comfort to me—this," she said.

"What is?"

"Why, everybody says the standard of honesty's gone down. It's nice to find someone belonging to our generation that had it even less."

"Rum comfort!"

"Human nature doesn't alter, Val. I believe in the young generation. We don't understand them—brought up in too settled times."

"That may be. My own dad wasn't too particular. But what am I to do about this?"

"Do you know his address?"

"He said the Brummell Club would find him—pretty queer haunt, if I remember. To come to sneaking things like that! It's upset me frightfully."

Holly looked at him lying on his back in bed. Catching her eyes on him, he said:

"But for you, old girl, I might have gone a holy mucker myself."

"Oh, no, Val! You're too open-air. It's the indoor people who go really wrong."

Val grinned.

"Something in that—the only exercise I ever saw that fellow take was in a punt. He used to bet like anything, but he didn't know a horse from a hedge-hog. Well, Mother must put up with it, I can't do anything."

Holly came up to his bed.

"Turn over, and I'll tuck you up."

Getting into bed herself, she lay awake, thinking of the man who had gone a holy mucker, and the contempt on his face—lined, dark, well-featured, with prematurely greying hair, and prematurely faded rings round the irises of the eyes; of his clothes, too, so preternaturally preserved, and the worn, careful school tie. She felt she knew him. No moral sense, and ingrained contempt for those who had. Poor Val! *He* hadn't so much moral sense that he need be despised for it! And yet——! With a good many risky male instincts, Val had been a loyal comrade all these years. If in philosophic reach or æsthetic taste he was not advanced, if he knew more of horses than of poetry, was he any the worse? She sometimes thought he was the better. The horse didn't change shape or colour every five years and start reviling its predecessor. The horse was a constant, kept you from going too fast, and had a nose to stroke—more than you could say of a poet. They had, indeed, only one thing in common—a liking for sugar. Since the publication of her novel Holly had become member of the 1930 Club. Fleur had put her up, and whenever she came to town, she studied modernity there. Modernity was nothing but speed! People who blamed it might as well blame telephone, wireless, flying machine, and quick lunch counter. Beneath that top-dressing of speed, modernity was old. Women had worn fewer clothes when Jane Austen began to write. Drawers—the historians said—were only nineteenth-century productions. And take modern talk! After South Africa the speed of it certainly took one's wind away; but the thoughts expressed were much her own thoughts as a girl, cut into breathless lengths, by car and telephone bell. Take modern courtships! They resulted in the same thing as under George the Second, but took longer to reach it, owing to the motor-cycle and the standing lunch. Take modern philosophy! People had no less real philosophy than Martin Tupper or Izaak Walton; only, unlike those celebrated ancients, they had no time to formulate it. As to a future life—modernity lived in hope, and not too much of that, as everyone had, from immemorial time. In fact, as a novelist naturally would, Holly jumped to conclusions. Scratch—she thought—the best of modern youth, and you would find Charles James Fox and Perdita in golf sweaters! A steady sound retrieved her thoughts. Val was asleep. How long and dark his eyelashes still were, but his mouth was open!

"Val," she said, very softly; "Val! Don't snore, dear!" ...

    *   *   *   *   *

A snuffbox may be precious, not so much for its enamel, its period, and its little brilliants, as because it has belonged to one's father. Winifred, though her sense of property had been well proved by her retention of Montague Dartie 'for poorer,' throughout so many years, did not possess her brother Soames' collecting instinct, nor, indeed, his taste in objects which George Forsyte had been the first to call 'of bigotry and virtue.' But the further Time removed her father James—a quarter of a century by now—the more she revered his memory. As some ancient general or philosopher, secured by age from competition, is acclaimed year by year a greater genius, so with James! His objection to change, his perfect domesticity, his power of saving money for his children, and his dread of not being told anything, were haloed for her more and more with every year that he spent underground. Her fashionable aspirations waning with the increase of adipose, the past waxed and became a very constellation of shining memories. The removal of this snuffbox—so tangible a reminder of James and Emily —tried her considerable equanimity more than anything that had happened to her for years. The thought that she had succumbed to the distinction of a voice on the telephone, caused her positive discomfort. With all her experience of distinction, she ought to have known better! She was, however, one of those women who, when a thing is done, admit the fact with a view to having it undone as soon as possible; and, having failed with Val, who merely said, "Awfully sorry, Mother, but there it is—jolly bad luck!" she summoned her brother.

Soames was little less than appalled. He remembered seeing James buy the box at Jobson's for hardly more than one-tenth of what it would fetch now. Everything seemed futile if, in such a way, one could lose what had been nursed for forty years into so really magnificent a state of unearned increment. And the fellow who had taken it was of quite good family, or so his nephew said! Whether the

honesty of the old Forsytes, in the atmosphere of which he
had been brought up and turned out into the world, had
been inherited or acquired—derived from their blood or
their Banks—he had never considered. It had been in their
systems just as the proverb "Honesty is the best policy" was
in that of the private banking which then obtained. A slight
reverie on banking was no uncommon affection of the mind
in one who could recall the repercussion of "Understart and
Darnett's" failure, and the disappearance one by one of all
the little, old Banks with legendary names. These great
modern affairs were good for credit and bad for novelists
—run on a Bank—there had been no better reading! Such
monster concerns couldn't 'go broke,' no matter what their
clients did; but whether they made for honesty in the individual, Soames couldn't tell. The snuffbox was gone, however; and if Winifred didn't take care, she wouldn't get it
back. How, precisely, she was to take care he could not at
present see; but he should advise her to put it into the hands
of somebody at once.

"But whose, Soames?"

"There's Scotland Yard," answered Soames, gloomily.
"I believe they're very little good, except to make a fuss.
There's that fellow I employed in the Ferrar case. He
charges very high."

"I shouldn't care so much," said Winifred, "if it hadn't
belonged to the dear Dad."

"Ruffians like that," muttered Soames, "oughtn't to be at
large."

"And to think," said Winifred, "that it was especially
to see him that Val came to stay here."

"Was it?" said Soames, gloomily. "I suppose you're sure
that fellow took it?"

"Quite. I'd had it out to polish only a quarter of an hour
before. After he went, I came back into the room at once,
to put it away, and it was gone. Val had been in the room
the whole time."

Soames dwelled for a moment, then rejected a doubt about his nephew, for, though connected by blood with that precious father of his, Montague Dartie, and a racing man to boot, he was half a Forsyte after all.

"Well," he said, "shall I send you this man—his name's Becroft—always looks as if he'd overshaved himself, but he's got a certain amount of *nous*. I should suggest his getting in touch with that fellow's club."

"Suppose he's already sold the box?" said Winifred.

"Yesterday afternoon? Should doubt that; but it wants immediate handling. I'll see Becroft as I go away. Fleur's overdoing it, with this canteen of hers."

"They say she's running it very well. I do think all these young women are so smart."

"Quick enough," grumbled Soames, "but steady does it in the long run."

At that phrase—a maxim never far away from the lips of the old Forsytes in her youthful days—Winifred blinked her rather too light eyelashes.

"That was always rather a bore, you know, Soames. And in these days, if you're not quick, things move past you, so."

Soames gathered his hat. "That snuffbox will, if we don't look sharp."

"Well, thank you, dear boy. I do hope we get it back. The dear Pater was so proud of it, and when he died it wasn't worth half what it is now."

"Not a quarter," said Soames, and the thought bored into him as he walked away. What was the use of having judgment, if anybody could come along and pocket the results! People sneered at property nowadays; but property was a proof of good judgment—it was one's *amour propre* half the time. And he thought of the *amour propre* Bosinney had stolen from him in those far-off days of trouble. Yes, even marriage—was an exercise of judgment—a pitting of yourself against other people. You 'spotted a winner,' as they called it, or you didn't—Irene hadn't been 'a winner'—not exactly! Ah! And he had forgotten to ask Winifred about that young Jon Forsyte who had suddenly come back into the wind. But about this snuffbox! The Brummell Club was some sort of betting place, he had heard; full of gamblers, and people who did and sold things on commisson, he shouldn't wonder. That was the vice of the day; that and the dole. Work? No! Sell things on commission—motor-cars, for choice. Brummell Club! Yes! This was the place! It had a window—he remembered. No harm, anyway, in asking if the fellow really belonged there! And entering, he enquired:

"Mr. Stainford a member here?"

"Yes. Don't know if he's in. Mr. Stainford been in, Bob?"

"Just come in."

"Oh!" said Soames, rather taken aback.

"Gentleman to see him, Bob."

A rather sinking sensation occurred within Soames.

"Come with me, sir."

Soames took a deep breath, and his legs moved. In an alcove off the entrance—somewhat shabby and constricted—he could see a man lolling in an old armchair, smoking a cigarette through a holder. He had a little red book in one hand and a small pencil in the other, and held them as still as if he were about to jot down a conviction that he had not got. He wore a dark suit with little lines; his legs were crossed, and Soames noted that one foot in a worn brown shoe, treed and polished against age to the point of pathos, was slowly moving in a circle.

"Gemman to see you, sir."

Soames now saw the face. Its eyebrows were lifted in a V reversed, its eyelids nearly covered its eyes. Together with the figure, it gave an impression of really remarkable languor. Thin to a degree, oval and pale, it seemed all shadow and slightly aquiline feature. The foot had become still, the whole affair still. Soames had the curious feeling of being in the presence of something arrogantly dead. Without time for thought, he began:

"Mr. Stainford, I think? Don't disturb yourself. My name is Forsyte. You called at my sister's in Green Street yesterday afternoon."

A slight contraction of the lines round that small mouth was followed by the words:

"Will you sit down?"

The eyes had opened now, and must once have been beautiful. They narrowed again, so that Soames could not help feeling that their owner had outlived everything except himself. He swallowed a qualm and resumed:

"I just wanted to ask you a question. During your call, did you by any chance happen to notice a Louis Quinze snuffbox on the table? It's—er—disappeared, and we want to fix the time of its loss."

As a ghost might have smiled, so did the man in the chair; his eyes disappeared still further.

"Afraid not."

With the thought, 'He's got it!' Soames went on:

"I'm sorry—the thing had virtue as an heirloom. It has obviously been stolen. I wanted to narrow down the issue. If you'd noticed it, we could have fixed the exact hour— on the little table just where you were sitting—blue enamel."

The thin shoulders wriggled slightly, as though resenting this attempt to place responsibility on them.

"Sorry I can't help you; I noticed nothing but some rather good marqueterie."

'Coolest card I ever saw,' thought Soames. 'Wonder if it's in his pocket.'

"The thing's unique," he said slowly. "The police won't have much difficulty. Well, thanks very much.

I apologise for troubling you. You knew my nephew at college, I believe. Good-morning."

"Good-morning."

From the door Soames took a stealthy glance. The figure was perfectly motionless, the legs still crossed, and above the little red book the pale forehead was poised under the smooth grizzling hair. Nothing to be made of that! But the fellow had it, he was sure.

He went out and down to the Green Park with a most peculiar feeling. Sneak thief! A gentleman to come to that! The Elderson affair had been bad, but somehow not pitiful like this. The whitened seams of the excellent suit, the traversing creases in the once admirable shoes, the faded tie exactly tied, were evidences of form preserved, day by day, from hand to mouth. They afflicted Soames. That languid figure! What *did* a chap do when he had no money and couldn't exert himself to save his life? Incapable of shame—that was clear! He must talk to Winifred again. And, turning on his heel, Soames walked back towards Green Street. Debouching from the Park, he saw on the opposite side of Piccadilly the languid figure. It, too, was moving in the direction of Green Street. Phew! He crossed over and followed. The chap had an air. He was walking like someone who had come into the world from another age—an age which set all its store on 'form.' He felt that 'this chap' would sooner part with life itself than exhibit interest in anything. Form! Could you carry contempt for emotion to such a pitch that you could no longer feel emotion? Could the lifted eyebrow become more important to you than all the movements of the heart and brain? Threadbare peacock's feathers walking, with no peacock inside! To show feeling was perhaps the only thing of which that chap would be ashamed. And, a little astonished at his own powers of diagnosis, Soames followed round corner after corner, till

he was actually in Green Street. By George! The chap
was going to Winifred's! 'I'll astonish his weak nerves!'
thought Soames. And, suddenly hastening, he said, rather
breathlessly, on his sister's very doorstep:

"Ah! Mr. Stainford! Come to return the snuffbox?"

With a sigh, and a slight stiffening of his cane on the
pavement, the figure turned. Soames felt a sudden compunction—as of one who has jumped out at a child in the
dark. The face, unmoved, with eyebrows still raised and
lids still lowered, was greenishly pale, like that of a man
whose heart is affected; a faint smile struggled on the
lips. There was fully half a minute's silence, then the
pale lips spoke.

"Depends. How much?"

What little breath was in Soames' body left him. The
impudence! And again the lips moved.

"You can have it for ten pounds."

"I can have it for nothing," said Soames, "by asking a
policeman to step here."

The smile returned. "You won't do that."

"Why not?"

"Not done."

"Not done!" repeated Soames. "Why on earth not?
Most barefaced thing I ever knew."

"Ten pounds," said the lips. "I want them badly."

Soames stood and stared. The thing was so sublime;
the fellow as easy as if asking for a match; not a flicker
on a face which looked as if it might pass into death at
any moment. Great art! He perceived that it was not
the slightest use to indulge in moral utterance. The choice
was between giving him the ten pounds or calling a policeman. He looked up and down the street.

"No—there isn't one in sight. I have the box here—
ten pounds."

Soames began to stammer. The fellow was exercising

on him a sort of fascination. And suddenly the whole thing tickled him. It was rich!

"Well!" he said, taking out two five-pound notes. "For brass—!"

A thin hand removed a slight protuberance from a side pocket.

"Thanks very much. Here it is! Good-morning!"

The fellow was moving away. He moved with the same incomparable languor; he didn't look back. Soames stood with the snuffbox in his hand, staring after him.

"Well," he said, aloud, "that's a specimen they can't produce now," and he rang Winifred's bell.

CHAPTER VII

MICHAEL HAS QUALMS

DURING the eight days of the General Strike Michael's somewhat hectic existence was relieved only by the hours spent in a House of Commons so occupied in meditating on what it could do, that it could do nothing. He had formed his own opinion of how to settle the matter, but as no one else had formed it, the result was inconspicuous. He watched, however, with a very deep satisfaction the stock of British character daily quoted higher at home and abroad; and with a certain uneasiness the stock of British intelligence becoming almost unsaleable. Mr. Blythe's continual remark: "What the bee aitch are they all about?" met with no small response in his soul. What *were* they about? He had one conversation with his father-in-law on the subject.

Over his egg Soames had said:

"Well, the Budget's dished."

Over his marmalade Michael answered:

"Used you to have this sort of thing in your young days, sir?"

"No," said Soames; "no Trade Unionism then, to speak of."

"People are saying this'll be the end of it. What's your opinion of the strike as a weapon, sir?"

"For the purposes of suicide, perfect. It's a wonder they haven't found that out long ago."

"I rather agree, but what's the alternative?"

"Well," said Soames, "they've got the vote."

"Yes, that's always said. But somehow Parliament seems to matter less and less; there's a directive sense in the country now, which really settles things before we get down to them in Parliament. Look at this strike, for instance; we can do nothing about it."

"There must be government," said Soames.

"Administration—of course. But all we seem able to do in Parliament is to discuss administration afterwards without much effect. The fact is, things swoop around too quick for us nowadays."

"Well," said Soames, "you know your own business best. Parliament always was a talking shop." And with that unconscious quotation from Carlyle—an extravagant writer whom he curiously connected with revolution—he looked up at the Goya, and added: "I shouldn't like to see Parliament done away with, though. Ever heard any more of that red-haired young woman?"

"Marjorie Ferrar? Oddly enough, I saw her yesterday in Whitehall. She told me she was driving for Downing Street."

"She spoke to you?"

"Oh, yes. No ill-feeling."

"H'm!" said Soames. "I don't understand this generation. Is she married?"

"No."

"That chap MacGown had a lucky escape—not that he deserved it. Fleur doesn't miss her evenings?"

Michael did not answer. He did not know. Fleur and he were on such perfect terms that they had no real knowledge of each other's thoughts. Then, feeling his father-in-law's grey eye gimletting into him, he said hastily:

"Fleur's all right, sir."

Soames nodded. "Don't let her overdo this canteen."

"She's thoroughly enjoying it—gives her head a chance."

"Yes," said Soames, "she's got a good little head, when she doesn't lose it." He seemed again to consult the Goya, and added:

"By the way, that young Jon Forsyte is over here—

they tell me——staying at Green Street, and stoking an engine or something. A boy-and-girl affair; but I thought you ought to know."

"Oh!" said Michael, "thanks. I hadn't heard."

"I don't suppose she's heard, either," said Soames guardedly; "I told them not to tell her. D'you remember, in America, up at Mount Vernon, when I was taken ill?"

"Yes, sir; very well."

"Well, I wasn't. Fact is, I saw that young man and his wife talking to you on the stairs. Thought it better that Fleur shouldn't run up against them. These things are very silly, but you never can tell."

"No," said Michael, drily; "you never can tell. I remember liking the look of him a good deal."

"H'm!" muttered Soames: "He's the son of his father, I expect."

And, from the expression on his face, Michael formed the notion that this was a doubtful advantage.

No more was said, because of Soames' lifelong conviction that one did not say any more than one need say; and of Michael's prejudice against discussing Fleur seriously, even with her father. She had seemed to him quite happy lately. After five-and-a-half years of marriage, he was sure that mentally Fleur liked him, that physically she had no objection to him, and that a man was not sensible if he expected much more. She consistently declined, of course, to duplicate Kit, but only because she did not want to be put out of action again for months at a time. The more active, the happier she was——over this canteen for instance, she was in her glory. If, indeed, he had realised that Jon Forsyte was being fed there, Michael would have been troubled; as it was, the news of the young man's reappearance in England made no great impression. The Country held the field of one's attention those strenuous days. The multiple evidence of patriotism exhilarated him

—undergraduates at the docks, young women driving cars, shopfolk walking cheerfully to their work, the swarm of 'specials,' the general 'carrying-on.' Even the strikers were good-humoured. A secret conviction of his own concerning England was being reinforced day by day, in refutation of the pessimists. And there was no place so un-English at the moment, he felt, as the House of Commons, where people had nothing to do but pull long faces and talk over 'the situation.'

The news of the General Strike's collapse caught him as he was going home after driving Fleur to the canteen. A fizz and bustle in the streets, and the words: "Strike Over" scrawled extempore at street corners, preceded the "End of the Strike—Official" of the hurrying newsvendors. Michael stopped his car against the curb and bought a news-sheet. There it was! For a minute he sat motionless with a choky feeling, such as he had felt when the news of the Armistice came through. A sword lifted from over the head of England! A source of pleasure to her enemies dried up! People passed and passed him, each with a news-sheet, or a look in the eye. They were taking it almost as soberly as they had taken the strike itself. 'Good old England! We're a great people when we're up against it!' he thought, driving his car slowly on into Trafalgar Square. A group of men, who had obviously been strikers, stood leaning against the parapet. He tried to read their faces. Glad, sorry, ashamed, resentful, relieved? For the life of him he could not tell. Some defensive joke seemed going the round of them.

'No wonder we're a puzzle to foreigners!' thought Michael: 'The least understood people in the world!'

He moved on slowly round the square, into Whitehall. Here were some slight evidences of feeling. The block was thick around the Cenotaph and the entrance to Downing Street; and little cheers kept breaking out. A 'special' was escorting a lame man across the street. As he came back, Michael saw his face. Why, it was Uncle Hilary! His mother's youngest brother, Hilary Charwell, Vicar of St. Augustine's-in-the-Meads.

"Hallo, Michael!"

"You a 'special,' Uncle Hilary? Where's your cloth?"

"My dear! Are you one of those who think the Church debarred from mundane pleasure? You're not getting old-fashioned, Michael?"

Michael grinned. He had a real affection for Uncle Hilary, based on admiration for his thin, long face, so creased and humorous, on boyish recollection of a jolly uncle, on a suspicion that in Hilary Charwell had been lost a Polar explorer, or other sort of first-rate adventurer.

"That reminds me, Michael; when are you coming round to see us? I've got a topping scheme for airing 'The Meads'."

"Ah!" said Michael; "overcrowding's at the bottom of everything, even this strike."

"Right you are, my son. Come along, then, as soon as you can. You fellows in Parliament ought always to see things at first hand. You suffer from auto-intoxication in that House. And now pass on, young man, you're impeding the traffic."

Michael passed on, grinning. Good old Uncle Hilary! Humanising religion, and living dangerously—had climbed all the worst peaks in Europe; no sense of his own importance and a real sense of humour. Quite the best type of Englishman! They had tried to make him a dignitary, but he had jibbed at the gaiters and hat-ropes. He was what they called a 'live wire' and often committed the most dreadful indiscretions; but everybody liked him, even his own wife. Michael dwelt for a moment on his Aunt May. Forty—he supposed—with three children and fourteen hundred things to attend to every day; shingled, and cheerful as a sandboy. Nice-looking woman, Aunt May!

Having garaged his car, he remembered that he had not
lunched. It was three o'clock. Munching a biscuit, he
drank a glass of sherry, and walked over to the House of
Commons. He found it humming in anticipation of a
statement. Sitting back, with his legs stretched out, he
had qualms. What things had been done in here! The
abolitions of Slavery and of Child Labour, the Married
Woman's Property Act, Repeal of the Corn Laws; but
could they be done nowadays? And if not—was it a life?
He had said to Fleur that you couldn't change your vocation
twice and survive. But did he want to survive? Failing
Foggartism—and Foggartism hadn't failed only because
it hadn't started—what did he really care about?

Leaving the world better than he found it? Sitting
there, he couldn't help perceiving a certain vagueness about
such an aspiration, even when confined to England. It was
the aspiration of the House of Commons; but in the ebb
and flow of Party, it didn't seem to make much progress.
Better to fix on some definite bit of administrative work,
stick to it, and get something done. Fleur wanted him to
concentrate on Kenya for the Indians. Again rather remote,
and having little to do with England. What definite work
was most needed in connection with England? Education?
Bunkered again! How tell what was the best direction
into which to turn education? When they brought in
State Education, for instance, they had thought the question
settled. Now people were saying that State education had
ruined the State. Emigration? Attractive, but negative.
Revival of agriculture? Well, the two combined were
Foggartism, and he knew by now that nothing but bitter
hardship would teach those lessons; you might talk till
you were blue in the face without convincing anyone but
yourself.

What then?

"I've got a topping scheme for airing 'The Meads'."
The Meads was one of the worst slum parishes in London.
'Clear the slums!' thought Michael; 'that's practical anyway!' You could smell the slums, and feel them. They
stank and bit and bred corruption. And yet the dwellers
therein loved them; or at least preferred them to slums
they knew not of! And slum-dwellers were such good
sorts! Too bad to play at shuttlecock with them! He
must have a talk with Uncle Hilary. Lots of vitality in
England still—numbers of red-haired children! But the
vitality got sooted as it grew up—like plants in a back
garden. Slum clearance, smoke abolition, industrial peace,
emigration, agriculture, and safety in the air! 'Them's
my sentiments!' thought Michael. 'And if that isn't a large
enough policy for any man, I'm——!'

He turned his face towards the Statement, and thought
of his uncle's words about this 'House.' Were they all
really in a state of auto-intoxication here—continual slow
poisoning of the tissues? All these chaps around him
thought they were doing things. And he looked at the
chaps. He knew most of them, and had great respect for
many, but collectively he could not deny that they looked
a bit dazed. His neighbour to the right was showing his
front teeth in an asphyxiated smile. 'Really,' he thought;
'it's heroic how we all keep awake day after day!'

CHAPTER VIII

SECRET

IT would not have been natural that Fleur should rejoice in the collapse of the General Strike. A national outlook over such a matter was hardly in her character. Her canteen was completing the re-establishment in her of the social confidence which the Marjorie Ferrar affair had so severely shaken; and to be thoroughly busy with practical matters suited her. Recruited by Norah Curfew, by herself, Michael, and his Aunt Lady Alison Charwell, she had a first-rate crew of helpers of all ages, most of them in Society. They worked in the manner popularly attributed to negroes; they craned at nothing—not even beetles. They got up at, or stayed up to, all hours. They were never cross and always cheery. In a word, they seemed inspired. The difference they had made in the appearance of the railway's culinary premises was startling to the Company. Fleur herself was 'on the bridge' all the time. On her devolved the greasing of the official wheels, the snipping off of red tape in numberless telephonic duels, and the bearding of the managerial face. She had even opened her father's pocket to supplement the shortcomings she encountered. The volunteers were fed to repletion, and—on Michal's inspiration—she had undermined the pickets with surreptitious coffee dashed with rum, at odd hours of their wearisome vigils. Her provisioning car, entrusted to Holly, ran the blockade, by leaving and arriving, as though Harridge's, whence she drew her supplies, were the last place in its thoughts.

"Let us give the strikers," said Michael, "every possible excuse to wink the other eye."

The canteen, in fact, was an unqualified success. She had not seen Jon again, but she lived in that peculiar mixture of fear and hope which signifies a real interest in life. On the Friday Holly announced to her that Jon's wife had arrived—might she bring her down next morning?

"Oh! yes," said Fleur: "What is she like?"

"Attractive—with eyes like a water-nymph's or so Jon thinks; but it's quite the best type of water-nymph."

"M-m!" said Fleur.

She was checking a list on the telephone next day when Holly brought Anne. About Fleur's own height, straight and slim, darker in the hair, browner in complexion, browner in the eye (Fleur could see what Holly had meant by "water-nymph") her nose a little too sudden, her chin pointed and her teeth very white, her successor stood. Did she know that Jon and she——?

And stretching out her free hand, Fleur said:

"I think it's awfully sporting of you as an American. How's your brother Francis?"

The hand she squeezed was brown, dry, warm; the voice she heard only faintly American, as if Jon had been at it.

"You were just too good to Francis. He always talks of you. If it hadn't been for you——"

"That's nothing. Excuse me. . . . Ye-es? . . . No! If the Princess comes, ask her to be good enough to come when they're feeding. Yes—yes—thank you! To-morrow? Certainly. . . . Did you have a good crossing?"

"Frightful! I was glad Jon wasn't with me. I do so hate being green, don't you?"

"I never am," said Fleur.

That girl had Jon to bend above her when she was green! Pretty? Yes. The browned face was very alive—rather like Francis Wilmot's, but with those enticing eyes, much more eager. What was it about those eyes that made them so unusual and attractive?—surely the suspicion of a squint! She had a way of standing, too—a trick of the neck, the head was beautifully poised. Lovely clothes, of course! Fleur's glance swept swiftly down to calves and ankles. Not thick, not crooked! No luck!

"I think it's just wonderful of you to let me come and help."

"Not a bit. Holly will put you wise."

"That sounds nice and homey."

"Oh! We all use your expressions now. Will you take her provisioning, Holly?"

When the girl had gone, under Holly's wing, Fleur bit her lip. By the uncomplicated glance of Jon's wife she guessed that Jon had not told her. How awfully young! Fleur felt suddenly as if she herself had never had a youth. Ah! If Jon had not been caught away from her! Her bitten lip quivered, and she buried it in the mouthpiece of the telephone.

Whenever again—three or four times—before the canteen was closed, she saw the girl, she forced herself to be cordial. Instinctively she felt that she must shut no doors on life just now. What Jon's reappearance meant to her she could not tell; but no one should put a finger this time in whatever pie she chose to make. She was mistress of her face and movements now, as she had never been when she and Jon were babes in the wood. With a warped pleasure she heard Holly's: "Anne thinks you wonderful, Fleur!" No! Jon had not told his wife about her. It was like him, for the secret had not been his alone! But how long would that girl be left in ignorance? On the day the canteen closed she said to Holly:

"No one has told Jon's wife that he and I were once in love, I suppose?"

Holly shook her head.

"I'd rather they didn't, then."

"Of course not, my dear. I'll see to it. The child's nice, I think."

"Nice," said Fleur, "but not important."

"You've got to allow for the utter strangeness of everything. Americans are generally important, sooner or later."

"To themselves," said Fleur, and saw Holly smile. Feeling that she had revealed a corner of her feelings, she smiled too.

"Well, so long as they get on. They do, I suppose?"

"My dear, I've hardly seen Jon, but I should say it's perfectly successful. Now the strike's over they're coming down to us at Wansdon."

"Good! Well, this is the end of the old canteen. Let's powder our noses and get out; Father's waiting for me with the car. Can we drop you?"

"No, thanks; I'll walk."

"What? The old *gêne*? Funny how hard things die!"

"Yes; when you're a Forsyte," murmured Holly: "You see, we don't show our feelings. It's airing them that kills feelings."

"Ah!" said Fleur: "Well, God bless you, as they say, and give Jon my love. I'd ask them to lunch, but you're off to Wansdon?"

"The day after to-morrow."

In the little round mirror Fleur saw her face mask itself more thoroughly, and turned to the door.

"I *may* look in at Aunt Winifred's, if I've time. So long!"

Going down the stairs she thought: 'So it's air that kills feelings!'

Soames, in the car, was gazing at Riggs' back. The fellow was as lean as a rail.

"Finished with that?" he said to her.

"Yes, dear."

"Good job, too. Wearing yourself to a shadow."

"Why? Do I look thin, Dad?"

"No," said Soames, "no. That's your mother. But you can't keep on at that rate. Would you like some air? Into the Park, Riggs."

Passing into that haven, he murmured:

"I remember when your grandmother drove here every day, regular as clockwork. People had habits, then. Shall we stop and have a look at that Memorial affair they made such a fuss about?"

"I've seen it, Dad."

"So have I," said Soames. "Stunt sculpture! Now, that St. Gaudens statue at Washington *was* something." And he looked at her sidelong. Thank goodness she didn't know of the way he had fended her off from young Jon Forsyte over there. She must have heard by now that the fellow was in London, and staying at her Aunt's, too! And now the strike was off, and normal railway services beginning again, he would be at a loose end! But perhaps he would go back to Paris; his mother was there still, he understood. It was on the tip of his tongue to ask. Instinct, however, potent only in his dealings with Fleur, stopped him. If she had seen the young man, she wouldn't tell him of it. She was looking somehow secret—or was that just imagination?

No! He couldn't see her thoughts. Good thing, perhaps! Who could afford to have his thoughts seen? The recesses, ramifications, excesses of thought! Only when sieved and filtered was thought fit for exposure. And again Soames looked sidelong at his daughter.

She was thinking, indeed, to purposes that would have upset him. How was she going to see Jon alone before he left for Wansdon? She could call to-morrow, of course, openly at Green Street, and probably *not* see him. She could ask him to lunch in South Square, but hardly without

his wife or her own husband. There was, in fact, no way
of seeing him alone except by accident. And she began
trying to plan one. On the point of perceiving that the
essence of an accident was that it could not be planned, she
planned it. She would go to Green Street at nine in the
morning to consult Holly and Anne on the canteen accounts. After such strenuous days Holly and Anne might
surely be breakfasting in bed. Val had gone back to Wansdon, Aunt Winifred never got up! Jon *might* be alone!
And she turned to Soames:

"Awfully sweet of you, Dad, to be airing me; I *am*
enjoying it."

"Like to get out and have a look at the ducks? The
swans have got a brood at Mapledurham again this year."

The swans! How well she remembered the six little
grey destroyers following the old swans over the green-
tinged water, that six-year-gone summer of her love!
Crossing the grass down to the Serpentine, she felt a sort
of creeping sweetness. But nobody—nobody should know
of what went on inside her. Whatever happened—and,
after all, most likely nothing would happen—she would
save face this time—strongest motive in the world, as
Michael said.

"Your grandfather used to bring me here when I was a
shaver," said her father's voice beside her. It did not
add: "And I used to bring that wife of mine when we
were first married." Irene! She had liked water and trees.
She had liked all beauty, and she hadn't liked him!

"Eton jackets. Sixty years ago and more. Who'd have
thought it then?"

"Who'd have thought what, Dad? That Eton jackets
would still be in?"

"That chap—Tennyson, wasn't it?—'The old order
changeth, giving place to new.' I can't see *you* in high
necks and skirts down to your feet, to say nothing of

bustles. Women then were defended up to the nines, but you knew just as much about them as you do now—and that's precious little."

"I wonder. Do you think people's passions are what they used to be, Dad?"

Soames brooded into his hand. Now, why had she said that? He had once told her that a grand passion was a thing of the past, and she had replied that she had one. And suddenly he was back in steamy heat, redolent of earth and potted pelargonium, kicking a hot water pipe in a greenhouse at Mapledurham. Perhaps she'd been right; there was always a lot of human nature about.

"Passions!" he said: "Well, you still read of people putting their heads under the gas. In old days they used to drown themselves. Let's go and have tea, at that kiosk place."

When they were seated, and the pigeons were enjoying his cake, he took a long look at her. She had her legs crossed—and very nice they were!—and just that difference in her body from the waist up, from so many young women he saw about. She didn't sit in a curve, but with a slight hollow in her back, giving the impression of backbone and a poise to her head and neck. She was shingled again—the custom had unexpected life—but, after all, her neck was remarkably white and round. Her face—short, with its firm rounded chin, very little powder and no rouge, with its dark-lashed white lids, clear-glancing hazel eyes, short, straight nose and broad low brow, with the chestnut hair over its ears, and its sensibly kissable mouth—really it was a credit!

"I should think," he said, "you'd be glad to have more time for Kit again. He's a rascal. What d'you think he asked me for yesterday—a hammer!"

"Yes; he's always breaking things up. I smack him as little as possible, but it's unavoidable at times—nobody else is allowed to. Mother got him used to it while we were away, so he looks on it as all in the day's work."

"Children," said Soames, "are funny things. We weren't made such a fuss of when I was young."

"Forgive me, Dad, but I think *you* make more fuss of him than anybody."

"What?" said Soames: "I?"

"You do exactly as he tells you. Did you give him the hammer?"

"Hadn't one—what should I carry hammers about for?"

Fleur laughed. "No; but you take him so seriously. Michael takes him ironically."

"The little chap's got a twinkle," said Soames.

"Mercifully. Didn't you spoil *me*, Dad?"

Soames gaped at a pigeon.

"Can't tell," he said. "Do you feel spoiled?"

"When I want things, I want things."

He knew that; but so long as she wanted the right things!

"And when I don't get them, I'm not safe."

"Who says that?"

"No one ever says it, but I know it."

H'm! What was she wanting now? Should he ask? And, as if attending to the crumbs on his lapel, he took 'a lunar.' That face of hers, whose eyes for a moment were off guard, was dark with some deep—he couldn't tell! Secret! That's what it was!

CHAPTER IX

RENCOUNTER

WITH the canteen accounts in her hand, Fleur stepped out between her tubbed bay-trees. A quarter to nine by Big Ben! Twenty odd minutes to walk across the Green Park! She had drunk her coffee in bed, to elude questions —and there, of course, was Dad with his nose glued to the dining-room window. She waved the accounts, and he withdrew his face as if they had flicked him. He was ever so good, but he shouldn't always be dusting her—she wasn't a piece of china!

She walked briskly. She had no honeysuckle sensations this morning, but felt hard and bright. If Jon had come back to England to stay, she must get him over. The sooner the better, without fuss! Passing the geraniums in front of Buckingham Palace, just out and highly scarlet, she felt her blood heating. Not walk so fast or she would arrive damp! The trees were far advanced; the Green Park, under breeze and sun, smelled of grass and leaves. Spring had not smelled so good for years. A longing for the country seized on Fleur. Grass and trees and water—her hours with Jon had been passed among them—one hour in this very Park, before he took her down to Robin Hill! Robin Hill had been sold to some peer or other, and she wished him joy of it—she knew its history as of some unlucky ship! That house had 'done in' her father, and Jon's father, yes—and his grandfather, she believed, to say nothing of herself. One would not be 'done in' again so easily! And, passing into Piccadilly, Fleur smiled at her green youth. In the early windows of the Club nicknamed by George Forsyte the 'Iseeum,' no one of his compeers sat as yet, above the moving humours of the street, sipping from glass or cup, and puffing his conclusions out in smoke.

Fleur could just remember him, her old Cousin George Forsyte, who used to sit there, fleshy and sardonic behind the curving panes; Cousine George, who had owned the 'White Monkey' up in Michael's study. Uncle Montague Dartie, too, whom she remembered because the only time she had seen him he had pinched her in a curving place, saying: "What are little girls made of?" so that she had clapped her hands when she heard that he had broken his neck, soon after; a horrid man, with fat cheeks and a dark moustache, smelling of scent and cigars. Rounding the last corner, she felt breathless. Geraniums were in her Aunt's window boxes—but not the fuchsias yet. Was *their* room the one she herself used to have? And, taking her hand from her heart, she rang the bell.

"Ah! Smither, anybody down?"

"Only Mr. Jon's down yet, Miss Fleur."

Why did hearts wobble? Sickening—when one was perfectly cool!

"He'll do for the moment, Smither. Where is he?"

"Having breakfast, Miss Fleur."

"All right; show me in. I don't mind having another cup myself."

Under her breath, she declined the creaking noun who was preceding her to the dining-room: "Smither: O Smither: Of a Smither: To a Smither: A Smither." Silly!

"Mrs. Michael Mont, Mr. Jon. Shall I get you some fresh coffee, Miss Fleur?"

"No, thank you, Smither." Stays creaked, the door was shut. Jon was standing up.

"Fleur!"

"Well, Jon?"

She could hold his hand and keep her pallor, though the blood was in *his* cheeks, no longer smudged.

"Did I feed you nicely?"

"Splendidly. How are you, Fleur? Not tired after all that?"

"Not a bit. How did you like stoking?"

"Fine! My engine-driver was a real brick. Anne will be so disappointed; she's having a lie-off."

"She was quite a help. Nearly six years, Jon; you haven't changed much."

"Nor you."

"Oh! *I* have. Out of knowledge."

"Well, I don't see it. Have you had breakfast?"

"Yes. Sit down and go on with yours. I came round to see Holly about some accounts. Is she in bed, too?"

"I expect so."

"Well, I'll go up directly. How does England feel, Jon?"

"Topping. Can't leave it again. Anne says she doesn't mind."

"Where are you going to settle?"

"Somewhere near Val and Holly, if we can get a place, to grow things."

"Still on growing things?"

"More than ever."

"How's the poetry?"

"Pretty dud."

Fleur quoted:

" 'Voice in the night crying, down in the old sleeping Spanish city darkened under her white stars.' "

"Good Lord! Do you remember that?"

"Yes."

His eyes were as straight, his lashes as dark as ever.

"Would you like to meet Michael, Jon, and see my infant?"

"Rather!"

"When do you go down to Wansdon?"

"To-morrow or the day after."

"Then, won't you both come and lunch to-morrow?"

"We'd love to."

"Half-past one. Holly and Aunt Winifred, too. Is your mother still in Paris?"

"Yes. She thinks of settling there."

"Well, Jon—things fall on their feet, don't they?"

"They do."

"Shall I give you some more coffee? Aunt Winifred prides herself on her coffee."

"Fleur, you do look splendid."

"Thank you! Have you been down to see Robin Hill?"

"Not yet. Some potentate's got it now."

"Does your—does Anne find things amusing here?"

"She's terribly impressed—says we're a nation of gentlemen. Did you ever think that?"

"Positively—no; comparatively—perhaps."

"It all smells so good here."

"The poet's nose. D'you remember our walk at Wansdon?"

"I remember everything, Fleur."

"That's honest. So do I. It took me some time to remember that I'd forgotten. How long did it take you?"

"Still longer, I expect."

"Well, Michael's the best male I know."

"Anne's the best female."

"How fortunate—isn't it? How old is she?"

"Twenty-one."

"Just right for you. Even if we hadn't been star-crossed, I was always too old for you. God! Weren't we young fools?"

"I don't see that. It was natural—it was beautiful."

"Still got ideals? Marmalade? It's Oxford."

"Yes. They can't make marmalade out of Oxford."

"Jon, your hair grows exactly as it used to. Have you noticed mine?"

"I've been trying to."

"Don't you like it?"

"Not so much, quite; and yet—"

"You mean I shouldn't look well out of the fashion. Very acute! You don't mind *her* being shingled, apparently."

"It suits Anne."

"Did her brother tell you much about me?"

"He said you had a lovely house; and nursed him like an angel."

"Not like an angel; like a young woman of fashion. There's still a difference."

"Anne was awfully grateful for that. She's told you?"

"Yes. But I'm afraid, between us, we sent Francis home rather cynical. Cynicism grows here; d'you notice it in me?"

"I think you put it on."

"My dear! I take it off when I talk to you. You were always an innocent. Don't smile—you were! That's why you were well rid of me. Well, I never thought I should see you again."

"Nor I. I'm sorry Anne's not down."

"You've never told her about me."

"How did you know that?"

"By the way she looks at me."

"Why should I tell her?"

"No reason in the world. Let the dead past—It's fun to see you again, though. Shake hands. I'm going up to Holly now."

Their hands joined over the marmalade on his plate.

"We're not children now, Jon. Till to-morrow, then! You'll like my house. *A revederci!*"

Going up the stairs she thought with resolution about nothing.

"Can I come in, Holly?"

"Fleur! My dear!"

That thin, rather sallow face, so charmingly intelligent, was propped against a pillow. Fleur had the feeling that, of all people, it was most difficult to keep one's thoughts from Holly.

"These accounts," she said. "I'm to see that official ass at ten. Did you order all these sides of bacon?"

The thin sallow hand took the accounts, and between the large grey eyes came a furrow.

"Nine? No—yes; that's right. Have you seen Jon?"

"Yes; he's the only early bird. Will you all come to lunch with us to-morrow?"

"If you think it'll be wise, Fleur."

"I think it'll be pleasant."

She met the search of the grey eyes steadily, and with secret anger. No one should see into her—no one should interfere!

"All right then, we'll expect you all four at one-thirty. I must run now."

She did run; but since she really had no appointment with any "official ass," she went back into the Green Park and sat down.

So that was Jon—now! Terribly like Jon—then! His eyes deeper, his chin more obstinate—that perhaps was all the difference. He still had his sunny look; he still believed in things. He still—admired her. Ye-es! A little wind talked above her in a tree. The day was surprisingly fine—the first really fine day since Easter! What should she give them for lunch? How should she deal with Dad? He must not be there! To have perfect command of oneself was all very well; to have perfect command of one's father was not so easy. A pattern of leaves covered her short skirt, the sun warmed her knees; she crossed them and leaned back. Eve's first costume—a pattern of leaves. . . . "Wise?" Holly had said. Who knew? Shrimp cocktails? No! English food. Pancakes—certainly! . . . To get rid of Dad, she must propose herself with Kit at Mapledurham for the day after; then he would go, to prepare for them. Her mother was still in France. The others would be gone to Wansdon. Nothing to wait for in town. A nice warm sun on her neck. A scent of grass— of honeysuckle! Oh! dear!

CHAPTER X

AFTER LUNCH

THAT the most pregnant function of human life is the meal, will be admitted by all who take part in these recurrent crises. The impossibility of getting down from table renders it the most formidable of human activities among people civilised to the point of swallowing not only their food but their feelings.

Such a conclusion at least was present to Fleur during that lunch. That her room was Spanish, reminded her that it was not with Jon she had spent her honeymoon in Spain. There had been a curious moment, too, before lunch; for, the first words Jon had spoken on seeing Michael, had been:

"Hallo! This is queer! Was Fleur with you that day at Mount Vernon?"

What was this? Had she been kept in the dark?

Then Michael had said:

"You remember, Fleur? The young Englishman I met at Mount Vernon."

" 'Ships that pass in the night!' " said Fleur.

Mount Vernon! So *they* had met there! And she had not!

"Mount Vernon is lovely. But you ought to see Richmond, Anne. We could go after lunch. You haven't been to Richmond for ages, I expect, Aunt Winifred. We could take Robin Hill on the way home, Jon."

"Your old home, Jon? Oh! Do let's!"

At that moment she hated the girl's eager face at which Jon was looking.

"There's the potentate," he said.

75

"Oh!" said Fleur, quickly, "He's at Monte Carlo. I read it yesterday. Could *you* come, Michael?"

"Afraid I've got a Committee. And the car can only manage five."

"It would be just too lovely!"

Oh! that American enthusiasm! It was comforting to hear her Aunt's flat voice opining that it would be a nice little run—the chestnuts would be out in the Park.

Had Michael really a Committee? She often knew what Michael really had, she generally knew more or less what he was thinking, but now she did not seem to know. In telling him last night of this invitation to lunch, she had carefully obliterated the impression by an embrace warmer than usual—he must not get any nonsense into his head about Jon! When, too, to her father she had said:

"Couldn't Kit and I come down to you the day after to-morrow; but you'll want a day there first, I'm afraid, if Mother's not there," how carefully she had listened to the tone of his reply:

"H'm! Ye—es! I'll go down to-morrow morning."

Had he scented anything; had Michael scented anything? She turned to Jon.

"Well, Jon, what d'you think of my house?"

"It's very like you."

"Is that a compliment?"

"To the house? Of course."

"Francis didn't exaggerate then?"

"Not a bit."

"You haven't seen Kit yet. We'll have him down. Coaker, please ask Nurse to bring Kit down, unless he's asleep. . . . He'll be three in July; quite a good walker already. It makes one frightfully old!"

The entrance of Kit and his silver dog caused a sort of cooing sound, speedily checked, for three of the women were of Forsyte stock, and the Forsytes did not coo. He stood there, blue and rather Dutch, with a slight frown and his hair bright, staring at the company.

"Come here, my son. This is Jon—your second cousin once removed."

Kit advanced.

"S'all I bwing my 'orse in?"

"Horse, Kit. No; shake hands."

The small hand went up; Jon's hand came down.

"You got dirty nails."

She saw Jon flush, heard Anne's: "Isn't he just too cunning?" and said:

"Kit, you're very rude. So would you have, if you'd been stoking an engine."

"Yes, old man, I've been washing them ever since, but I can't get them clean."

"Why?"

"It's got into the skin."

"Le' me see."

"Go and shake hands with your great-aunt, Kit."

"No."

"Dear little chap," said Winifred. "Such a bore, isn't it, Kit?"

"Very well, then, go out again, and get your manners, and bring them in."

"All wight."

His exit, closed in by the silver dog, was followed by a general laugh; Fleur said, softly:

"Little wretch—poor Jon!" And through her lashes she saw Jon give her a grateful look. . . .

In this mid-May fine weather the view from Richmond Hill had all the width and leafy charm which had drawn so many Forsytes in phaetons and barouches, in hansom cabs and motor cars from immemorial time, or at least from the days of George the Fourth. The winding river shone discreetly, far down there; and the trees of the encompassing landscape, though the oaks were still goldened, had just begun to have a brooding look; in July they would be heavy and blueish. Curiously, few houses showed among the trees and fields; very scanty evidence of man, within twelve miles of London! The spirit of an older England seemed to have fended jerry-builders from a prospect sacred to the ejaculations of four generations.

Of those five on the terrace Winifred best expressed that guarding spirit, with her:

"Really, it's a very pretty view!"

A view—a view! And yet a view was not what it had been when old Jolyon travelled the Alps with that knapsack of brown leather and square shape, still in his grandson Jon's possession; or Swithin above his greys, rolling his neck with consequence toward the lady by his side, had pointed with his whip down at the river and pouted: "A pooty little view!" Or James, crouched over his long knees in some gondola, had examined the Grand Canal at Venice with doubting eyes, and muttered: "They never told me the water was this colour!" Or Nicholas, taking his constitutional at Matlock, had opined that the gorge was the finest in England. No, a view was not what it had been! George Forsyte and Montague Dartie, with their backs to it, quizzically contemplating the Liberty ladies brought down to be fed, had started that rot; and now the young folk didn't use the expression, but just ejaculated: "Christ!" or words to that effect.

But there was Anne, of course, like an American, with clasped hands, and:

"Isn't it too lovely, Jon? It's sort of romantic!"

And so to the Park, where Winifred chanted automatically at sight of the chestnuts, and every path and patch of fern and fallen tree drew from Holly or Jon some riding recollection.

"Look, Anne, that's where I threw myself off my pony as a kid when I lost my stirrup and got so bored with being bumped."

Or: "Look, Jon! Val and I had a race down that avenue. Oh! and there's the log we used to jump. Still there!"

And Anne was in ecstasies over the deer and the grass, so different from the American varieties.

To Fleur the Park meant nothing.

"Jon," she said, suddenly, "what are you going to do to get in at Robin Hill?"

"Tell the lodge-keeper that I want to show my wife where I lived as a boy; and give him a couple of good reasons. I don't want to see the house, all new furniture and that."

"Couldn't we go in at the bottom, through the coppice?" and her eyes added: "As we did that day."

"We might come on someone, and get turned back."

The couple of good reasons secured their top entrance to the grounds; the 'family' was not 'in residence.'

Bosinney's masterpiece wore its mellowest aspect. The sun-blinds were down, for the sun was streaming on its front, past the old oak tree, where was now no swing. In Irene's rose-garden, which had replaced old Jolyon's fernery, buds were forming, but only one rose was out.

" 'Rose, you Spaniard!' " Something clutched Fleur's heart. What was Jon thinking—what remembering, with those words and that frown? Just here she had sat between his father and his mother, believing that she and Jon would live here some day; together watch the roses bloom, the old oak drop its leaves; together say to their guests: "Look! There's the Grand Stand at Epsom—see? Just above those poplars!"

And now she could not even walk beside him, who was playing guide to that girl, his wife! Beside her aunt she walked instead. Winifred was extremely intrigued. She had never yet seen this house, which Soames had built with the brains of young Bosinney; which Irene, with 'that unfortunate little affair of hers' had wrecked; this house where Old Uncle Jolyon, and Cousin Jolyon had died;

and Irene, so ironically, had lived and had this boy Jon—
a nice boy, too; this house of Forsyte song and story. It
was very distinguished and belonged to a peer now, which,
since it had gone out of the family, seemed suitable. In the
walled fruit-garden, she said to Fleur:

"Your grandfather came down here once, to see how it
was getting on. I remember his saying: 'It'll cost a pretty
penny to keep up.' And I should think it does. But it was
a pity to sell it. Irene's doing, of course! She never cared
for the family. Now, if only——" But she stopped short
of the words: "you and Jon had made a match of it."

"What on earth would Jon have done, Auntie, with a
great place like this so near London? He's a poet."

"Yes," murmured Winifred—not very quick, because
in her youth quickness had not been fashionable. "There's
too much glass, perhaps." And they went down through
the meadow.

The coppice! Still there at the bottom of the field. But
Fleur lingered now, stood by the fallen log, waited till she
could say:

"Listen! The cuckoo, Jon!"

The cuckoo's song, and the sight of bluebells under the
larch trees! Beside her Jon stood still! Yes, and the Spring
stood still. There went the song—over and over!

"It was *here* we came on your mother, Jon, and our
stars were crossed. Oh, Jon!"

Could so short a sound mean so much, say so much, be
so startling? His face! She jumped on to the log at once.

"No ghosts, my dear!"

And, with a start, Jon looked up at her.

She put her hands on his shoulders and jumped down.
And among the bluebells they went on. And the bird sang
after them.

"That bird repeats himself," said Fleur.

CHAPTER XI

PERAMBULATION

THE instinct in regard to his daughter, which by now formed part of his protective covering against the machinations of Fate, had warned Soames, the day before, that Fleur was up to something when she went out while he was having breakfast. Seen through the window waving papers at him, she had an air of unreality, or at least an appearance of not telling him anything. As something not quite genuine in the voice warns a dog that he is about to be left, so was Soames warned by the ostentation of those papers. He finished his breakfast, therefore, too abruptly for one constitutionally given to marmalade, and set forth to Green Street. Since that young fellow Jon was staying there, this fashionable locality was the seat of any reasonable uneasiness. If, moreover, there was a place in the world where Soames could still unbutton his soul, it was his sister Winifred's drawing-room, on which in 1879 he himself had impressed so deeply the personality of Louis Quinze that, in spite of jazz and Winifred's desire to be in the heavier modern fashion, that monarch's incurable levity was still to be observed.

Taking a somewhat circuitous course and looking in at the Connoisseurs' Club on the way, Soames did not arrive until after Fleur's departure. The first remark from Smither confirmed the uneasiness which had taken him forth.

"Mr. Soames! Oh! What a pity—Miss Fleur's just gone! And nobody down yet but Mr. Jon."

"Oh!" said Soames. "Did she see him?"

"Yes, sir. He's in the dining-room, if you'd like to go in."

Soames shook his head.

"How long are they staying, Smither?"

"Well, I did hear Mrs. Val say they were all going back to Wansdon the day after to-morrow. We shall be all alone again in case you were thinking of coming to us, Mr. Soames."

Again Soames shook his head. "Too busy," he said.

"What a beautiful young lady Miss Fleur 'as grown, to be sure; such a colour she 'ad this morning!"

Soames gave vent to an indeterminate sound. The news was not to his liking, but he could hardly say so in front of an institution. One could never tell how much Smither knew. She had creaked her way through pretty well every family secret in her time, from the days when his own matrimonial relations supplied Timothy's with more than all the gossip it required. Yes, and were not his matrimonial relations, twice-laid, still supplying the raw material? Curiously sinister it seemed to him just then, that the son of his supplanter Jolyon should be here in this house, the nearest counterfeit of that old homing centre of the Forsytes, Timothy's in the Bayswater Road. What a perversity there was in things! And, repeating the indeterminate sound, he said:

"By the way, I suppose that Mr. Stainford never came here again?"

"Oh, yes, Mr. Soames; he called yesterday to see Mr. Val; but Mr. Val was gone."

"He did—did he?" said Soames, round-eyed. "What did he take this time?"

"Oh! Of course I knew better than to let him in."

"You didn't give him Mr. Val's address in the country?"

"Oh, no, sir; he knew it."

"Deuce he did!"

"Shall I tell the mistress you're here, Mr. Soames? She must be nearly down by now."

"No; don't disturb her."

"I am that sorry, sir; it's always such a pleasure to her to see you."

Old Smither bridling! A good soul! No such domestics nowadays! And, putting on his hat, Soames touched its brim, murmuring:

"Well, good-bye, Smither. Give her my love!" and went out.

'So!' he thought, 'Fleur's seen that boy!' The whole thing would begin over again! He had known it! And, very slowly, with his hat rather over his eyes, he made for Hyde Park Corner. This was for him a moment in deep waters, when the heart must be hardened to this dangerous decision or to that. With the tendency for riding past the hounds inherited from his father James in all matters which threatened the main securities of life, Soames rushed on in thought to the ruin of his daughter's future, wherein so sacredly was embalmed his own.

"Such a colour she 'ad this morning!" When she waved those papers at him, she was pale enough—too pale! A confounded chance! Breakfast time, too—worst time in the day—most intimate! His naturally realistic nature apprehended all the suggestions that lay in breakfast. Those who breakfasted alone together, slept together as often as not. Putting things into her head! Yes; and they were not boy and girl now! Well, it all depended on what their feelings were, if they still had any. And who was to know? Who, in heaven's name, was to know? Automatically he had begun to encompass the Artillery Memorial. A great white thing which he had never yet taken in properly, and didn't know that he wanted to. Yet somehow it was very real, and suited to his mood—faced things; nothing high-flown about that gun—short, barking brute of a thing; or those dark men—drawn and devoted under their steel hats! Nothing pretty-pretty about that memorial—no angels' wings there! No Georges and no dragons, nor horses on the prance; no panoply, and no *panache!* There it 'sot'— as they used to say—squatted like a great white toad on the nation's life. Concreted thunder. Not an illusion about it! Good thing to look at once a day, and see what you'd got to avoid. 'I'd like to rub the noses of those Crown Princes and military cocks-o'-the-walk on it,' thought Soames, 'with their—what was it?—"fresh and merry wars!"' And, crossing the road in the sunshine, he passed into the Park, moving towards Knightsbridge.

But about Fleur? Was he going to take the bull by the horns, or to lie low? Must be one thing or the other. He walked rapidly now, concentrated in face and movement, stalking as it were his own thoughts with a view to finality. He passed out at Knightsbridge, and after unseeing scrutiny of two or three small shops where in his time he had picked up many a bargain, for himself or shopman, he edged past Tattersall's. That hung on—they still sold horses there, he believed! Horses had never been in his line, but he had not lived in Montpellier Square without knowing the habitués of Tattersall's by sight. Like everything else that was crusted, they'd be pulling it down before long, he shouldn't wonder, and putting up some motor place or cinema!

Suppose he talked to Michael? No! Worse than useless. Besides, he couldn't talk about Fleur and that boy to anyone —thereby hung too long a tale; and the tale was his own. Montpellier Square! He had turned into the very place, whether by design he hardly knew. It hadn't changed—but was all slicked up since he was last there, soon after the war. Builders and decorators must have done well lately —about the only people who had. He walked along the right side of the narrow square, where he had known tur- bulence and tragedy. There the house was, looking much as it used to, not quite so neat, and a little more florid. Why had he ever married that woman? What had made him so set on it? Well! She had done her best to deter him. But—God!—how he had wanted her! To this day he could recognise that. And at first—at first, he had thought, and perhaps she had thought—but who could tell? —*he* never could! And then slowly—or was it quickly? —the end; a ghastly business! He stood still by the square railings, and stared at the doorway that had been his own, as if from its green paint and its brass number he might receive inspiration how to choke love in his own daughter for the son of his own wife—yes, how to choke it before it spread and choked her?

And as, on those days and nights of his first married life, returning home, he had sought in vain for inspiration how to awaken love, so now no inspiration came to tell him how to strangle love. And, doggedly, he turned out of the little square.

In a way it was ridiculous to be fussing about the matter; for, after all, Michael was a good young fellow, and her marriage far from unhappy, so far as he could see. As for young Jon, presumably he had married for love; there hadn't been anything else to marry for, he believed —unless he had been misinformed, the girl and her brother had been museum pieces, two Americans without money to speak of. And yet—there was the moon, and he could not forget how Fleur had always wanted it. A desire to have what she hadn't yet got was her leading characteristic. Impossible, too, to blink his memory of her, six years ago —to forget her body crumpled and crushed into the sofa in the dark that night when he came back from Robin Hill and broke the news to her. Perusing with his mind the record since, Soames had an acute and comfortless feeling that she had, as it were, been marking time, that all her fluttering activities, even the production of Kit, had been in the nature of a makeshift. Like the age to which she belonged, she had been lifting her feet up and down without getting anywhere, because she didn't know where she wanted to get. And yet, of late, since she had been round the world, he had seemed to notice something quieter and more solid in her conduct, as if settled purposes were pushing up, and she were coming to terms at last with her daily life. Look, for instance, at the way she had tackled this canteen! And, turning his face homeward, Soames had a vision of a common not far from Mapledurham, where some fool had started a fire which had burned the gorse, and of the grass pushing up, almost impudently green and young, through the charred embers of that conflagration. Rather like things generally, when you thought of it! The war had burned them all out, but things, yes, and people, too—one noticed —were beginning to sprout a bit, as if they felt again it might be worth while. Why, even he himself had regained some of his old connoisseur's desire to have nice things! It all depended on what you saw ahead, on whether you could eat and drink because to-morrow you didn't die. With this Dawes Settlement and Locarno business, and the General Strike broken, there might even be another long calm, like the Victorian, which would make things possible. He was seventy-one, but one could always dwell on Timothy, who had lived to be a hundred, fixed star in shifting skies. And Fleur—only twenty-four—might almost outlive the century if she, or, rather the century, took care and bottled up its unruly passions, its disordered longings, and all that silly rushing along to nowhere in particular. If they steadied down, the age might yet become a golden, or a platinum, age at any rate. Even he might live to see the income tax at half-a-crown. 'No,' he thought, confused between his daughter and the age; 'she mustn't go throwing her cap over the windmill. It's short-sighted!' And, his blood warmed by perambulation, he became convinced that he would not speak to her, but lie low, and trust to that common-sense, of which she surely had her share—oh, yes! 'Just keep my eyes open, and speak to no one,' he thought; 'least said, soonest mended.'

He had come again to the Artillery Memorial; and for the second time he moved around it. No! A bit of a blot —it seemed to him, now—so literal and heavy! Would that great white thing help Consols to rise? Some thing with wings might, after all, have been preferable. Some encouragement to people to take shares or go into domestic service; help, in fact, to make life liveable, instead of re-minding them all the time that they had already once been blown to perdition and might again be. Those Artillery fellows—he had read somewhere—loved their guns, and wanted to be reminded of them. But did anybody else love their guns, or want reminder? Not those Artillery fellows would look at this every day outside St. George's Hospital, but Tom, Dick, Harry, Peter, Gladys, Joan and Marjorie. 'Mistake!' thought Soames; 'and a pretty heavy one. Something sedative, statue of Vulcan, or somebody on a horse; that's what's wanted!' And remembering George III. on a horse, he smiled grimly. Anyway, there the thing was, and would have to stay! But it was high time artists went back to nymphs and dolphins, and other evidences of a settled life.

When at lunch Fleur suggested that he would want a day's law at Mapledurham before she and Kit came down, he again felt there was something behind; but, relieved enough at getting her, he let 'the sleeping dog' lie; nor did he mention his visit to Green Street.

"The weather looks settled," he said. "You want some sun after that canteen. They talk about these ultra-violet rays. Plain sunshine used to be good enough. The doctors'll be finding something extra-pink before long. If they'd only let things alone!"

"Darling, it amuses them."

"Re-discovering what our grandmothers knew so well that we've forgotten 'em, and calling 'em by fresh names! A thing isn't any more wholesome to eat, for instance, because they've invented the word "vitamin." Why, your grandfather ate an orange every day of his life, because his old doctor told him to, at the beginning of the last century. Vitamins! Don't you let Kit get faddy about his food. It's a long time before he'll go to school—that's one comfort. School feeding!"

"Did they feed you so badly, Dad?"

"Badly! How we grew up, I don't know. We ate our principal meal in twenty minutes, and were playing football ten minutes after. But nobody thought about digestion, then."

"Isn't that an argument for thinking of it now?"

"A good digestion," said Soames, "is the whole secret of life." And he looked at his daughter. Thank God! *She* wasn't peaky. So far as he knew, her digestion was excellent. She might fancy herself in love, or out of it; but so long as she was unconscious of her digestion, she would come through. "The thing is to walk as much as you can, in these days of cars," he added.

"Yes," said Fleur, "I had a nice walk this morning."

Was she challenging him over her apple charlotte? If so, he wasn't going to rise.

"So did I," he said. "I went all about. We'll have some golf down there."

She looked at him for a second, then said a surprising thing:

"Yes, I believe I'm getting middle-aged enough for golf."

Now what did she mean by that?

CHAPTER XII

PRIVATE FEELINGS

ON the day of the lunch party and the drive to Robin
Hill, Michael really had a Committee, but he also
had his private feelings and wanted to get on terms with
them. There are natures in which discovery of what
threatens happiness perverts to prejudice all judgment of
the disturbing object. Michael's was not such. He had taken
a fancy to the young Englishman met at the home of that
old American George Washington, partly, indeed, because
he *was* English; and, seeing him now seated next to Fleur,
—second cousin and first love—he was unable to revise the
verdict. The boy had a nice face, and was better-looking
than himself; he had attractive hair, a strong chin, straight
eyes, and a modest bearing; there was no sense in blinking
facts like those. The Free Trade in love, which obtained
amongst pleasant people, forbade Michael to apply the
cruder principles of Protection even in thoughts. Fortunately, the boy was married to this slim and attractive girl,
who looked at one—as Mrs. Val had put it to him—like
a guaranteed-pure water-nymph! Michael's private feelings were therefore more concerned with Fleur than with
the young man himself. But hers was a difficult face to
read, a twisting brain to follow, a heart hard to get at;
and—was Jon Forsyte the reason why? He remembered
how in Cork Street this boy's elderly half-sister—that fly-
away little lady, June Forsyte—had blurted out to him that
Fleur ought to have married her younger brother—first he
had ever heard of it. How painfully it had affected him
with its intimation that he played but second fiddle in the
life of his beloved! He remembered, too, some cautious and
cautionary allusions by "old Forsyte." Coming from that

model of secrecy and suppressed feelings, they, too, had made on Michael a deep and lasting impression, reinforced by his own failure to get at the bottom of Fleur's heart. He went to his Committee with but half his mind on public matters. What had nipped that early love affair in the bud and given him his chance? Not sudden dislike, lack of health, or lack of money—not relationship, for Mrs. Val Dartie had married her second cousin apparently with everyone's consent. Michael, it will be seen, had remained quite ignorant of the skeleton in Soames' cupboard. Such Forsytes as he had met, reticent about family affairs, had never mentioned it; and Fleur had never even spoken of her first love, much less of the reason why it had come to naught. Yet, there must have been some reason; and it was idle to try and understand her present feelings without knowing what it was!

His Committee was on birth control in connection with the Ministry of Health; and, while listening to arguments why he should not support for other people what he practised himself, he was visited by an idea. Why not go and ask June Forsyte? He could find her in the telephone book —there could be but one with such a name.

"What do *you* say, Mont?"

"Well, sir, if we won't export children to the Colonies or speed up emigration somehow, there's nothing for it but birth control. In the upper and middle classes we're doing it all the time, and blinking the moral side, if there is one; and I really don't see how we can insist on a moral side for those who haven't a quarter of our excuse for having lots of children."

"My dear Mont," said the chairman, with a grin, "aren't you cutting there at the basis of all privilege?"

"Very probably," said Michael, with an answering grin. "I think, of course, that child emigration is much better, but nobody else does, apparently."

Everybody knew that 'young Mont' had a 'bee in his bonnet' about child emigration, and there was little disposition to encourage it to buzz. And, since no one was more aware than Michael of being that crank in politics, one who thought you could not eat your cake and have it, he said no more. Presently, feeling that they would go round and round the mulberry bush for some time yet, and sit on the fence after, he excused himself and went away.

He found the address he wanted: "Miss June Forsyte, Poplar House, Chiswick," and mounted a Hammersmith 'bus.

How fast things seemed coming back to the normal! Extraordinarily difficult to upset anything so vast, intricate, and elastic as a nation's life. The 'bus swung along among countless vehicles and pedestrian myriads, and Michael realised how firm were those two elements of stability in the modern state, the common need for eating, drinking, and getting about; and the fact that so many people could drive cars. 'Revolution?' he thought: 'There never was a time when it had less chance. Machinery's dead agin it.' Machinery belonged to the settled state of things, and every day saw its reinforcement. The unskilled multitude and the Communistic visionaries, their leaders, only had a chance now where machinery and means of communication were still undeveloped, as in Russia. Brains, ability, and technical skill were by nature on the side of capital and individual enterprise, and were gaining ever more power.

"Poplar House" took some finding, and, when found, was a little house supporting a large studio with a north light. It stood, behind two poplar trees, tall, thin, white, like a ghost. A foreign woman opened to him. Yes. Miss Forsyte was in the studio with Mr. Blade! Michael sent up his card, and waited in a draught, extremely ill at ease; for now that he was here he could not imagine

why he had come. How to get the information he wanted
without seeming to have come for it, passed his compre-
hension; for it was the sort of knowledge that could only
be arrived at by crude questioning.

Finding that he was to go up, he went, perfecting his
first lie. On entering the studio, a large room with green-
canvassed walls, pictures hung or stacked, the usual daïs,
a top light half curtained, and some cats, he was conscious
of a fluttering movement. A little light lady in flowing
green, with short silver hair, had risen from a footstool,
and was coming towards him.

"How do you do? You know Harold Blade, of course?"

The young man, at whose feet she had been sitting,
rose and stood before Michael, square, somewhat lowering,
with a dun-coloured complexion and heavily charged eyes.

"You must know his wonderful Rafaelite work."

"Oh, yes!" said Michael, whose conscience was saying:
"Oh, no!"

The young man said, grimly: "He doesn't know me
from Adam."

"No, really," muttered Michael. "But do tell me, why
Rafaelite? I've always wanted to know."

"Why?" exclaimed June. "Because he's the only man
who's giving us the old values; he's re-discovered them."

"Forgive me, I'm such a dud in art matters—I thought
the academicians were still in perspective!"

"*They!*" cried June, and Michael winced at the passion
in the word. "Oh, well—if you still believe in them——"

"But I don't," said Michael.

"Harold is the only Rafaelite; people are grouping
round him, of course, but he'll be the last, too. It's always
like that. A great painter makes a school, but the schools
never amount to anything."

Michael looked with added interest at the first and last
Rafaelite. He did not like the face, but it had a certain
epileptic quality.

"Might I look round? Does my father-in-law know your work, I wonder? He's a great collector, and always on the look-out."

"Soames!" said June, and again Michael winced. "He'll be collecting Harold when we're all dead. Look at that!"

Michael turned from the Rafaelite, who was shrugging his thick shoulders. He saw what was clearly a portrait of June. It was entirely recognisable, very smooth, all green and silver, with a suggestion of halo round the head.

"Pure primary line and colour—d'you think they'd hang *that* in the Academy?"

'Seems to me exactly what they would hang,' thought Michael, careful to keep the conclusion out of his face.

"I like the suggestion of a halo," he murmured.

The Rafaelite uttered a short, sharp laugh.

"I'm going for a walk," he said; "I'll be in to supper. Good-bye!"

"Good-bye!" said Michael, with a certain relief.

"Of course," said June when they were alone, "he's the *only* person who could paint Fleur. He'd get her modern look so perfectly. Would she sit to him? With everybody against him, you know, he has *such* a struggle."

"I'll ask her. But do tell me—why is everybody against him?"

"Because he's been through all these empty modern crazes, and come back to pure form and colour. They think he's a traitor, and call him academic. It's always the way when a man has the grit to fly against fashion and follow his own genius. I can see exactly what he'd do with Fleur. It would be a great chance for him, because he's very proud, and this would be a proper commission from Soames. Splendid for her, too, of course. She ought to jump at it—in ten years' time he'll be *the* man."

Michael, who doubted if Fleur would "jump at it," or Soames give the commission, replied cautiously: "I'll sound her. . . . By the way, your sister Holly and your young brother and his wife were lunching with us to-day."

"Oh!" said June, "I haven't seen Jon yet." And, looking at Michael with her straight blue eyes, she added:

"Why did you come to see me?"

Under that challenging stare Michael's diplomacy wilted.

"Well," he said, "frankly, I want you to tell me why Fleur and your young brother came to an end with each other."

"Sit down," said June, and resting her pointed chin on her hand, she looked at him with eyes moving a little from side to side, as might a cat's.

"I'm glad you asked me straight out; I hate people who beat about the bush. Don't you know about Jon's mother? She was Soames' first wife, of course."

"Oh!" said Michael.

"Irene," and, as she spoke the name, Michael was aware of something deep and primitive stirring in that little figure. "Very beautiful—they didn't get on; she left him —and years later she married my father, and Soames divorced her. I mean Soames divorced her and she married my father. They had Jon. And then, when Jon and Fleur fell in love, Irene and my father were terribly upset, and so was Soames—at least, he ought to have been."

"And then?" asked Michael, for she was silent.

"The children were told; and my father died in the middle of it all; and Jon sacrificed himself and took his mother away, and Fleur married you."

So that was it! In spite of the short, sharp method of the telling, he could feel tragic human feeling heavy in the tale. Poor little devils!

"I always thought it was too bad," said June, suddenly. "Irene ought to have put up with it. Only—only——" and she stared at Michael, "they wouldn't have been happy. Fleur's too selfish. I expect she saw that."

Michael raised an indignant voice.

"Yes," said June; "you're a good sort, I know—too good for her."

"I'm not," said Michael, sharply.

"Oh, yes, you are. She isn't bad, but she's a selfish little creature."

"I wish you'd remember——"

"Sit down! Don't mind what I say. I only speak the truth, you know. Of course, it was all horrible; Soames and my father were first cousins. And those children were awfully in love."

Again Michael was conscious of the deep and private feeling within the little figure; conscious, too, of something deep and private stirring withing himself.

"Painful!" he said.

"I don't know," June went on, abruptly, "I don't know; perhaps it was all for the best. You're happy, aren't you?"

With that pistol to his head, he stood and delivered.

"I am. But is she?"

The little green-and-silver figure straightened up. She caught his hand and gave it a squeeze. There was something almost terribly warm-hearted about the action, and Michael was touched. He had only seen her twice before!

"After all, Jon's married. What's his wife like?"

"Looks charming—nice, I think."

"An American!" said June, deeply. "Well, Fleur's half French. I'm glad you've got a boy."

Never had Michael known anyone whose words conveyed so much unintended potency of discomfort! Why was she glad he had a boy? Because it was an insurance—against what?

"Well," he mumbled, "I'm very glad to know at last what it was all about."

"You ought to have been told before; but you don't know still. Nobody can know what family feuds and feelings are like, who hasn't had them. Though I was angry about those children, I admit that. You see, I was the first to back Irene against Soames in the old days. I wanted her to leave him at the beginning of everything. She had a beastly time; he was such a—such a slug about his precious rights, and no proper pride either. Fancy forcing yourself on a woman who didn't want you!"

"Ah!" Michael muttered. "Fancy!"

"People in the 'eighties and 'nineties didn't understand how disgusting it was. Thank goodness, they do now!"

"Do they?" murmured Michael. "I wonder!"

"Of course they do."

Michael sat corrected.

"Things are much better in that way than they were—not nearly so stuffy and farmyardy. I wonder Fleur hasn't told you all about it."

"She's never said a word."

"Oh!"

That sound was as discomforting as any of her more elaborate remarks. Clearly she was thinking what he himself was thinking: that it had gone too deep with Fleur to be spoken of. He was not even sure that Fleur knew whether he had ever heard of her affair with Jon.

And, with a sudden shrinking from any more discomforting sounds, he rose.

"Thanks awfully for telling me. I must buzz off now, I'm afraid."

"I shall come and see Fleur about sitting to Harold. It's too good a chance for him to miss. He simply must get commissions."

"Of course!" said Michael; he could trust Fleur's powers of refusal better than his own.

"Good-bye, then!"

But when he got to the door and looked back at her standing alone in that large room, he felt a pang—she

seemed so light, so small, so fly-away, with her silver hair
and her little intent face—still young from misjudged
enthusiasm. He had got something out of her, too, left
nothing with her; and he had stirred up some private
feeling of her past, some feeling as strong, perhaps stronger,
than his own.

She looked dashed lonely! He waved his hand to her.

Fleur had returned when he got home, and Michael
realised suddenly, that in calling on June Forsyte he had
done a thing inexplicable, save in relation to her and Jon!

'I must write and ask that little lady not to mention
it,' he thought. To let Fleur know that he had been fussing about her past would never do.

"Had a good time?" he said.

"Very. Young Anne reminds me of Francis, except for
her eyes."

"Yes; I liked the looks of those two when I saw them
at Mount Vernon. That was a queer meeting, wasn't it?"

"The day father was unwell?"

He felt that she knew the meeting had been kept from
her. If only he could talk to her freely; if only she would
blurt out everything!

But all she said was: "I feel at a bad loose end, Michael,
without the canteen."

CHAPTER XIII

SOAMES IN WAITING

TO say that Soames preferred his house by the river when his wife was not there, would be a crude way of expressing a far from simple equation. He was glad to be still married to a handsome woman and very good housekeeper, who really could not help being French and twenty-five years younger than himself. But the fact was, that when she was away from him, he could see her good points so much better than when she was not. Though fond of mocking him in her French way, she had, he knew, lived into a certain regard for his comfort, and her own position as his wife. Affection? No, he did not suppose she had affection for him, but she liked her home, her bridge, her importance in the neighbourhood, and doing things about the house and garden. She was like a cat. And with money she was admirable—making it go further and buy more than most people. She was getting older, too, all the time, so that he had lost serious fear that she would overdo some friendship or other, and let him know it. That Prosper Profond business of six years ago, which had been such a squeak, had taught her discretion.

It had been quite unnecessary really for him to go down a day before Fleur's arrival; his household ran on wheels too well geared and greased. On his fifteen acres, with the new dairy and cows across the river, he grew everything now except flour, fish, and meat of which he was but a sparing eater. Fifteen acres, if hardly "land," represented a deal of produce. The establishment was, in fact, typical of countless residences of the unlanded well-to-do.

Soames had taste, and Annette, if anything, had more,

especially in food, so that a better fed household could scarcely have been found.

In this bright weather, the leaves just full, the may-flower in bloom, bulbs not yet quite over, and the river re-learning its summer smile, the beauty of the prospect was not to be sneezed at. And Soames on his green lawn walked a little and thought of why gardeners seemed always on the move from one place to another. He couldn't seem to remember ever having seen an English gardener other-wise than about to work. That was, he supposed, why peo-ple so often had Scotch gardeners. Fleur's dog came out and joined him. The fellow was getting old, and did little but attack imaginary fleas. Soames was very particu-lar about real fleas, and the animal was washed so often that his skin had become very thin—a golden brown re-triever, so rare that he was always taken for a mongrel. The head gardener came by with a spud in his hand.

"Good afternoon, sir."

"Good afternoon," replied Soames. "So the strike's over!"

"Yes, sir. If they'd attend to their business, it'd be better."

"It would. How's your asparagus?"

"Well, I'm trying to make a third bed, but I can't get the extra labour."

Soames gazed at his gardener, who had a narrow face, rather on one side, owing to the growth of flowers. "What?" he said. "When there are about a million and a half people out of employment?"

"And where they get to, I can't think," said the gar-dener.

"Most of them," said Soames, "are playing instruments in the streets."

"That's right, sir—my sister lives in London. I could get a boy, but I can't trust him."

"Why don't you do it yourself?"

"Well, sir, I expect it'll come to that; but I don't want to let the garden down, you know." And he moved the spud uneasily.

"What have you got that thing for? There isn't a weed about the place."

The gardener smiled. "It's something cruel," he said, "the way they spring up when you're not about."

"Mrs. Mont will be down to-morrow," muttered Soames; "I shall want some good flowers in the house."

"Very little at this time of year, sir."

"I never knew a time of year when there was much. You must stir your stumps and find something."

"Very good, sir," said the gardener, and walked away.

'Where's he going now?' thought Soames. 'I never knew such a chap. But they're all the same.' He supposed they did work some time or other; in the small hours, perhaps—precious small hours! Anyway, he had to pay 'em a pretty penny for it! And, noticing the dog's head on one side, he said:

"Want a walk?"

They went out of the gate together, away from the river. The birds were in varied song, and the cuckoos obstreperous.

They walked up to the bit of common land where there had been a conflagration in the exceptionally fine Easter weather. From there one could look down at the river winding among poplars and willows. The prospect was something like that in a long river landscape by Daubigny which he had seen in an American's private collection—a very fine landscape, he never remembered seeing a finer. He could mark the smoke from his own kitchen chimney, and was more pleased than he would have been marking the smoke from any other. He had missed it a lot last year —all those months, mostly hot—touring the world with

Fleur from one unhomelike place to another. Young Michael's craze for emigration! Soames was Imperialist enough to see the point of it in theory; but in practice every place out of England seemed to him so raw, or so extravagant. An Englishman was entitled to the smoke of his own kitchen chimney. Look at the Ganges—monstrous great thing, compared with that winding silvery thread down there! The St. Lawrence, the Hudson, the Pótomac —as he still called it in thought—had all pleased him, but, comparatively, they were sprawling pieces of water. And the people out there were a sprawling lot. They had to be, in those big places. He moved down from the common through a narrow bit of wood where rooks were in a state of some excitement. He knew little about the habits of birds, not detached enough from self for the study of creatures quite unconnected with him; but he supposed they would be holding a palaver about food—worm-currency would be depressed, or there had been some inflation or other—fussy as the French over their wretched franc. Emerging, he came down opposite the lock-keeper's cottage. There, with the scent of the wood-smoke threading from its low and humble chimney, the weir murmuring, the blackbirds and the cuckoos calling, Soames experienced something like asphyxiation of the proprietary instincts. Opening the handle of his shooting-stick, he sat down on it, to contemplate the oozy green on the sides of the emptied lock and dabble one hand in the air. Ingenious things—locks! Why not locks in the insides of men and women, so that their passions could be damned to the proper moment, then used, under control, for the main traffic of life, instead of pouring to waste over weirs and down rapids? The tongue of Fleur's dog licking his dabbled hand interrupted this somewhat philosophic reflection. Animals were too human nowadays, always wanting to have notice taken of them; only that afternoon he had

seen Annette's black cat look up into the plaster face of
his Naples Psyche, and mew faintly—wanting to be taken
up into its lap, he supposed—only the thing hadn't one.

The lock-keeper's daughter came out to take some garments off a line. Women in the country seemed to do
nothing but hang clothes on lines and take them off again!
Soames watched her, neat-handed, neat-ankled, in neat
light-blue print, with a face like a Botticelli—lots of faces
like that in England! She would have a young man, or
perhaps two—and they would walk in that wood, and sit
in damp places and all the rest of it, and imagine themselves happy, he shouldn't wonder; or she would get up
behind him on one of those cycle things and go tearing
about the country with her dress up to her knees. And her
name would be Gladys or Doris, or what not! She saw
him, and smiled. She had a full mouth that looked pretty
when it smiled. Soames raised his hat slightly.

"Nice evening!" he said.

"Yes, sir."

Very respectful!

"River's still high."

"Yes, sir."

Rather a pretty girl! Suppose he had been a lock-
keeper, and Fleur had been a lock-keeper's daughter—hanging clothes on a line, and saying, "Yes, sir!" Well, he
would as soon be a lock-keeper as anything else in a humble
walk of life—watching water go up and down, and living
in that pretty cottage, with nothing to worry about, except
—except his daughter! And he checked an impulse to say
to the girl: "Are you a good daughter?" Was there such
a thing nowadays—a daughter that thought of you first,
and herself after?

"These cuckoos!" he said, heavily.

"Yes, sir."

She was taking a somewhat suggestive garment off the

line now, and Soames lowered his eyes, he did not want to embarrass the girl—not that he saw any signs. Probably you couldn't embarrass a girl nowadays! And, rising, he closed the handle of his shooting-stick.

"Well, it'll keep fine, I shouldn't wonder."

"Yes, sir."

"Good evening."

"Good evening, sir."

Followed by the dog, he moved along towards home. Butter wouldn't melt in her mouth; but how would she talk to her young man? Humiliating to be old! On an evening like this, one should be young again, and walk in a wood with a girl like that; and all that had been faun-like in his nature pricked ears for a moment, licked lips, and with a shrug and a slight sense of shame, died down.

It had always been characteristic of Soames, who had his full share of the faun, to keep the fact carefully hidden. Like all his family, except, perhaps, his cousin George and his uncle Swithin, he was secretive in matters of sex; no Forsyte talked sex, or liked to hear others talk it; and when they felt its call, they gave no outward sign. Not the Puritan spirit, but a certain refinement in them forbade the subject, and where they got it from they did not know!

After his lonely dinner he lit his cigar and strolled out again. It was really warm for May, and still light enough for him to see his cows in the meadow beyond the river. They would soon be sheltering for the night, under that hawthorn hedge. And here came the swans, with their grey brood in tow; handsome birds, going to bed on the island!

The river was whitening; the dusk seemed held in the trees, waiting to spread and fly up into a sky just drained of sunset. Very peaceful, and a little eerie—the hour be-tween! Those starlings made a racket—disagreeable beg-gars; there could be no real self-respect with such short tails! The swallows went by, taking 'night-caps' of gnats and early moths; and the poplars stood so still—just as if listening—that Soames put up his hand to feel for breeze. Not a breath! And then, all at once—no swallows flying, no starlings; a chalky hue over river, over sky! The lights sprang up in the house. A night-flying beetle passed him, booming. The dew was falling—he felt it; must go in. And, as he turned, quickly, dusk softened the trees, the sky, the river. And Soames thought: 'Hope to goodness there'll be no mysteries when she comes down to-morrow. I don't want to be worried!' Just she and the little chap; it might be so pleasant, if that old love trouble with its gnarled roots in the past and its bitter fruits in the future were not present, to cast a gloom. . . .

He slept well, and next morning could settle to nothing but the arrangement of things already arranged. Several times he stopped dead in the middle of this task to listen for the car and remind himself that he must not fuss, or go asking things. No doubt she had seen young Jon again yesterday, but he must not ask.

He went up to his picture gallery and unhooked from the wall a little Watteau, which he had once heard her admire. He took it downstairs and stood it on an easel in her bedroom—a young man in full plum-coloured skirts and lace ruffles, playing a tambourine to a young lady in blue, with a bare bosom, behind a pet lamb. Charming thing! She could take it away when she went, and hang it with the Fragonards and Chardin in her drawing-room. Standing by the double-poster, he bent down and sniffed at the bed linen. Not quite as fragrant as it ought to be. That woman, Mrs. Edger—his housekeeper—had forgotten the pot-pourri bags; he knew there would be something! And, going to a store closet, he took four little bags with tiny mauve ribbons from a shelf, and put them into the bed. He wandered thence into the bathroom. He didn't know whether she would like those salts—they were Annette's new specialty, and smelt too strong for *his* taste. Otherwise it seemed all right; the soap was "Roger and Gallet," and the waste worked. All these new gadgets—half of them didn't; there was nothing like the old-fashioned thing that pulled up with a chain! Great change in washing during his lifetime. He couldn't quite remember pre-bathroom days; but he could well recall how his father used to say regularly: "They never gave me a bath when I was a boy. First house of my own, I had one put in—people used to come and stare at it—in 1840. They tell me the doctors are against washing now; but I don't know." James had been dead a quarter of a century, and the doctors had turned their coats several times since. Fact was, people enjoyed baths; so it didn't really matter what view the doctors took! Kit enjoyed them—some children didn't. And, leaving the bathroom, Soames stood in front of the flowers the gardener had brought in—among them, three special early roses. Roses were the fellow's forte, or rather his weak point—he cared for nothing else; that was the worst of people nowadays, they specialized so that there was no relativity between things, in spite of its being the fashionable philosophy, or so they told him. He took up a rose and sniffed at it deeply. So many different kinds now—he had lost track! In his young days one could tell them—La France, Maréchal Niel, and Gloire de Dijon—nothing else to speak of; you never heard of *them* now. And at this reminder of the mutability of flowers and the ingenuity of human beings, Soames felt slightly exhausted. There was no end to things!

She was late, too! That fellow Riggs—for he had left the car to bring her down, and had come by train himself —would have got punctured, of course; he was always getting punctured if there was any reason why he shouldn't. And for the next half-hour Soames fidgeted about so that he was deep in nothing in his picture gallery at the very top of the house and did not hear the car arrive. Fleur's voice roused him from thoughts of her.

"Hallo!" he said, peering down the stairs, "where have *you* sprung from? I expected you an hour ago."

"Yes, dear, we had to get some things on the way. How lovely it all looks! Kit's in the garden."

"Ah!" said Soames, descending. "Did you get a rest yester——" and he pulled up in front of her.

She bent her face forward for a kiss, and her eyes looked beyond him. Soames put his lips on the edge of her cheekbone. She was away, somewhere! And, as his lips mumbled her soft skin slightly, he thought: 'She's not thinking of me—why should she? She's young.'

PART II

CHAPTER I

SON OF SLEEPING DOVE

WHETHER or not the character of Englishmen in general is based on chalk, it is undeniably present in the systems of our jockeys and trainers. Living for the most part on Downs, drinking a good deal of water, and concerned with the joints of horses, they are almost professionally calcareous, and at times distinguished by bony noses and chins.

The chin of Greenwater, the retired jockey in charge of Val Dartie's stable, projected, as if in years of race-riding it had been bent on prolonging the efforts of his mounts and catching the judge's eye. His thin, commanding nose dominated a mask of brown skin and bone, his narrow brown eyes glowed slightly, his dark hair was smooth and brushed back; he was five feet seven inches in height, and long seasons, during which he had been afraid to eat, had laid a look of austerity over such natural liveliness, as may be observed in—say—a water-wagtail. A married man with two children, he was endeared to his family by the taciturnity of one who had been intimate with horses for thirty-five years. In his leisure hours he played the piccolo. No one in England was more reliable.

Val, who had picked him up on his retirement from the pig-skin in 1921, thought him an even better judge of men than of horses, incapable of trusting them further than he could see them, and that not very far. Just now it was particularly necessary to trust no one, for there was in the stable a two-year-old colt, Rondavel, by Kaffir out of Sleeping Dove, of whom so much was expected, that nothing whatever had been said about him. On the Mon-

day of Ascot week Val was the more surprised, then, to
hear his trainer remark:

"Mr. Dartie, there was a son of a gun watching the
gallop this morning."

"The deuce there was!"

"Someone's been talking. When they come watching a
little stable like this—something's up. If you take my advice, you'll send the colt to Ascot and let him run his
chance on Thursday—won't do him any harm to smell
a racecourse. We can ease him after, and bring him again
for Goodwood."

Aware of his trainer's conviction that the English racehorse, no less than the English man, liked a light prepara-
tion nowadays, Val answered:

"Afraid of overdoing him?"

"Well, he's fit now, and that's a fact. I had Sinnet
shake him up this morning, and he just left 'em all standing. Fit to run for his life, he is; wish you'd been
there."

"Oho!" said Val, unlatching the door of the box.
"Well, my beauty?"

The Sleeping Dove colt turned his head, regarding his
owner with a certain lustrous philosophy. A dark grey,
with one white heel and a star, he stood glistening from
his morning toilet. A good one! The straight hocks and
ranginess of St. Simon crosses in his background! Scope,
and a rare shoulder for coming down a hill. Not exactly
what you'd call a 'picture'—his lines didn't quite 'flow,'
but great character. Intelligent as a dog, and game as an
otter! Val looked back at his trainer's intent face.

"All right, Greenwater. I'll tell the missus—we'll go in
force. Who can you get to ride at such short notice?"

"Young Lamb."

"Ah!" said Val, with a grin; "you've got it all cut and
dried, I see."

Only on his way back to the house did he recollect a possible 'hole in the ballot' of secrecy. . . . Three days after the General Strike collapsed, before Holly and young Jon and his wife had returned, he had been smoking a second pipe over his accounts, when the maid had announced:

"A gentleman to see you, sir."

"What name?"

"Stainford, sir."

Checking the impulse to say, "And you left him in the hall!" Val passed hurriedly into that part of the house.

His old college pal was contemplating a piece of plate over the stone hearth.

"Hallo!" said Val.

His unemotional visitor turned round.

Less threadbare than in Green Street, as if something had restored his credit, his face had the same crow's-footed, contemptuous calm.

"Ah, Dartie!" he said. "Joe Lightson, the bookie, told me you had a stable down here. I thought I'd look you up on my way to Brighton. How has your Sleeping Dove yearling turned out?"

"So-so," said Val.

"When are you going to run him? I thought, perhaps, you'd like me to work your commission. I could do it much better than the professionals."

Really, the fellow's impudence was sublime!

"Thanks very much; but I hardly bet at all."

"Is that possible? I say, Dartie, I didn't mean to bother you again, but if you could let me have a 'pony,' it would be a great boon."

"Sorry, but I don't keep 'ponies' about me down here."

"A cheque——"

Cheque—not if he knew it!

"No," said Val firmly. "Have a drink?"

"Thanks very much!"

Pouring out the drink at the sideboard in the dining-room, with one eye on the stilly figure of his guest, Val took a resolution.

"Look here, Stainford——" he began, then his heart failed him. "How did you get here?"

"By car, from Horsham. And that reminds me. I haven't a sou with me to pay for it."

Val winced. There was something ineffably wretched about the whole thing.

"Well," he said, "here's a fiver, if that's any use to you; but really I'm not game for any more." And, with a sudden outburst, he added: "I've never forgotten, you know, that I once lent you all I had at Oxford when I was deuced hard pressed myself, and you never paid it back, though you came into shekels that very term."

The well-shaped hand closed on the fiver; a bitter smile opened the thin lips.

"Oxford! Another life! Well, good-bye, Dartie—I'll get on; and thanks! Hope you'll have a good season."

He did not hold out his hand. Val watched his back, languid and slim, till it was out of sight. . . .

Yes! That memory explained it! Stainford must have picked up some gossip in the village—not likely that they would let a 'Sleeping Dove' lie! It didn't much matter; since Holly would hardly let him bet at all. But Green-water must look sharp after the colt. Plenty of straight men racing; but a lot of blackguards hanging about the sport. Queer how horses collected blackguards—most beautiful creatures God ever made! But beauty was like that —look at the blackguards hanging round pretty women! Well, he must let Holly know. They could stay, as usual, at old Warmson's Inn, on the river; from there it was only a fifteen-mile drive to the course. . . .

The 'Pouter Pigeon' stood back a little from the river Thames, on the Berkshire side, above an old-fashioned

garden of roses, stocks, gillyflowers, poppies, phlox drum-
mondi, and sweet-williams. In the warm June weather
the scents from that garden and from sweetbriar round the
windows drifted into an old brick house painted cream-
colour. Late Victorian service in Park Lane under James
Forsyte, confirmed by a later marriage with Emily's maid
Fifine, had induced in Warmson, indeed, such complete
knowledge of what was what, that no river inn had greater
attractions for those whose taste had survived modernity.
Spotless linen, double beds warmed with copper pans, even
in summer; cider, home-made from a large orchard, and
matured in rum casks—the inn was a veritable feather-bed
to all the senses. Prints of "Mariage à la Mode," "Rake's
Progress," "The Nightshirt Steeplechase," "Run with the
Quorn," and large functional groupings of Victorian celeb-
rities with their names attached to blank faces on a key
chart, decorated the walls. Its sanitation and its port were
excellent. Pot-pourri lay in every bedroom, old pewter
round the coffee room, clean napkins at every meal. And
a poor welcome was assured to earwigs, spiders, and the
wrong sort of guest . . . Warmson, one of those self-
contained men who spread when they take inns, pervaded
the house, with a red face set in small, grey whiskers, like
a sun of just sufficient warmth.

To young Anne Forsyte all was "just too lovely."
Never in her short life, confined to a large country, had she
come across such defiant cosiness—the lush peace of the
river, the songs of birds, the scents of flowers, the rustic
arbour, the drifting lazy sky, now blue, now white, the
friendly fat spaniel, and the feeling that to-morrow and
to-morrow and to-morrow would for ever be the same
as yesterday.

"It's a poem, Jon."

"Slightly comic. When everything's slightly comic, you
don't tire."

"I'd certainly never tire of this."

"We don't grow tragedy in England, Anne."

"Why?"

"Well, tragedy's extreme; and we don't like extremes. Tragedy's dry and England's damp."

She was leaning her elbows on the wall at the bottom of the garden, and, turning her chin a little in her hand, she looked round and up at him.

"Fleur Mont's father lives on the river, doesn't he? Is that far from here?"

"Mapledurham? I should think about ten miles."

"I wonder if we shall see her at Ascot. I think she's lovely."

"Yes," said Jon.

"I wonder you didn't fall in love with her, Jon."

"We were kids when I knew her."

"I think she fell in love with you."

"Why?"

"By the way she looks at you. . . . She isn't in love with Mr. Mont; she just likes him."

"Oh!" said Jon.

Since in the coppice at Robin Hill Fleur had said "Jon!" in so strange a voice, he had known queer moments. There was that in him which could have caught her, balanced there on the log with her hands on his shoulders, and gone straight back into the past with her. There was that in him which abhorred the notion. There was that in him which sat apart and made a song about them both, and that in him which said: Get to work and drop all these silly feelings! He was, in fact, confused. The past, it seemed, did not die, as he had thought, but lived on beside the present, and sometimes, perhaps, became the future. Did one live for what one had not got? There was a wrinkling in his soul, and feverish draughts crept about within him. The whole thing was on his conscience—for if Jon had anything, he had a conscience.

"When we get our place," he said, "we'll have all these old-fashioned flowers. They're much the sweetest!"

"Ah! Yes, do let's get a home, Jon. Only are you sure you want one? Wouldn't you like to travel and write poetry?"

"It's not a job. Besides, my verse isn't good enough. You want the mood of Hatteras J. Hopkins:

" 'Now, severed from my kind by my contempt,
   I live apart and beat my lonely drum.' "

"I wish you weren't modest, Jon."

"It's not modesty, Anne; it's a sense of the comic."

"Couldn't we get a swim before dinner? It would be fine."

"I don't know what the regulations are here."

"Let's bathe first and find out afterwards."

"All right. You go and change. I'll get this gate open."

A fish splashed, a long white cloud brushed the poplar tops beyond the water. Just such an evening, six years ago, he had walked the towing-path with Fleur, had separated from her, waited to see her look back and wave her hand. He could see her still—that special grace, which gave her movements a lingering solidity within the memory. And now—it was Anne! And Anne in water was a dream! . . .

Above the 'Pouter Pigeon' the sky was darkening; cars in their garages were still; no boats passed, only the water moved, and the river wind talked vaguely in the rushes and among the leaves. All within was cosy. On their backs lay Warmson and his Fifine, singing a little through their noses. By a bedside light Holly read 'The Worst Journey in the World,' and beside her Val dreamed that he was trying to stroke a horse's nose, shortening under his hand to the size of a leopard's. And Anne slept with her eyes hidden against Jon's shoulder, and Jon lay staring at the crannies through which the moonlight eddied.

And in his stable at Ascot the son of Sleeping Dove, from home for the first time, pondered on the mutability of equine affairs, closing and opening his eyes, and breathing without sound in the strawy dark, above the black cat he had brought to bear him company.

CHAPTER II

SOAMES GOES RACING

TO Winifred Dartie the début of her son's Sleeping Dove colt on Ascot Cup Day seemed an occasion for the gathering of such members of her family as were permitted to go racing by the primary caution in their blood; but it was almost a shock to her when Fleur telephoned: "Father's coming; he's never been to Ascot, and doesn't know that he wants to go."

"Oh!" she said, "then you'll have to have two of my Enclosure tickets. Jack can fend for himself. But what about Michael?"

"Michael can't come; he's deep in slums—got a new slogan: 'Broader gutters!'"

"He's so good," said Winifred. "Let's go down early enough to lunch before racing, dear. I think we'd better drive."

"Father's car is up—we'll call for you."

"Delightful!" said Winifred. "Has your father got a grey top hat? No? Oh! But he simply must wear one; they're all the go this year. Don't say anything, just get him one. He wears seven-and-three-quarters; and dear, tell them to heat the hat and squash it in at the sides—otherwise they're always too round for him. And he needn't bring any money to speak of; Jack will do all our betting for us."

Fleur thought that it was not likely father would have a bet; he had said he just wanted to see what the thing was like.

"He's so funny about betting," said Winifred, "like your grandfather."

Not that it had been altogether funny in the case of
James, who had been called on to pay the racing debts of
Montague Dartie three times over.

With Soames and Winifred on the back seats, Fleur and
Imogen on the front seats, and Jack Cardigan alongside
Riggs, they took a circuitous road by way of Harrow to
avoid the traffic, and emerged into it just at the point
where for the first time it became thick. Soames, who had
placed his grey top hat on his knee, put it on, and said:

"Just like Riggs!"

"Oh, no, Uncle!" said Imogen. "It's Jack's doing.
When he's got to go through Eton, he always likes to go
through Harrow first."

"Oh! Ah!" said Soames. "He was there. I should like
Kit's name put down."

"How nice!" said Imogen: "Our boys would still be
there when he goes. You look so well in that hat, Uncle."

Soames took it off again.

"White elephant," he said. "Can't think what made
Fleur get me the thing!"

"My dear," said Winifred, "it'll last you for years.
Jack's had his ever since the war. The great thing is to
prevent the moth getting into it, between seasons. What
a lot of cars! I do think it's wonderful that so many
people should have the money in these days."

The sight of so much money flowing down from town
would have been more exhilarating to Soames if he had
not been wondering where on earth they all got it. With
the coal trade at a standstill, and factories closing down all
over the place, this display of wealth and fashion, however
reassuring, seemed to him almost indecent.

Jack Cardigan, from his front seat, had begun explaining a thing he called the 'tote.' It seemed to be a machine
that did your betting for you. Jack Cardigan was a funny
fellow; he made a life's business of sport; there wasn't

another country that could have produced him! And, leaning forward, Soames said to Fleur:

"You've not got a draught there?"

She had been very silent all the way, and he knew why.
Ten to one if young Jon Forsyte wouldn't be at Ascot!
Twice over at Mapledurham he had noticed letters ad-
dressed by her to:

> "Mrs. Val Dartie,
> Wansdon,
> Sussex."

She had seemed to him very fidgety or very listless all
that fortnight. Once, when he had been talking to her
about Kit's future, she had said: "I don't think it matters, Dad, whatever one proposes—he'll dispose; parents
don't count now: look at me!"

And he had looked at her, and left it at that.

He was still contemplating the back of her head when
they drew into an enclosure and he was forced to expose
his hat to the public gaze. What a crowd! Here, on the
far side of the course, were rows of people all jammed
together, who, so far as he could tell, would see nothing,
and be damp one way or another throughout the afternoon.
If that was pleasure! He followed the others across the
course, in front of the Grand Stand. So those were 'the
bookies'! Funny lot, with 'their names painted clearly
on each,' so that people could tell them apart, just as well,
for they all seemed to him the same, with large necks and
red faces, or scraggy necks and lean faces, one of each kind
in every firm, like a couple of music-hall comedians. And,
every now and then, in the pre-racing hush, one of them
gave a sort of circular howl and looked hungrily at space.
Funny fellows! Soames was glad to pass into the Royal
Enclosure where bookmakers did not seem to be admitted.
Numbers of grey top hats here! This was the place—he

had heard—to see pretty women. He was looking for them when Winifred pressed his arm.

"Look, Soames—the Royal Procession!"

Thus required to gape at those horse-drawn carriages at which everybody else would be gaping, Soames averted his eyes, and became conscious that Winifred and he were alone!

"What's become of the others?" he said.

"Gone to the paddock, I expect."

"What for?"

"To look at the horses, dear."

Soames had forgotten the horses.

"Fancy driving up like that, at this time of day!" he muttered.

"I think it's so amusing!" said Winifred. "Shall we go to the paddock, too?"

Soames, who had not intended to lose sight of his daughter, followed her towards whatever the paddock might be.

It was one of those days when nobody could tell whether it was going to rain, so that he was disappointed by the dresses, and the women's looks. He saw nothing to equal his daughter, and was about to make a disparaging remark, when a voice behind him said:

"Look, Jon! There's Fleur Mont!"

Placing his foot on Winifred's, Soames stood still. There, and wearing a grey top hat, too, was that young chap between his wife and his sister. A memory of tea at Robin Hill, with his cousin Jolyon, that boy's father, twenty-seven years ago, assailed Soames—and of how Holly and Val had come in and sat looking at him as if he were a new kind of bird. There they went, those three, into a ring of people who were staring at nothing so far as he could see. And there, close to them, were those other three, Jack Cardigan, Fleur, and Imogen.

"My dear," said Winifred, "you *did* tread on my toe."

"I didn't mean to," muttered Soames. "Come over to the other side—there's more room."

It seemed horses were being led round; but it was at his daughter that Soames wanted to gaze from behind Winifred's shoulder. She had not yet seen the young man, but was evidently looking for him—her eyes were hardly ever on the horses—no great wonder in that, perhaps, for they all seemed alike to Soames, shining and snakey, quiet as sheep, with boys holding on to their heads. Ah! A stab went through his chest, for she had suddenly come to life; and, as suddenly, seemed to hide her resurrection even from herself! How still she stood—ever so still, gazing at that young fellow talking to his wife.

"That's the favourite, Soames. At least, Jack said he would be. What do you think of him?"

"Much like the others—got four legs."

Winifred laughed. Soames was so amusing!

"Jack's moving; if we're going to have a bet, I think we'd better go back, dear. I know what I fancy."

"I don't fancy anything," said Soames. "Weak-minded, I call it; as if they could tell one horse from another!"

"Oh! but you'd be surprised," said Winifred; "you must get Jack to——"

"No, thank you."

He had seen Fleur move and join those three. But faithful to his resolve to show no sign, he walked glumly back into the Enclosure. What a monstrous noise they were making now in the ring next door! And what a pack of people in that great Stand! Up there, on the top of it, he could see what looked like half-a-dozen lunatics frantically gesticulating—some kind of signalling, he supposed. Suddenly, beyond the railings at the bottom of the lawn, a flash of colour passed. Horses—one, two, three; a dozen or more—all labelled with numbers, and with little bright men sitting on their necks like monkeys. Down they went

—and soon they'd come back, he supposed; and a lot of
money would change hands. And then they'd do it again,
and the money would change back. And what satisfaction
they all got out of it, he didn't know! There were men
who went on like that all their lives he believed—thousands
of them: must be lots of time and money to waste in the
country! What was it Timothy had said: "Consols are
going up!" They hadn't; on the contrary, they were down
a point, at least, and would go lower before the Coal
Strike was over. Jack Cardigan's voice said in his ear:

"What are you going to back, Uncle Soames?"

"How should I know?"

"You must back something, to give you an interest."

"Put something on for Fleur, and leave me alone,"
said Soames; "I'm too old to begin."

And, opening the handle of his racing stick, he sat down
on it. "Going to rain," he added, gloomily. He sat there
alone; Winifred and Imogen had joined Fleur down by
the rails with Holly and her party—Fleur and that young
man side by side. And he remembered how, when Bosinney had been hanging round Irene, he, as now, had made
no sign, hoping against hope that by ignoring the depths
beneath him he could walk upon the waters. Treacherous-
ly they had given way then and engulfed him; would they
again—would they again? His lip twitched; and he put out
his hand. A little drizzle fell on the back of it.

"They're off!"

Thank goodness—the racket had ceased! Funny change
from din to hush. The whole thing funny—a lot of
grown-up children! Somebody called out shrilly at the top
of his voice—there was a laugh—then noise began swelling
from the stand; heads were craning round him. "The
favourite wins!" "Not he!" More noise; a thudding—
a flashing past of colour! And Soames thought: 'Well,
that's over!' Perhaps everything was like that really. A

hush—a din—a flashing past—a hush! All life a race, a
spectacle—only you couldn't see it! A venture and a paying-up! And beneath his new hat he passed his hand down
over one flat cheek, and then the other. A paying-up! He
didn't care who paid up, so long as it wasn't Fleur!
But there it was—some debts could not be paid by proxy!
What on earth was Nature about when she made the human
heart!

The afternoon wore on, and he saw nothing of his
daughter. It was as if she suspected his design of watching
over her. There was the "horse of the century" running
in the Gold Cup, and he positively mustn't miss that—
they said. So again Soames was led to the ring where the
horses were moving round.

"That the animal?" he said, pointing to a tall mare,
whom, by reason of two white ankles, he was able to distinguish from the others. Nobody answered him, and he
perceived that he was separated from Winifred and the
Cardigans by three persons, all looking at him with a
certain curiosity.

"Here he comes!" said one of them. Soames turned his
head. Oh! So *this* was the horse of the century, was it?—
this bay fellow—same colour as the pair they used to drive
in the Park Lane barouche. His father always had bays,
because old Jolyon had browns, and Nicholas blacks, and
Swithin greys, and Roger—he didn't remember what Roger
used to have—something a bit eccentric—piebalds, he
shouldn't wonder. Sometimes they would talk about horses,
or, rather, about what they had given for them; Swithin
had been a judge, or so he said—Soames had never believed
it, he had never believed in Swithin at all. But he could
perfectly well remember George being run away with by
his pony in the Row, and pitched into a flowerbed—no one
had ever been able to explain how; just like George, with
his taste for the grotesque! He himself had never taken

any interest in horses! Irene, of course, had loved riding—
she would! She had never had any after she married
him. . . . A voice said:

"Well, what do you think of him, Uncle Soames?"

Val, with his confounded grin; Jack Cardigan, too, and
a thin, brown-faced man with a nose and chin. Soames
said guardedly:

"Nice enough nag."

If they thought they were going to get a rise out of him!

"Think he'll stay, Val? It's the deuce of a journey."

"He'll stay all right."

"Got nothing to beat," said the thin brown man.

"The Frenchman, Greenwater."

"No class, Captain Cardigan. He's not all the horse they
think him, but he can't lose to-day."

"Well, I hope to God he beats the Frenchman; we want
a Cup or two left in the country."

Something responded within Soames' breast. If it was
against a Frenchman, he would do his best to help.

"Put me five pounds on him," he said, suddenly, to
Jack Cardigan.

"Good for you, Uncle Soames. He'll start about evens.
See his head and his forehand and the way he's let down—
lots of heart room. Not quite so good behind the saddle,
but a great horse, I think."

"Which is the Frenchman?" asked Soames. "That!
Oh! Ah! I don't like *him*. I want to see this race."

Jack Cardigan gripped his arm—the fellow's fingers
were like iron.

"You come along with me!" he said. Soames went,
was put up higher than he had been yet, given Imogen's
glasses—a present from himself—and left there. He was
surprised to find how well and far he could see. What a
lot of cars, and what a lot of people! 'The national pastime'—didn't they call it! Here came the horses walking

past, each led by a man. Well! they were pretty creatures, no doubt! An English horse against a French horse—that gave the thing some meaning. He was glad Annette was still with her mother in France, otherwise she'd have been here with him. Now they were cantering past. Soames made a real effort to tell one from the other, but except for their numbers, they were so confoundedly alike. "No," he said to himself, "I'll just watch those two, and that tall horse"—its name had appealed to him, Pons Asinorum. Rather painfully he got the colours of the three by heart and fixed his glasses on the wheeling group out there at the starting point. As soon as they were off, however, all he could see was that one horse was in front of the others. Why had he gone to the trouble of learning the colours? On and on and on he watched them, worried because he could make nothing of it, and everybody else seemed making a good deal. Now they were rounding into the straight. "The favourite's coming up!" "Look at the Frenchman!" Soames could see the colours now. Those two! His hand shook a little and he dropped his glasses. Here they came—a regular ding-dong! Dash it—he wasn't—England wasn't! Yes, by George! No! Yes! Entirely without approval his heart was beating painfully. 'Absurd!' he thought. 'The Frenchman!' "No! the favourite wins! He wins!" Almost opposite, the horse was shooting out. Good horse! Hooray! England for ever! Soames covered his mouth just in time to prevent the words escaping. Somebody said something to him. He paid no attention; and, carefully putting Imogen's glasses into their case, took off his grey hat and looked into it. There was nothing there except a faint discoloration of the buff leather where he had perspired.

CHAPTER III

THE TWO-YEAR-OLDS

THE toilet of the two-year-olds was proceeding in the more unfrequented portions of the paddock.

"Come and see Rondavel saddled, Jon," said Fleur.

And, when he looked back, she laughed.

"No, you've got Anne all day and all night. Come with me for a change."

On the far side of the paddock the son of Sleeping Dove was holding high his intelligent head, and his bit was being gently jiggled, while Greenwater with his own hands adjusted the saddle.

"A racehorse has about the best time of anything on earth," she heard Jon say. "Look at his eye—wise, bright, not bored. Draft horses have a cynical, long-suffering look —racehorses never. He likes his job; that keeps him spirity."

"Don't talk like a pamphlet, Jon. Did you expect to see me here?"

"Yes."

"And it didn't keep you away? How brave!"

"Must you say that sort of thing?"

"What then? You notice, Jon, that a racehorse never stands over at the knee; the reason is, of course, that he isn't old enough. By the way, there's one thing that spoils your raptures about them. They're not free agents."

"Is anyone?"

How set and obstinate his face!

"Let's see him walk round."

They joined Val, who said gloomily:

"D'you want to have anything on?"

"Do *you*, Jon?" said Fleur.

"Yes; a tenner."

"So will I then. Twenty pounds between us, Val."

Val sighed.

"Look at him! Ever see a two-year-old more self-contained? I tell you that youngster's going far. And I'm confined to a miserable 'pony'! Damn!"

He left them and spoke to Greenwater.

"More self-contained," said Fleur. "Not a modern quality, is it, Jon?"

"Perhaps, underneath."

"Oh! You've been in the backwoods too long. Francis, too, was wonderfully primitive; so, I suppose, is Anne. You should have tried New York, judging by their literature."

"I don't judge by literature; I don't believe there's any relation between it and life."

"Let's hope not, anyway. Where shall we see the race from?"

"The Enclosure rails. It's the finish I care about. I don't see Anne."

Fleur closed her lips suddenly on the words: "Damn Anne."

"We can't wait for them," she said. "The rails soon fill up."

On the rails they were almost opposite the winning post, and they stood there silent, in a queer sort of enmity— it seemed to Fleur.

"Here they come!"

Too quickly and too close to be properly taken in, the two-year-olds came cantering past.

"Rondavel goes well," said Jon. "And I like that brown."

Fleur noted them languidly, too conscious of being alone with him—really alone, blocked off by strangers from any

knowing eye. To savour that loneliness of so few minutes
was tasking all her faculties. She slipped her hand through
his arm, and forced her voice.

"I'm awfully worked up, Jon. He simply must win."

Did he know that in focussing his glasses he left her
hand uncaged?

"I can't make them out from here." Then his arm re-
caged her hand against his side. Did he know? What did
he know?

"They're off!"

Fleur pressed closer.

Silence—din—shouting of this name—that name! But
pressure against him was all it meant to Fleur. Past they
came, a flourishing flash of colour; but she saw nothing of
it, for her eyes were closed.

"By Gosh!" she heard him say: "He's won."

"Oh, Jon!"

"I wonder what price we got?"

Fleur looked at him, a spot of red in each pale cheek,
and her eyes very clear.

"Price? Did you really mean that, Jon?"

And, though he was behind her, following to the paddock she knew from the way his eyes were fixed on her,
that he had not meant it.

They found their party reunited all but Soames. Jack
Cardigan was explaining that the price obtained was un-
accountably short, since there was no stable money on to
speak of; somebody must have known something; he seemed
to think that this was extremely reprehensible.

"I suppose Uncle Soames hasn't been going for the
gloves," he said. "Nobody's seen him since the Gold Cup.
Wouldn't it be ripping if we found he's kicked over and
had a 'monkey' on?"

Fleur said uneasily:

"I expect Father got tired and went to the car. We'd
better go too, Auntie, and get away before the crowd."

She turned to Anne. "When shall we see you again?" She saw the girl look at Jon, and heard him say glumly:

"Oh! sometime."

"Yes, we'll fix something up. Good-bye, my dear! Good-bye, Jon! Tell Val I'm very glad." And, with a farewell nod, she led the way. Of a sort of rage in her heart she gave no sign, preparing normality for her father's eyes.

Soames, indeed, was in the car. Excitement over the Gold Cup—so contrary to his principles—had caused him to sit down in the Stand. And there he had remained during the next two races, idly watching the throng below, and the horses going down fast and coming back faster. There, quietly, in the isolation suited to his spirit, he could, if not enjoy, at least browse on a scene strikingly unfamiliar to him. The national pastime—he knew that everybody had 'a bit on' something now-a-days. For one person who ever went racing there were twenty—it seemed—who didn't, and yet knew at least enough to lose their money. You couldn't buy a paper, or have your hair cut, without being conscious of that. All over London, and the South, the Midlands and the North, in all classes, they were at it, supporting horses with their bobs and dollars and sovereigns. Most of them—he believed—had never seen a racehorse in their lives—hardly a horse of any sort; racing was a sort of religion, he supposed, and now that they were going to tax it, an orthodox religion. Some primeval nonconformity in the blood of Soames shuddered a little. He had no sympathy, of course, with those leather-lunged chaps down there under their queer hats and their umbrellas, but the feeling that they were now made free of heaven—or at least of that synonym of heaven the modern State—ruffled him. It was almost as if England were facing realities at last—Very dangerous! They would be licensing prostitution next! To tax what were called vices was to admit that they were part of human nature. And though, like a Forsyte, he had long known them to be so, to admit it was, he felt, too French. To acknowledge the limitations of human nature was a sort of defeatism; when you once began that, you didn't know where you'd stop. Still, from all he could see, the tax would bring in a pretty penny—and pennies were badly needed; so, he didn't know, he wasn't sure. He wouldn't have done it himself, but he wasn't prepared to turn out the Government for having done it. They had recognised, too, no doubt, as he did, that gambling was the greatest make-weight there was against revolution; so long as a man could bet he had always a chance of getting something for nothing, and that desire was the real driving force behind any attempt to turn things upside down. Besides you had to move with the times uphill or downhill, and it was difficult to tell one from the other. The great thing was to avoid extremes.

From this measured reflection he was abruptly transferred to feelings unmeasured. Fleur and that young fellow were walking across the lawn of the Enclosure! From under the brim of his grey hat he watched them painfully, reluctantly admitting that they made as pretty a couple as any there. They came to a stand on the rails—not talking; and to Soames, who, when moved, was exceptionally taciturn, this seemed a bad sign. Were things really going wrong, then—was passion forming within its still cocoon to fly on butterfly wings for its brief hour? What was going on within the silence of those two? The horses were passing now; and the grey, they said, was his own nephew's? Why did the fellow have horses? He had known how it would be when Fleur said she was going to Ascot. He regretted now having come. No, he didn't! Better to know what there was to be known. In the press of people to the rails he could no longer see more than the young man's grey hat, and the black-and-white covering of his daughter's head. For a minute the race diverted him: might

as well see Val's horse well beaten. They said he thought
a lot of it; and Soames thought the less of its chance for
that. Here they came, all in a bunch—thundering great
troop, and that grey—a handy colour, you couldn't miss
it.—Why, he was winning! Hang it—he had won!

"H'm!" he said, aloud: "that's my nephew's horse!"

Since nobody replied, he hoped they hadn't heard; and
back went his eyes to the Enclosure rails. Those two were
coming away silently—Fleur a little in front. Perhaps—
perhaps, after all, they didn't get on, now! Must hope for
the best. By George, but he felt tired! He would go to
the car, and wait.

And there in the dusk of it he was sitting when they
came, full of bubble and squeak—something very little-
headed about people when they'd won money. For they
had all won money, it seemed!

"And you didn't back him, Uncle Soames?"

"I was thinking of other things," said Soames, gazing at
his daughter.

"We thought you were responsible for the shockin' bad
price."

"Why!" said Soames, gloomily. "Did you expect me
to bet against him?"

Jack Cardigan threw back his head and laughed.

"I don't see anything funny," muttered Soames.

"Nor do I, Jack," said Fleur. "Why should Father
know anything about racing?"

"I beg your pardon, Sir, I'll tell you all about it."

"God forbid!" said Soames.

"No, but it's rather queer. D'you remember that chap
Stainford, who sneaked the Mater's snuff-box?"

"I do."

"Well it seems he paid Val a visit at Wansdon, and Val
thinks he picked up the idea that Rondavel was a real
good one. There was a chap watching the gallop last Mon-

day. That's what decided them to run the colt to-day. They were going to wait for Goodwood. Too late, though; somebody's made a pot over him. We only got fours."

Is was all Greek to Soames, except that the languid ruffian Stainford had somehow been responsible a *second* time for bringing about a meeting between Fleur and Jon; for he knew from Winifred that Val and his *ménage* had gone to stay at Green Street during the Strike on purpose to see Stainford. He wished to goodness he had called a policeman that day, and had the fellow shut up.

They were a long time getting out of the traffic—owing to the perversity of "that chap Riggs," and did not reach South Square till seven o'clock. They were greeted by the news that Kit had a temperature. Mr. Mont was with him. Fleur flew up. Having washed off his day, Soames settled himself in the 'parlour' to wait uneasily for their report. Fleur used to have temperatures, and not infrequently they led to something. If Kit's didn't lead to anything serious, it might be good for her—keeping her thoughts at home. He lay back in his chair opposite the Fragonard—a delicate thing, but with no soul in it, like all the works of that period—wondering why Fleur had changed the style of this room from Chinese to Louis Quinze. Just for the sake of change, he supposed. These young people had no continuity; some microbe in the blood —of the 'idle rich,' and the 'idle poor,' and everybody else, so far as he could see. Nobody could be got to stay anywhere—not even in their graves, judging by all those séances. If only people would attend quietly to their business, even to that of being dead! They had such an appetite for living, that they had no life. A beam of sunlight, smoky with dust-motes, came slanting in on to the wall before him—pretty thing, a beam of sunlight, but a terrible lot of dust, even in a room spick-and-spandy as this. And to think that a thing smaller than one of those dust-motes could give a child a temperature. He hoped to goodness Kit had nothing catching. And his mind went over the illnesses of childhood—mumps, measles, chicken-pox, whooping-cough. Fleur had caught them all, but never scarlet fever. And Soames began to fidget. Surely Kit was too young to have got scarlet fever. But nurses were so careless—you never knew! And suddenly he began to wish for Annette. What was she doing out in France all this time? She was useful in illness; had some very good prescriptions. He *would* say that for the French—their doctors were clever when you could get them to take an interest. The stuff they had given him for his lumbago at Deauville had been first-rate. And after his visit the little doctor chap had said: "I come for the money to-morrow!" or so it had sounded. It seemed he had meant: "I come in the morning to-morrow." They never could speak anything but their own confounded language, and looked aggrieved when you couldn't speak it yourself.

They had kept him a long time there without news before Michael came in.

"Well?"

"Well, sir, it looks uncommonly like measles."

"H'm! Now, how on earth did he get that?"

"Nurse has no idea; but Kit's awfully sociable. If there's another child in sight, he goes for him."

"That's bad," said Soames. "You've got slums at the back here."

"Ah!" said Michael: "Slums to the right of us, slums to the left of us, slums to the front of us—how can you wonder?"

Soames stared. "They're not notifiable," he said, "thank goodness!"

"Slums?"

"No. Measles." If he had a dread, it was a notifiable disease, with the authorities poking their noses in, and having up the drains as likely as not. "How's the little chap feeling?"

"Very sorry for himself."

"In my opinion," said Soames, "there's a great deal more in fleas than they think. That dog of his may have picked up a measley flea. I wonder the doctors don't turn their attention to fleas."

"I wonder they don't turn their attention to slums," said Michael; "that's where the fleas come from."

Again Soames stared. Had his son-in-law got slums in his bonnet now? His manifestations of public spirit were very disturbing. Perhaps he'd been going round those places, and brought the flea in himself, or some infection or other.

"Have you sent for the doctor?"

"Yes; he'll be here any minute."

"Is he any good, or just the ordinary cock-and-bull type?"

"The same man we had for Fleur."

"Oh! Ah! I remember—too much manner, but shrewd. Doctors!"

There was silence in the polished room, while they waited for the bell to ring; and Soames brooded. Should he tell Michael about the afternoon? His mouth opened once, but nothing came out. Over and over again his son-in-law had surprised him by the view he took of things. And he only stared at Michael, who was gazing out of the window—queer face the young fellow had; plain, and yet attractive, with those pointed ears and eyebrows running up on the outside—wasn't always thinking of himself like good-looking young men seemed to be. Good-looking men were always selfish; got spoiled, he supposed. He would give a penny for the young fellow's thoughts.

"Here he is!" said Michael, jumping up.

Soames was alone again. How long alone, he didn't know, for he was tired, and, in spite of his concern, he dozed. The opening of the door roused him in time to assume anxiety before Fleur spoke.

"It's almost certainly measles, Dad."

"Oh!" said Soames, blankly. "What about nursing?"

"Nurse and I, of course."

"That'll mean you can't get about."

"And aren't you glad?" her face seemed to say. How she read his thoughts!

God knew he wasn't glad of anything that troubled her —and yet!

"Poor little chap!" he said, evasively: "Your mother must come back. I must try and find him something that'll take his attention off."

"Don't trouble, Dad; he's too feverish, poor darling. Dinner's ready. I'm having mine upstairs."

Soames rose and went up to her.

"Don't you be worrying," he said. "All children——"

Fleur put her arm out.

"Not too near, Dad. No, I won't worry."

"Give him my love," said Soames. "He won't care for it."

Fleur looked at him. Her lips smiled a very little. Her eyelids winked twice. Then she turned and went out, and Soames thought:

'She—poor little thing! I'm no use!' It was of her, not of his grandson, that he thought.

CHAPTER IV

IN THE MEADS

THE Meads of St. Augustine had, no doubt, once on a time been flowery, and burgesses had walked there of a Sunday, plucking summer nosegays. If there were a flower now, it would be found on the altar of the Reverend Hilary's church, or on Mrs. Hilary's dining-table. The rest of a numerous population had heard of these unnatural products, and, indeed, seeing them occasionally in baskets, would utter the words: "Aoh! Look at the luv-ly flahers!"

When Michael visited his uncle, according to promise, on Ascot Cup Day, he was ushered hurriedly into the presence of twenty little Augustinians on the point of being taken in a covered motor van for a fortnight among flowers in a state of nature. His Aunt May was standing among them. She was a tall woman with bright brown shingled hair going grey, and the slightly rapt expression of one listening to music. Her smile was very sweet, and this, with the puzzled twitch of her delicate eyebrows, as who should say placidly: "What next, I wonder?" endeared her to everyone. She had emerged from a Rectory in Huntingdonshire, in the early years of the century, and had married Hilary at the age of twenty. He had kept her busy ever since. Her boys and girls were all at school now, so that in term time she had merely some hundreds of Augustinians for a family. Hilary was wont to say: "May's a wonder. Now that she's had her hair off, she's got so much time on her hands that we're thinking of keeping guinea-pigs. If she'd only let me grow a beard, we could really get a move on."

She greeted Michael with a nod and a twitch.

"Young London, my dear," she said, privately, "just off to Leatherhead. Rather sweet, aren't they?"

Michael, indeed, was surprised by the solidity and neatness of the twenty young Augustinians. Judging by the streets from which they came and the mothers who were there to see them off, their families had evidently gone 'all out' to get them in condition for Leatherhead.

He stood grinning amiably, while they were ushered out on the glowing pavement between the unrestrained appreciation of their mothers and sisters. Into the van, open only at the rear, they were piled, with four young ladies to look after them.

"Four-and-twenty blackbirds baked in a pie," murmured Michael.

His aunt laughed.

"Yes, poor little dears, won't they be hot! But aren't they good?" She lowered her voice. "And d'you know what they'll say when they come back after their fortnight? 'Oh! yes, we liked it all very much, thank you, but it was rather slow. We like the streets better.' Every year it's the same."

"Then, what's the use of sending them, Aunt May?"

"It does them good physically; they look sturdy enough, but they aren't really strong. Besides, it seems so dreadful they should never see the country. Of course we country-bred folk, Michael, never can realise what London streets are to children—very nearly Heaven, you know."

The motor van moved to an accompaniment of fluttered handkerchiefs and shrill cheering.

"The mothers love them to go," said his aunt; "it's kind of distinguished. Well, that's that! What would you like to see next? The street we've just bought, to gut and re-gut? Hilary'll be there with the architect."

"Who owned the street?" asked Michael.

"He lived in Capri. I don't suppose he ever saw it. He

died the other day, and we got it rather reasonably, considering how central we are, here. Sites are valuable."

"Have you paid for it?"

"Oh! no." Her eyebrows twitched. "Post-dated a
cheque on Providence."

"Good Lord!"

"We had to have the street. It was such a chance.
We've paid the deposit, and we've got till September to
get the rest."

"How much?" said Michael.

"Thirty-two thousand."

Michael gasped.

Oh! We shall get it, dear, Hilary's wonderful in that
way. Here's the street."

It was a curving street of which, to Michael, slowly
passing, each house seemed more dilapidated than the last.
Grimy and defaced, with peeling plaster, broken rails and
windows, and a look of having been abandoned to its fate
—like some half-burnt-out ship—it hit the senses and the
heart with its forlornness.

"What sort of people live here, Aunt May?"

"All sorts—three or four families to each house. Covent
Garden workers, hawkers, girls in factories, out-of-works
—every kind. The unmentionable insect abounds, Michael.
The girls are wonderful—they keep their clothes in paper
bags. Many of them turn out quite neat. If they didn't,
of course, they'd get the sack, poor dears."

"But is it possible," said Michael, "that people can *want*
to go on living here?"

His aunt's brows became intricate.

"It isn't a question of want, my dear. It's a simple eco-
nomic proposition. Where else *can* they live so cheaply?
It's more than that, even; where else can they go at all,
if they're turned out? The Authorities demolished a street
not long ago up there, and built that great block of work-

men's flats; but the rents were prohibitive to the people
who had been living in the street, and they simply melted
away to other slums. Besides, you know, they don't like
those barracky flats, and I don't wonder. They'd much
rather have a little house, if they can; or the floor of a
house if they can't. Or even a room. That's in the English nature, and it will be till they design workmen's dwell-
ings better. The English like to live low down: I suppose
because they always have. Oh! Here's Hilary!"

Hilary Charwell, in a dark grey Norfolk suit, a turn-
down collar open at the neck, and no hat, was standing in
the doorway of a house, talking to another spare man with
a thin, and, to Michael, very pleasant face.

"Well, Michael, my boy, what think you of Slant
Street? Each one of these houses is going to be gutted and
made as bright as a new pin."

"How long will they keep bright, Uncle Hilary?"

"Oh! That's all right," said Hilary, "judging by our
experiments so far. Give 'em a chance, and the people
are only too glad to keep their houses clean. It's wonderful what they do, as it is. Come in and see, but don't touch
the walls. May, you stay and talk to James. An Irish lady
in here; we haven't many. Can I come in, Mrs.
Corrigan?"

"Sure an' ye can. Plased to see your rivirence, though
ut's not tidy I am this mornin'."

A broad woman, with grizzled black hair and brawny
arms, had paused in whatever she was doing to a room in-
conceivably crowded and encrusted. Three people evidently slept in the big bed, and one in a cot; cooking seemed
to go on at the ordinary small black hearth, over which,
on a mantel-board, were the social trophies of a lifetime.
Some clothes were hung on a line. The patched and greasy
walls had no pictures.

"My nephew, Mr. Michael Mont, Mrs. Corrigan; he's
a Member of Parliament."

The lady put her arms akimbo.

"Indeed, an' is he, then?"

It was said with an infinite indulgence that went to Michael's heart. "An' is ut true your rivirence has bought the street? An' what would ye be doing with ut? Ye won't be after turning us out, I'm thinking."

"Not for the world, Mrs. Corrigan."

"Well, an' I knew that. I said to them: 'It's cleaning our insides he'll maybe doing, but he'll never be after putting us out.'"

"When the turn of this house comes, Mrs. Corrigan—I hope before very long—we'll find you good lodgings till you can come back here to new walls and floors and ceilings, a good range, no more bugs, and proper washing arrangements."

"Well, an' wouldn't that be the day I'd like to see!"

"You'll see it fast enough. Look Michael, if I put my finger through there, the genuine article will stalk forth! It's you that can't knock holes in your walls, Mrs. Corrigan."

"An' that's the truth o' God," replied Mrs. Corrigan. "The last time Corrigan knocked a peg in, 'twas terrible— the life there was in there!"

"Well, Mrs. Corrigan, I'm delighted to see you looking so well. Good morning, and tell Corrigan if his donkey wants a rest any time, there'll be room in our paddock. Will you be going hopping this year?"

"We will that," replied Mrs. Corrigan. "Good-day to your rivirence; good-day, sorr!"

On the bare, decrepit landing Hilary Charwell said: "Salt of the earth, Michael. But imagine living in that atmosphere! Luckily, they're all 'snoof'."

"What?" said Michael, taking deep breaths of the somewhat less complicated air.

"It's a portmanteau syllable for 'Got no sense of smell

to speak of.' And wanted, too. One says 'deaf,' 'blind,' 'dumb'—why not 'snoof'?"

"Excellent! How long do you reckon it'll take you to convert this street, Uncle Hilary?"

"About three years."

"And how are you going to get the money?"

"Win, wangle and scrounge it. In here there are three girls who serve in 'Petter and Poplin's.' They're all out, of course. Neat, isn't it? See their paper bags?"

"I say, Uncle, would you blame a girl for doing anything to get out of a house like this?"

"No," said the Reverend Hilary, "I would not, and that's the truth o' God."

"That's why I love you, Uncle Hilary. You restore my faith in the Church."

"My dear boy," said Hilary, "the old Reformation was nothing to what's been going on in the Church lately. You wait and see! Though I confess a little wholesome Disestablishment would do us all no harm. Come and have lunch, and we'll talk about my slum conversion scheme. We'll bring James along."

"You see," he resumed, when they were seated in the Vicarage dining-room, "there must be any amount of people who would be glad enough to lay out a small proportion of their wealth at two per cent., with the prospect of a rise to four as time went on, if they were certain that it meant the elimination of the slums. We've experimented and we find that we can put slum houses into proper living condition for their existing population at a mere fraction over the old rents, and pay two per cent. on our outlay. If we can do that here, it can be done in all slum centres, by private Slum Conversion Societies such as ours, working on the principle of not displacing the existing slum population. But what's wanted, of course, is money—a General Slum Conversion fund—Bonds at two per cent., with bonuses, repayable in twenty years, from which the Societies could draw funds as they need them for buying and converting slum property."

"How will you repay the Bonds in twenty yaars?"

"Oh! Like the Government—by issuing more."

"But," said Michael, "the local Authorities have very wide powers, and much more chance of getting the money."

Hilary shook his head.

"Wide powers, yes; but they're slow, Michael—the snail is a fast animal compared with them; besides, they only displace, because the rents they charge are too high. Also it's not in the English character, my dear. Somehow we don't like being 'done for' by officials, or being answerable to them. There's lots of room, of course, for slum area treatment by Borough Councils, and they do lots of good work, but by themselves, they'll never scotch the evil. You want the human touch; you want a sense of humour, and faith; and that's a matter for private effort in every town where there are slums."

"And who's going to start this general fund?" asked Michael, gazing at his aunt's eyebrows, which had begun to twitch.

"Well," said Hilary, twinkling, "I thought that might be where you came in. That's why I asked you down today, in fact."

"The deuce!" said Michael almost leaping above the Irish stew on his plate.

"Exactly!" said his uncle; "but couldn't you get together a Committee of both Houses to issue an appeal? From the work we've done James can give you exact figures. They could see for themselves what's happened here. Surely, Michael, there must be ten just men who could be got to move in a matter like this——"

" 'Ten Apostles'," said Michael, faintly.

"Well, but there's no real need to bring Christ in— nothing remote or sentimental; you could approach them from any angle. Old Sir Timothy Fanfield, for example, would love to have a 'go' at slum landlordism. Then we've electrified all the kitchens so far, and mean to go on doing it—so you could get old Shropshire on that. Besides, there's no need to confine the Committee to the two Houses —Sir Thomas Morsell, or, I should think, any of the big doctors, would come in; you could pinch a brace of bankers with Quaker blood in them; and there are always plenty of retired Governor Generals with their tongues out. Then if you could rope in a member of the Royal Family to head it—the trick would be done."

"Poor Michael!" said his aunt's soft voice: "Let him finish his stew, Hilary."

But Michael had dropped his fork for good; he saw another kind of stew before him.

"The General Slum Conversion Fund," went on Hilary, "affiliating every Slum Conversion Society in being or to be, so long as it conforms to the principle of not displacing the present inhabitant. Don't you see what a pull that gives us over the inhabitants?—we start them straight, and we jolly well see that they don't let their houses down again."

"But can you?" said Michael.

"Ah! you've heard stories of baths being used for coal and vegetables, and all that. Take it from me, they're exaggerated, Michael. Anyway, that's where we private workers come in with a big advantage over municipal authorities. They have to drive, we try to lead."

"Let me hot up your stew, dear?" said his aunt.

Michael refused. He perceived that it would need no hotting up! Another crusade! His Uncle Hilary had always fascinated him with his crusading blood—at the time of the Crusades the name had been Kéroual, and, now spelt Charwell, was pronounced Cherwell, in accordance with the sound English custom of worrying foreigners.

"I'm not approaching you, Michael, with the inducement that you should make your name at this, because, after all, you're a gent!"

"Thank you!" murmured Michael; "always glad of a kind word."

"No. I'm suggesting that you ought to do something, considering your luck in life."

"I quite agree," said Michael, humbly. "The question seems to be: Is this the something?"

"It is, undoubtedly," said his uncle, waving a salt-spoon on which was engraved the Charwell crest. "What else can it be?"

"Did you never hear of Foggartism, Uncle Hilary?"

"No; what's that?"

"My aunt!" said Michael.

"Some blanc-mange, dear?"

"Not you, Aunt May! But did you really never hear of it, Uncle Hilary?"

"Foggartism? Is it that fog-abating scheme one reads about?"

"It is not," said Michael. "Of course, you're sunk in misery and sin here. Still, it's almost too thick. *You've* heard of it, Aunt May?"

His aunt's eyebrows became intricate again.

"I think," she said, "I do remember hearing someone say it was balderdash!"

Michael groaned: "And you, Mr. James?"

"It's to do with the currency, isn't it?"

"And here," said Michael, "we have three intelligent, public-spirited persons, who've never heard of Foggartism —and I've heard of nothing else for over a year."

"Well," said Hilary, "had you heard of my slum-conversion scheme?"

"Certainly not."

"I think," said his aunt, "it would be an excellent thing

if you'd smoke while I make the coffee. Now I do remember, Michael: Your mother did say to me that she
wished you would get over it. I'd forgotten the name.
It had to do with taking town-children away from their
parents."

"Partly," said Michael, with gloom.

"You have to remember, dear, that the poorer people are,
the more they cling to their children."

"Vicarious joy in life," put in Hilary.

"And the poorer children are, the more they cling to
their gutters, as I was telling you."

Michael buried his hands in his pockets.

"There is no good in me," he said, stonily. "You've
pitched on a stumer, Uncle Hilary."

Both Hilary and his wife got up very quickly, and each
put a hand on his shoulder.

"My dear boy!" said his aunt.

"God bless you!" said Hilary: "Have a 'gasper.'"

"All right," said Michael, grinning, "it's wholesome."

Whether or not it was the "gasper" that was wholesome,
he took and lighted it from his uncle's.

"What is the most pitiable sight in the world, Aunt May
—I mean, next to seeing two people dance the Charleston?"

"The most pitiable sight?" said his aunt, dreamily. "Oh!
I think—a rich man listening to a bad gramophone."

"Wrong!" said Michael. "The most pitiable sight in
the world is a politician barking up the right tree. Behold
him!"

"Look out, May! Your machine's boiling. She makes
very good coffee, Michael—nothing like it for the grumps.
Have some, and then James and I will show you the houses
we've converted. James—come with me a moment."

"Noted for his pertinacity," muttered Michael, as they
disappeared.

"Not only noted, Michael—dreaded."

"Well, I would rather be Uncle Hilary than anybody I know."

"He *is* rather a dear," murmured his aunt. "Coffee?"

"What does he really believe, Aunt May?"

"Well, he hardly has time for that."

"Ah! that's the new hope of the Church. All the rest is just as much an attempt to improve on mathematics as Einstein's theory. Orthodox religion was devised for the cloister, Aunt May, and there aren't any cloisters left."

"Religion," said his aunt, dreamily, "used to burn a good many people, Michael, not in cloisters."

"Quite so, when it emerged from cloisters, religion used to be red-hot politics; then it became caste feeling, and now it's a cross-word puzzle—You don't solve *them* with your emotions."

His aunt smiled.

"You have a dreadful way of putting things, my dear."

"In our 'suckles,' Aunt May, we do nothing but put things—it destroys all motive power. But about this slum business: do you really advise me to have 'a go'?"

"Not if you want a quiet life."

"I don't know that I do. I did, after the war; but not now. But, you see, I've tried Foggartism and everybody's too sane to look at it. I really can't afford to back another loser. Do you think there's a chance of getting a national move on?"

"Only a sporting chance, dear."

"Would you take it up then, if you were me?"

"My dear, I'm prejudiced—Hilary's heart is so set on it; but it does seem to me that there's no other cause I'd so gladly fail in. Well, not that exactly; but there really is nothing so important as giving our town dwellers decent living conditions."

"It's rather like going over to the enemy," muttered Michael. "Our future oughtn't to be so bound up in the towns."

"It *will* be, whatever's done. 'A bird in the hand,' and such a big bird, Michael. Ah! Here's Hilary!"

Hilary and his architect took Michael forth again into the Meads. The afternoon had turned drizzly, and the dismal character of that flowerless quarter was more than ever apparent. Up street, down street, Hilary extolled the virtues of his parishoners. They drank, but not nearly so much as was natural in the circumstances; they were dirty, but he would be dirtier under their conditions. They didn't come to church—who on earth would expect them to? They assaulted their wives to an almost negligible extent; were extraordinarily good, and extremely unwise, to their children. They had the most marvellous faculty for living on what was not a living wage. They helped each other far better than those who could afford to; never saved a bean, having no beans to save, and took no thought for a morrow which might be worse than to-day. Institutions they abominated. They were no more moral than was natural in their overcrowded state. Of philosophy they had plenty, of religion none that he could speak of. Their amusements were cinemas, streets, gaspers, public houses, and Sunday papers. They liked a tune, and would dance if afforded a chance. They had their own brand of honesty, which required special study. Unhappy? Not precisely, having given up a future state in this life or in that—realists to their encrusted fingernails. English? Well, nearly all, and mostly London-born. A few country folk had come in young, and would never go out old.

"You'd like them, Michael; nobody who really knows them can help liking them. And now, my dear fellow, good-bye, and think it over. The hope of England lies in you young men. God bless you!"

And with these words in his ears, Michael went home, to find his little son sickening for measles.

CHAPTER V

MEASLES

THE diagnosis of Kit's malady was soon verified, and Fleur went into purdah.

Soames' efforts to distract his grandson arrived almost every day. One had the ears of a rabbit, with the expression of a dog, another the tail of a mule detachable from the body of a lion, the third made a noise like many bees; the fourth, though designed for a waistcoat, could be pulled out tall. The procuring of these rarities, together with the choicest mandarine oranges, muscatel grapes, and honey that was not merely "warranted" pure, occupied his mornings in town. He was staying at Green Street, whereto the news, judiciously wired, had brought Annette. Soames, who was not yet entirely resigned to a spiritual life, was genuinely glad to see her. But after one night, he felt he could spare her to Fleur. It would be a relief to feel that she had her mother with her. Perhaps by the end of her seclusion that young fellow would be out of her reach again. A domestic crisis like this might even put him out of her head. Soames was not philosopher enough to gauge in-round the significance of his daughter's yearnings. To one born in 1855 love was a purely individual passion, or if it wasn't, ought to be. It did not occur to him that Fleur's longing for Jon might also symbolise the craving in her blood for life, the whole of life, and nothing but life; that Jon had represented her first serious defeat in the struggle for the fulness of perfection; a defeat that might yet be wiped out. The modern soul, in the intricate turmoil of its sophistication, was to Soames a book which, if not sealed, had its pages still uncut. 'Crying for the moon' had become a principle when he was already much too old for principles. Recognition of the limits of human life and happiness was in his blood, and had certainly been fostered by his experience. Without, exactly, defining existence as "making the best of a bad job," he would have contended that though, when you had almost everything, you had better ask for more, you must not fash yourself if you did not get it. The virus of a time-worn religion which had made the really irreligious old Forsytes say their prayers to the death, in a muddled belief that they would get something for them after death, still worked inhibitively in the blood of their prayerless offspring, Soames; so that, although fairly certain that he would get nothing after death, he still believed that he would not get everything before death. He lagged, in fact, behind the beliefs of a new century in whose "make-up" resignation played no part— a century which either believed, with spiritualism, that there were plenty of chances to get things after death, or that, since one died for good and all, one must see to it that one had everything before death. Resignation! Soames would have denied, of course, that he believed in any such thing; and certainly he thought nothing too good for his daughter! And yet, somehow, he felt in his bones that there *was* a limit, and Fleur did not—this little distinction, established by the difference in their epochs, accounted for his inability to follow so much of her restive search.

Even in the nursery, grieved and discomforted by the feverish miseries of her little son, Fleur continued that search. Sitting beside his cot, while he tossed and murmured and said he was "so 'ot," her spirit tossed and murmured and said so, too. Except that, by the doctor's orders, bathed and in changed garments, she went for an hour's walk each day, keeping to herself, she was entirely out of the world, so that the heart from which she suffered had no anodyne but that of watching and ministering to Kit.

Michael was "ever so sweet" to her; and the fact that she wanted another in his place could never have been guessed from her manner. Her resolution to give nothing away was as firm as ever, but it was a real relief not to encounter the gimletting affection of her father's eye. She wrote to no one; but she received from Jon a little letter of condolence.

"Wansdon.

"June 22.

"Dear Fleur,

"We are so awfully sorry to hear of Kit's illness. It must be wretched for you. We do hope the poor little chap is over the painful part by now. I remember my measles as two beastly days, and then lots of things that felt nice and soothing all the way down. But I expect he's too young to be conscious of anything much except being thoroughly uncomfy.

"Rondavel, they say, is all the better for his race. It was jolly seeing it together.

"Good-bye, dear Fleur; with all sympathy,

Your affectionate friend,

"Jon."

She kept it—as she had kept his old letters—but not, like them, about her; there had come to be a dim, round mark on the "affectionate friend" which looked as if it might have dropped from an eye; besides, Michael was liable to see her in any stage of costume. So she kept it in her jewel box, whereof she alone had the key.

She read a good deal to Kit in those days, but still more to herself, conscious that of late she had fallen behind the forward march of literature, and seeking for distraction in an attempt to be up-to-date, rather than in the lives of characters too lively to be alive. They had so much soul, and that so contortionate, that she could not even keep her attention on them long enough to discover why they were not

alive. Michael brought her book after book, with the
words, "This is supposed to be clever," or "Here's the last
Nazing," or "Our old friend Calvin again—not quite so
near the ham-bone this time, but as near as makes no matter." And she would sit with them on her lap and feel
gradually that she knew enough to be able to say: "Oh!
yes, I've read 'The Gorgons'—it's marvellously Proustian."
Or " 'Love—the Chameleon'?—well, it's better than her
'Green Cave,' but not up to 'Souls in the Nude.' " Or,
"You *must* read 'The Whirligig,' my dear—it gets quite
marvellously nowhere."

She held some converse with Annette, but of the guarded
character, suitable between mothers and daughters after a
certain age; directed, in fact, towards elucidating problems
not unconnected with garb. The future—according to Annette—was dark. Were skirts to be longer or shorter by
the autumn? If shorter, she herself would pay no attention; it might be all very well for Fleur, but she had
reached the limit herself—at her age she would *not* go
above the knee. As to the size of hats—again there was no
definite indication. The most distinguished cocotte in Paris
was said to be in favour of larger hats, but forces were
working in the dark against her—motoring and Madame
de Michel-Ange *"qui est toute pour la vieille cloche."*
Fleur wanted to know whether she had heard anything
fresh about shingling. Annette, who was not yet shingled,
but whose neck for a long time had trembled on the block,
confessed herself *"desespérée."* Everything now depended
on the Basque cap. If women took to them, shingling would
stay; if not, hair might come in again. In any case the
new tint would be pure gold; *"Et ça sera impossible. Ton
père aurait une apoplexie. En tout cas, chérie, je crains que
je suis condamnée aux cheveux longs, jusqu'au jugement
dernier. Eh bien, peutêtre, on me donnera une bonne petite
marque à cause de cela."*

"If you want to shingle, Mother, I should. It's just father's conservatism—he doesn't really know what he likes. It would be a new sensation for him."

Annette grimaced. *"Ma chère; je n'en sais rien, ton père est capable de tout."*

The man "capable of anything" came every afternoon for half an hour, and would remain seated before the Fragonard, catechising Michael or Annette, and then say, rather suddenly:

"Well, give my love to Fleur; I'm glad the little chap's better!" Or, "That pain he's got will be wind, I expect. But I should have what's-his-name see to it. Give my love to Fleur." And in the hall he would stand a moment by the coat-sarcophagus, listening. Then, adjusting his hat, he would murmur what sounded like: "Well, there it is!" or: "She doesn't get enough air," and go out.

And from the nursery window Fleur would see him, departing at his glum and measured gait, with a compunctious relief. Poor old Dad! Not his fault that he symbolised for her just now the glum and measured paces of domestic virtue. Soames' hope, indeed, that enforced domesticity might cure her, was not being borne out. After the first two or three anxious days, while Kit's temperature was still high, it worked to opposite ends. Her feeling for Jon, in which now was an element of sexual passion, lacking before her marriage, grew, as all such feelings grow, without air and exercise for the body and interest for the mind. It flourished like a plant transferred into a hothouse. The sense of having been defrauded fermented in her soul. Were they never to eat of the golden apple—she and Jon? Was it to hang there, always out of reach—amid dark, lustrous leaves, quite unlike an apple-tree's? She took out her old water-colour box—long now since it had seen the light—and coloured a fantastic tree with large golden fruits.

Michael caught her at it.

"That's jolly good," he said. "You ought to keep up your water-colours, old thing."

Rigid, as if listening for something behind the words, Fleur answered: "Sheer idleness!"

"What's the fruit?"

Fleur laughed.

"Exactly! But this is the soul of a fruit-tree, Michael —not its body!"

"I might have known," said Michael, ruefully. "Anyway, may I have it for my study when it's done? It's got real feeling."

Fleur felt a queer gratitude. "Shall I label it 'The Uneatable Fruit'?"

"Certainly not—it looks highly luscious; you'd have to eat it over a basin, like a mango."

Fleur laughed again.

"Steward!" she said. And, to Michael bending down to kiss her, she inclined her cheek. At least he should guess nothing of her feelings. And, indeed, the French blood in her never ran cold at one of whom she was fond but did not love; the bitter spice which tinctured the blood of most of the Forsytes preserved the jest of her position. She was still the not unhappy wife of a good comrade and best of fellows, who, whatever she did herself, would never do anything ungenerous or mean. Fastidious recoilings from unloved husbands of which she read in old-fashioned novels, and of which she knew her father's first wife had been so guilty, seemed to her rather ludicrous. Promiscuity was in the air; a fidelity of the spirit so logical that it extended to the motions of the body, was paleolithic, or at least Victorian and 'middle-class.' Fulness of life could never be reached on those lines. And yet the frank paganism, advocated by certain masters of French and English literature, was also debarred from Fleur, by its austerely logical habit of going the whole hog. There wasn't enough necessary virus in her blood, no sex mania about Fleur; indeed, hereunto, that obsession had hardly come her way at all. But now—new was the feeling, as well as old, that she had for Jon; and the days went by in scheming how, when she was free again, she could see him and hear his voice and touch him as she had touched him by the enclosure rails while the horses went flashing by.

CHAPTER VI

FORMING A COMMITTEE

IN the meantime Michael was not so unconscious as she thought, for when two people live together, and one of them is still in love, he senses change as a springbok will scent drought. Memories of that lunch, and of his visit to June, were still unpleasantly green. In his public life—that excellent anodyne for its private counterpart—he sought distraction, and made up his mind to go 'all out' for his Uncle Hilary's slum-conversion scheme. Having amassed the needed literature, he began considering to whom he should go first, well aware that public bodies are centrifugal. Round what fine figure of a public man should he form his committee? Sir Timothy Fanfield and the Marquess of Shropshire would come in usefully enough later, but, though well known for their hobbies, they 'cut no ice' with the general public. A certain magnetism was needed. There was none in any banker he could think of, less in any lawyer or cleric, and no reforming soldier could be otherwise than discredited, until he had carried his reforms, by which time he would be dead. He would have liked an admiral, but they were all out of reach. Retired Prime Ministers were in too lively request, besides being tarred with the brush of Party; and literary idols would be too old, too busy with themselves, too lazy, or too erratic. There remained doctors, business men, governor generals, dukes, and newspaper proprietors. It was at this point that he consulted his father.

Sir Lawrence, who had also been coming to South Square almost daily during Kit's illness, focussed the problem with his eyeglass, and said nothing for quite two minutes.

"What do you mean by magnetism, Michael? The rays of a setting or of a rising sun?"

"Both, if possible, Dad."

"Difficult," said his progenitor, "difficult. One thing's certain—you can't afford cleverness."

"How?"

"The public have suffered from it too much. Besides, we don't really like it in this country, Michael. Character, my dear, character!"

Michael groaned.

"Yes, I know," said Sir Lawrence, "awfully out of date with you young folk." Then, raising his loose eyebrow abruptly so that his eyeglass fell on to the problem, he added: "Eureka! Wilfred Bentworth! The very man —last of the squires—reforming the slums. It's what you'd call a stunt."

"Old Bentworth?" repeated Michael, dubiously.

"He's only my age—sixty-eight, and got nothing to do with politics."

"But isn't he stupid?"

"There speaks your modern! Rather broad in the beam, and looking a little like a butler with a moustache, but— stupid? No. Refused a peerage three times. Think of the effect of that on the public!"

"Wilfred Bentworth? I should never have thought of him—always looked on him as the professional honest man," murmured Michael.

"But he *is* honest!"

"Yes, but when he speaks, he always alludes to it."

"That's true," said Sir Lawrence, "but one must have a defect. He's got twenty thousand acres, and knows all about fatting stock. He's on a railway board; he's the figurehead of his county's cricket, and chairman of a big hospital. Everybody knows him. He has Royalty to shoot; goes back to Saxon times; and is the nearest thing to John

Bull left. In any other country he'd frighten the life out of any scheme, but in England—well, if you can get him, Michael, your job's half done."

Michael looked quizzically at his parent. Did Bart quite understand the England of to-day? His mind roved hurriedly over the fields of public life. By George! He did!

"How shall I approach him, Dad? Will you come on the committee yourself? You know him; and we could go together."

"If you'd really like to have me," said Sir Lawrence, almost wistfully, "I will. It's time I did some work again."

"Splendid! I think I see your point about Bentworth. Beyond suspicion—has too much already to have anything to gain, and isn't clever enough to take in anyone if he wanted to."

Sir Lawrence nodded. "Add his appearance; that counts tremendously in a people that have given up the land as a bad job. We still love to think of beef. It accounts for a good many of our modern leaderships. A people that's got away from its base, and is drifting after it knows not what, wants beam, beef, beer—or at least port—in its leaders. There's something pathetic about that, Michael. What's to-day—Thursday? This'll be Bentworth's board day. Shall we strike while the iron's hot? We'll very likely catch him at Burton's."

"Good!" said Michael, and they set forth.

"This club," murmured Sir Lawrence, as they were going up the steps of Burton's Club, "is confined to travellers, and I don't suppose Bentworth's ever travelled a yard. That shows how respected he is. No, I'm wronging him. I remember he commanded his yeomanry in the Boer War. 'The Squire' in the Club, Smileman?"

"Yes, Sir Lawrence; just come in."

The "last of the squires" was, indeed, in front of the tape. His rosy face, with clipped white moustache, and hard, little, white whiskers, was held as if the news had come to him, not he to the news. Banks might inflate and Governments fall, wars break out and strikes collapse, but there would be no bending of that considerable waist, no flickering in the steady blue stare from under eyebrows a little raised at their outer ends. Rather bald, and clipped in what hair was left, never did man look more perfectly shaved; and the moustache ending exactly where the lips ended, gave an extreme firmness to the general good humour of an open-air face.

Looking from him to his own father—thin, quick, twisting, dark, as full of whims as a bog is of snipe—Michael was impressed. A whim, to Wilfred Bentworth, would be strange fowl indeed! 'However he's managed to keep out of politics,' thought Michael, 'I can't conceive.'

"'Squire'—my son—a suckling statesman. We've come to ask you to lead a forlorn hope. Don't smile! You're 'for it,' as they say in this Bonzoid age. We propose to shelter ourselves behind you in the breach."

"Eh! What? Sit down! What's all this?"

"It's a matter of the slums, 'if you know what I mean,' as the lady said. But go ahead, Michael!"

Michael went ahead. Having developed his uncle's thesis and cited certain figures, he embroidered them with as much picturesque detail as he could remember, feeling rather like a fly attacking the flanks of an ox and watching his tail.

"When you drive a nail into the walls, sir," he ended, "things come out."

"Good God!" said the squire suddenly. "Good God!"

"One doubts the good, there," put in Sir Lawrence.

The squire stared.

"Irreverent beggar," he said. "I don't know Charwell, they say he's cracked."

"Hardly that," murmured Sir Lawrence; "merely unusual, like most members of really old families."

The early English specimen in the chair before him twinkled.

"The Charwells, you know," went on Sir Lawrence, "were hoary when that rascally lawyer, the first Mont, founded us under James the First."

"Oh!" said the squire. "Are you one of *his* precious creations? I didn't know."

"You're not familiar with the slums, sir?" said Michael, feeling that they must not wander in the mazes of descent.

"What! No. Ought to be, I suppose. Poor devils!"

"It's not so much," said Michael, cunningly, "the humanitarian side, as the deterioration of stock, which is so serious."

"M'm?" said the squire. "Do you know anything about stock-breeding?"

Michael shook his head.

"Well, you can take it from me that it's nearly all heredity. You could fat a slum population, but you can't change their character!"

"I don't think there's anything very wrong with their character," said Michael. "The children are predominantly fair, which means, I suppose, that they've still got the Anglo-Saxon qualities."

He saw his father cock an eye. "Quite the diplomat!" he seemed saying.

"Whom have you got in mind for this committee?" asked the squire, abruptly.

"My father," said Michael; "and we'd thought of the Marquess of Shropshire——"

"Very long in the tooth."

"But very spry," said Sir Lawrence. "Still game to electrify the world."

"Who else?"

"Sir Timothy Fanfield——"

"That fire-eating old buffer! Yes?"

"Sir Thomas Morsell——"

"M'm!"

Michael hurried on: "Or any other medical man you thought better of, sir."

"There are none. Are you sure about the bugs?"

"Absolutely!"

"Well, I should have to see Charwell. I'm told he can gammon the hind-leg off a donkey."

"Hilary's a good fellow," put in Sir Lawrence; "a really good fellow, 'squire.'"

"Well, Mont, if I take to him, I'll come in. I don't like vermin."

"A great national movement, sir," began Michael, "and nobody——"

The squire shook his head.

"Don't make any mistake," he said. "May get a few pounds, perhaps—get rid of a few bugs; but national movements—no such things in this country." . . .

"Stout fellow," said Sir Lawrence when they were going down the steps again; "never been enthusiastic in his life. He'll make a splendid chairman. I think we've got him, Michael. You played your bugs well. We'd better try the Marquess next. Even a duke will serve under Bentworth, they know he's of older family than themselves, and there's something about him."

"Yes, what is it?"

"Well, he isn't thinking about himself; he never gets into the air; and he doesn't give a damn for anyone or anything."

"There must be something more than that," said Michael.

"Well, there is. The fact is, he thinks as England really thinks, and not as it thinks it thinks."

"By Jove!" said Michael. "'Some' diagnosis! Shall we dine, sir?"

"Yes, let's go to the Parthenæum! When they made me a member there, I used to think I should never go in, but d'you know, I use it quite a lot. It's more like the East than anything else in London. A Yogi could ask for nothing better. I go in and I sit in a trance until it's time for me to come out again. There isn't a sound; nobody comes near me. There's no vulgar material comfort. The prevailing colour is that of the Ganges. And there's more inaccessible wisdom in the place than you could find anywhere else in the West. We'll have the club dinner. It's calculated to moderate all transports. Lunch, of course, you can't get if you've a friend with you. One must draw the line somewhere at hospitality."

"Now," he resumed, when they had finished moderating their transports, "let's go and see the Marquess! I haven't set eyes on the old boy since that Marjorie Ferrar affair. We'll hope he hasn't got gout." . . .

In Curzon Street, they found that the Marquess had finished dinner and gone back to his study.

"Don't wake him if he's asleep," said Sir Lawrence.

"The Marquess is never asleep, Sir Lawrence."

He was writing when they were ushered in, and stopped to peer at them round the corner of his bureau.

"Ah, young Mont!" he said. "How pleasant!" Then paused rather abruptly. "Nothing to do with my granddaughter, I trust?"

"Far from it, Marquess. We just want your help in a public work on behalf of the humble. It's a slum proposition, as the Yanks say."

The Marquess shook his head.

"I don't like interfering with the humble; the humbler people are, the more one ought to consider their feelings."

"We're absolutely with you there, sir; but let my son explain."

"Sit down, then." And the Marquess rose, placed his

foot on his chair, and leaning his elbow on his knee, inclined his head to one side. For the second time that evening Michael plunged into explanation.

"Bentworth?" said the Marquess. "His shorthorns are good; a solid fellow, but behind the times."

"That's why we want you, Marquess."

"My dear young Mont, I'm too old."

"It's precisely because you're so young that we came to you."

"Frankly, sir," said Michael, "we thought you'd like to be on the committee of appeal, because in my uncle's policy there's electrification of the kitchens; we must have someone who's an authority on that and can keep it to the fore."

"Ah!" said the Marquess. "Hilary Charwell—I once heard him preach in St. Paul's—most amusing! What do the slum-dwellers say to electrification?"

"Nothing till it's done, of course, but once it's done, it's everything to them, sir."

"H'm!" said the Marquess. "H'm! It would appear that there are no flies on your uncle."

"We hope," pursued Michael, "that, with electrification, there will soon be no flies on anything else."

The Marquess nodded. "It's the right end of the stick. I'll think of it. My trouble is that I've no money; and I don't like appealing to others without putting down something substantial myself."

The two Monts looked at each other; the excuse was patent, and they had not foreseen it.

"I suppose," went on the Marquess, "you don't know anyone who would buy some lace—*point de Venise*, the real stuff? Or," he added, "I've a Morland——"

"Have you, sir?" cried Michael. "My father-in-law was saying only the other day that he wanted a Morland."

"Has he a good home for it?" said the Marquess, rather wistfully. "It's a white pony."

"Oh, yes, sir; he's a real collector."

"Any chance of its going to the nation, in time?"

"Quite a good chance, I think."

"Well, perhaps he'd come and look at it. It's never changed hands so far. If he would give me the market price, whatever that may be, it might solve the problem."

"That's frightfully good of you, sir."

"Not at all," said the Marquess. "I believe in electricity, and I detest smoke; this seems a movement in the right direction. It's a Mr. Forsyte, I think. There was a case—my granddaughter; but that's a past matter. I trust you're friends again?"

"Yes, sir; I saw her about a fortnight ago, and it was quite O.K."

"Nothing lasts with you modern young people," said the Marquess; "the younger generation seems to have forgotten the war already. Is that good, I wonder? What do *you* say, Mont?"

"'*Tout casse, tout passe,*' Marquess."

"Oh! I don't complain," said the Marquess; "rather the contrary. By the way—on this committee you'll want a new man with plenty of money."

"Can you suggest one, sir?"

"My next-door neighbour—a man called Montross—I think his real name is shorter—might possibly serve. He's made millions, I believe, out of the elastic band—has some patent for making them last only just long enough. I see him sometimes gazing longingly at me—I don't use them, you know. Perhaps if you mention my name. He has a wife, and no title at present. I should imagine he might be looking for a public work."

"He sounds," said Sir Lawrence, "the very man. Do you think we might venture now?"

"Try!" said the Marquess, "try. A domestic character, I'm told. It's no use doing things by halves; an immense amount of money will be wanted if we are to electrify any considerable number of kitchens. A man who would help substantially towards that would earn his knighthood much better than most people."

"I agree," said Sir Lawrence; "a real public service. I suppose we mustn't dangle the knighthood?"

The Marquess shook the head that was resting on his hand.

"In these days—no," he said. "Just the names of his colleagues. We can hardly hope that he'll take an interest in the thing for itself."

"Well, thank you ever so much, sir. We'll let you know whether Wilfred Bentworth will take the chair, and how we progress generally."

The Marquess took his foot down and inclined his head at Michael.

"I like to see young politicians interesting themselves in the future of England, because, in fact, no amount of politics will prevent her having one. By the way, have you had your own kitchen electrified?"

"My wife and I are thinking of it, sir."

"Don't think!" said the Marquess. "Have it done!"

"We certainly shall, now."

"We must strike while the strike is on," said the Marquess. "If there is anything shorter than the public's memory, I am not aware of it."

"Phew!" said Sir Lawrence, on the next doorstep; "the old boy's spryer than ever. I take it we may assume that the name here was originally Moss. If so, the question is: 'Have we the wits for this job?'"

And, in some doubt, they scrutinised the mansion before them.

"We had better be perfectly straightforward," said Michael. "Dwell on the slums, mention the names we hope to get, and leave the rest to him."

"I think," said his father, "we had better say 'got,' not 'hope to get.'"

"The moment we mention the names, Dad, he'll know we're after his dibs."

"He'll know that in any case, my boy."

"I suppose there's no doubt about the dibs?"

"Montross, Ltd.! They're not confined to elastic bands."

"I should like to make a perfectly plain appeal to his generosity, Dad. There's a lot of generosity in that blood, you know."

"We can't stand just here, Michael, discussing the make-up of the chosen. Ring the bell!"

Michael rang.

"Mr. Montross at home? Thank you. Will you give him these cards, and ask if we might see him for a moment?"

The room into which they were ushered was evidently accustomed to this sort of thing, for, while there was nothing that anyone could take away, there were chairs in which it was possible to be quite comfortable, and some valuable but large pictures and busts.

Sir Lawrence was examining a bust, and Michael a picture, when the door was opened, and a voice said: "Yes, gentlemen?"

Mr. Montross was of short stature, and somewhat like a thin walrus who had once been dark but had gone grey; his features were slightly aquiline, he had melancholy brown eyes, and big drooping grizzly moustaches and eyebrows.

"We were advised to come to you, sir," began Michael at once, "by your neighbour, the Marquess of Shropshire. We're trying to form a committee to issue an appeal for a national fund to convert the slums." And for the third time he plunged into detail.

"And why do you come to *me*, gentlemen?" said Mr. Montross, when he had finished.

Michael subdued a stammer.

"Because of your wealth, sir," he said, simply.

"Good!" said Mr. Montross. "You see, I began in the slums, Mr. Mont—is it?—yes, Mr. Mont—I began there —I know a lot about those people, you know. I thought perhaps you came to me because of that."

"Splendid, sir," said Michael, "but of course we hadn't an idea."

"Well, those people are born without a future."

"That's just what we're out to rectify, sir."

"Take them away from their streets and put them in a new country, then—perhaps; but leave them to their streets ——" Mr. Montross shook his head. "I know them, you see, Mr. Mont; if these people thought about the future, they could not go on living. And if you do not think about the future, you cannot have one."

"How about yourself?" said Sir Lawrence.

Mr. Montross turned his gaze from Michael to the cards in his hand, then raised his melancholy eyes.

"Sir Lawrence Mont, isn't it?—I am a Jew—that is different. A Jew will rise from any beginnings, if he is a real Jew. The reason the Polish and the Russian Jews do not rise so easily you can see from their faces—they have too much Slav or Mongol blood. The pure Jew like me rises."

Sir Lawrence and Michael exchanged a glance. "We like this fellow," it seemed to say.

"I was a poor boy in a bad slum," went on Mr. Montross, intercepting the glance, "and I am now—well, a millionaire; but I have not become that, you know, by throwing away my money. I like to help people that will help themselves."

"Then," said Michael, with a sigh, "there's nothing in this scheme that appeals to you, sir?"

"I will ask my wife," answered Mr. Montross, also with

a sigh. "Good-night, gentlemen. Let me write to you."

The two Monts moved slowly towards Mount Street in the last of the twilight.

"Well?" said Michael.

Sir Lawrence cocked his eyebrow.

"An honest man," he said; "it's fortunate for us he has a wife."

"You mean——?"

"The potential Lady Montross will bring him in. There was no other reason why he should ask her. That makes four, and Sir Timothy's a 'sitter'; slum landlords are his *bêtes noires*. We only want three more. A bishop one can always get, but I've forgotten which it is for the moment; we *must* have a big doctor, and we ought to have a banker, but perhaps your uncle, Lionel Charwell, will do; he knows all about the shady side of finance in the courts, and we could make Alison work for us. And now, my dear, good-night! I don't know when I've felt more tired."

They parted at the corner, and Michael walked towards Westminster. He passed under the spikes of Buckingham Palace Gardens, and along the stables leading to Victoria Street. All this part had some very nice slums, though of late he knew the authorities had been 'going for them.' He passed an area where they had 'gone' for them to the extent of pulling down a congery of old houses. Michael stared up at the remnants of walls mosaicked by the un-stripped wall papers. What had happened to the tribe out-driven from these ruins; whereto had they taken the tragic lives of which they made such cheerful comedy? He came to the broad river of Victoria Street and crossed it, and, taking a route that he knew was to be avoided, he was soon where women encrusted with age sat on doorsteps for a breath of air, and little alleys led off to unplumbed depths. Michael plumbed them in fancy, not in fact. He stood quite a while at the end of one, trying to imagine what it must be like to live there. Not succeeding, he walked briskly on, and turned into his own square, and to his own habitat with its bay-treed tubs, its Danish roof, and almost hopeless cleanliness. And he suffered from the feeling which besets those who are sensitive about their luck.

'Fleur would say,' he thought, perching on the coat-sarcophagus, for he, too, was tired, 'that those people having no æsthetic sense and no tradition to wash up to, are at least as happy as we are. She'd say that they get as much pleasure out of living from hand to mouth (and not too much mouth), as we do from baths, jazz, poetry and cocktails; and she's generally right.' Only, what a confession of defeat! If that were really so, to what end were they all dancing? If life with bugs and flies were as good as life without bugs and flies, why Keating's powder and all the other aspirations of the poets? Blake's New Jerusalem was, surely, based on Keating, and Keating was based on a sensitive skin. To say, then, that civilisation was skin-deep, wasn't cynical at all. People possibly had souls, but they certainly had skins, and progress was real only if thought of in terms of skin!

So ran the thoughts of Michael, perched on the coat-sarcophagus; and meditating on Fleur's skin, so clear and smooth, he went upstairs.

She had just had her final bath, and was standing at her bedroom window. Thinking of—what? The moon over the square?

"Poor prisoner!" he said, and put his arm round her.

"What a queer sound the town makes at night, Michael. And, if you think, it's made up of the seven million separate sounds of people going their own separate ways."

"And yet—the whole lot are going one way."

"We're not going any way," said Fleur, "there's only pace."

"There must be direction, my child, underneath."

"Oh! Of course, change."

"For better or worse; but that's direction in itself."

"Perhaps only to the edge, and over we go."

"Gadarene swine!"

"Well, why not?"

"I admit," said Michael unhappily, "it's all hair-trig-gerish; but there's always common-sense."

"Common-sense—in face of passions!"

Michael slackened his embrace. "I thought you were always on the side of common-sense. Passion? The passion to have? Or the passion to know?"

"Both," said Fleur. "That's the present age, and I'm a child of it. You're not, you know, Michael."

"Query!" said Michael, letting go of her waist. "But if you want to have or know anything particular, Fleur, I'd like to be told."

There was a moment of stillness, before he felt her arm slipping through his, and her lips against his ear.

"Only the moon, my dear. Let's go to bed."

CHAPTER VII

TWO VISITS

ON the very day that Fleur was freed from her nursing she received a visit from the last person in her thoughts. If she had not altogether forgotten the existence of one indelibly associated with her wedding-day, she had never expected to see her again. To hear the words: "Miss June Forsyte, ma'am," and find her in front of the Fragonard, was like experiencing a very slight earthquake.

The silvery little figure had turned at her entrance, extending a hand clad in a fabric glove.

"It's a flimsy school, that," she said, pointing her chin at the Fragonard; "but I like your room. Harold Blade's pictures would look splendid here. Do you know his work?"

Fleur shook her head.

"Oh! I should have thought any——" The little lady stopped, as if she had seen a brink.

"Won't you sit down?" said Fleur. "Have you still got your gallery off Cork Street?"

"That? Oh, no! It was a hopeless place. I sold it for half what my father gave for it."

"And what became of that Polo-American—Boris Strumo something—you were so interested in?"

"He! Oh! Gone to pieces utterly. Married, and does purely commercial work. He gets big prices for his things —no good at all. So Jon and his wife——" Again she stopped, and Fleur tried to see the edge from which she had saved her foot.

"Yes," she said, looking steadily into June's eyes, which were moving from side to side, "Jon seems to have abandoned America for good. I can't see his wife being happy over here."

"Ah!" said June. "Holly told me you went to America, yourself. Did you see Jon over there?"

"Not quite."

"Did you like America?"

"It's very stimulating."

June sniffed.

"Do they buy pictures? I mean, do you think there'd be a chance for Harold Blade's work there?"

"Without knowing the work——"

"Of course, I forgot; it seems so impossible that you don't know it."

She leaned towards Fleur and her eyes shone.

"I do so want you to sit to him, you know; he'd make such a wonderful picture of you. Your father simply must arrange that. With your position in Society, Fleur, especially after that case last year,"—Fleur winced, if imperceptibly—"it would be the making of poor Harold. He's such a genius," she added, frowning; "you *must* come and see his work."

"I should like to," said Fleur. "Have you seen Jon yet?"

"No. They're coming on Friday. I hope I shall like her. As a rule, I like all foreigners, except the Americans and the French. I mean—with exceptions, of course."

"Naturally," said Fleur. "What time are you generally in?"

"Every afternoon between five and seven are Harold's hours for going out—he has my studio, you know. I can show you his work better without him; he's so touchy—all real geniuses are. I want him to paint Jon's wife, too. He's extraordinary with women."

"In that case, I think you should let Jon see him and his work first."

June's eyes stared up at her for a moment, and flew off to the Fragonard.

"When will your father come?" she asked.

"Perhaps it would be best for me to come first."

"Soames naturally likes the wrong thing," said June, thoughtfully; "but if *you* tell him you want to be painted ——he's sure to——he always spoils you——"

Fleur smiled.

"Well, I'll come. Perhaps not this week." And, in thought, she added: 'And perhaps, yes—Friday.'

June rose. "I like your house, and your husband. Where is he?"

"Michael? Slumming, probably; he's in the thick of a scheme for their conversion."

"How splendid! Can I see your boy?"

"I'm afraid he's only just over measles."

June sighed. "It does seem long since I had measles. I remember Jon's measles so well; I got him his first adventure books." Suddenly she looked up at Fleur: "Do you like his wife? I think it's ridiculous his being married so young. I tell Harold he must never marry; it's the end of adventure." Her eyes moved from side to side, as if she were adding: "Or the beginning, and I've never had it." And suddenly she held out both hands.

"I shall expect you. I don't know whether he'll like your hair!"

Fleur smiled.

"I'm afraid I can't grow it for him. Oh! Here's my father coming in!" She had seen Soames pass the window.

"I don't know that I want to see him unless it's necessary," said June.

"I expect he'll feel exactly the same. If you just go out, he won't pay any attention."

"Oh!" said June, and out she went.

Through the window Fleur watched her moving as if she had not time to touch the ground.

A moment later Soames came in.

"What's that woman want here?" he said. "She's a stormy petrel."

"Nothing much, dear; she has a new painter, whom she's trying to boost."

"Another of her lame ducks! She's been famous for them all her life—ever since——" He stopped short of Bosinney's name. "She'd never go anywhere without wanting something," he added. "Did she get it?"

"Not more than I did, dear!"

Soames was silent, feeling vaguely that he had been near the proverb, "The kettle and the pot." What was the use, indeed, of going anywhere unless you wanted something? It was one of the cardinal principles of life.

"I went to see that Morland," he said; "it's genuine enough. In fact, I bought it." And he sank into a reverie. . . .

Acquainted by Michael with the fact that the Marquess of Shropshire had a Morland he wanted to sell, he had said at once: "I don't know that I want to buy one."

"I thought you did, sir, from what you were saying the other day. It's a white pony."

"That, of course," said Soames. "What does he want for it?"

"The market price, I believe."

"There isn't such a thing. Is it genuine?"

"It's never changed hands, he says."

Soames brooded aloud. "The Marquess of Shropshire—that's that red haired baggage's grandfather, isn't it?"

"Yes, but perfectly docile. He'd like you to see it, he said."

"I daresay," said Soames, and no more at the moment. . .

"Where's this Morland?" he asked a few days later.

"At Shropshire House—in Curzon Street, sir."

"Oh! Ah! Well, I'll have a look at it."

Having lunched at Green Street, where he was still staying, he walked round the necessary corners, and sent in his
card, on which he had pencilled the words: "My son-in-
law, Michael Mont, says you would like me to see your
Morland."

The butler came back, and, opening a door, said:

"In here, sir. The Morland is over the sideboard."

In that big dining-room, where even large furniture
looked small, the Morland looked smaller, between two
still-lifes of a Dutch size and nature. It had a simple
scheme—white pony in stable, pigeon picking up some
grains, small boy on upturned basket eating apple. A glance
told Soames that it was genuine, and had not even been restored—the chiaroscuro was considerable. He stood, back
to the light, looking at it attentively. Morland was not so
sought after as he used to be; on the other hand, his pictures were distinctive and of a handy size. If one had not
much space left, and wanted that period represented, he
was perhaps the most repaying after Constable—good Old
Cromes being so infernally rare. A Morland was a Morland, as a Millet was a Millet; and would never be anything else. Like all collectors in an experimental epoch,
Soames was continually being faced with the advisability
of buying not only what was what, but what would remain what. Such modern painters as were painting modern
stuff, would, in his opinion, be dead as door-nails before he
himself was; besides, however much he tried, he did not
like the stuff. Such modern painters, like most of the academicians, as were painting ancient stuff, were careful fellows, no doubt, but who could say whether any of them
would live? No! The only safe thing was to buy the dead,
and only the dead who were going to live, at that. In this
way—for Soames was not alone in his conclusions—the
early decease of most living painters was ensured. They
were already, indeed, saying that hardly one of them could
sell a picture for love or money.

He was looking at the pony through his curved thumb and forefinger when he heard a slight sound; and, turning, saw a short old man in a tweed suit, apparently looking at him in precisely the same way.

Dropping his hand, and deciding not to say "His Grace," or whatever it was, Soames muttered:

"I was looking at the tail—some good painting in that."

The Marquess had also dropped his hand, and was consulting the card between his other thumb and forefinger.

"Mr. Forsyte? Yes. My grandfather bought it from the painter. There's a note on the back. I don't want to part with it, but these are lean days. Would you like to see the back?"

"Yes," said Soames; "I always look at their backs."

"Sometimes," said the Marquess, detaching the Morland with difficulty, " the best part of the picture."

Soames smiled down the further side of his mouth; he did not wish the old fellow to receive a false impression that he was 'kowtowing,' or anything of that sort.

"Something in the hereditary principle, Mr. Forsyte," the Marquess went on, with his head on one side, "when it comes to the sale of heirlooms."

"Oh! I can see it's genuine," said Soames, "without looking at the back."

"Then, if you do want to buy, we can have a simple transaction between gentlemen. You know all about values, I hear."

Soames put his head to the other side, and looked at the back of the picture. The old fellow's words were so disarming, that for the life of him he could not tell whether or not to be disarmed.

" 'George Morland to Lord George Ferrar,' " he read, " 'for value received—£80. 1797.' "

"He came into the title later," said the Marquess. "I'm glad Morland got his money—great rips, our grandfathers, Mr. Forsyte; days of great rips, those."

Subtly flattered by the thought that "Superior Dosset" was a great rip, Soames expanded slightly.

"Great rip, Morland," he said. "But there were real painters then, people could buy with confidence—they can't now."

"I'm not sure," said the Marquess, "I'm not sure. The electrification of art may be a necessary process. We're all in a movement, Mr. Forsyte."

"Yes," said Soames, glumly; "but we can't go on at this rate—it's not natural. We shall be standing-pat again before long."

"I wonder. We must keep our minds open, mustn't we?"

"The pace doesn't matter so much," said Soames, astonished at himself, "so long as it leads somewhere."

The Marquess resigned the picture to the sideboard, and putting his foot up on a chair, leaned his elbow on his knee.

"Did your son-in-law tell you for what I wanted the money? He has a scheme for electrifying slum kitchens. After all, we *are* cleaner and more humane than our grandfathers, Mr. Forsyte. Now, what do you think would be a fair price?"

"Why not get Dumetrius' opinion?"

"The Haymarket man? Is his opinion better than yours?"

"That I can't say," said Soames, honestly. "But if you mentioned my name, he'd value the picture for five guineas, and might make you an offer himself."

"I don't think I should care for it to be known that I was selling pictures."

"Well," said Soames, "I don't want you to get less than perhaps you could. But if I told Dumetrius to buy me a Morland, five hundred would be my limit. Suppose I give you six."

The Marquess tilted up his beard. "That would be too generous, perhaps. Shall we say five-fifty?"

Soames shook his head.

"We won't haggle," he said. "Six. You can have the cheque now, and I'll take it away. It will hang in my gallery at Mapledurham."

The Marquess took his foot down, and sighed.

"Really, I'm very much obliged to you. I'm delighted to think it will go to a good home."

"If you care to come and see it at any time——" Soames checked himself. An old fellow with one foot in the House of Lords and one in the grave, and no difference between them, to speak of—as if he'd want to come!

"That would be delightful," said the Marquess, with his eyes wandering, as Soames had suspected they would. "Have you your own electric plant there?"

"Yes," and Soames took out his cheque-book. "May I have a taxi called? If you hang the still-lifes a little closer together, this won't be missed."

With that doubtful phrase in their ears, they exchanged goods, and Soames, with the Morland, returned to Green Street in a cab. He wondered a little on the way whether or not the Marquess had 'done' him, by talking about a transaction between gentlemen. Agreeable old chap in his way, but quick as a bird looking through his thumb and finger like that! . . .

And now, in his daughter's 'parlour' he said:

"What's this about Michael electrifying slum kitchens?"

Fleur smiled, and Soames did not approve of its irony.

"Michael's over head and ears."

"In debt?"

"Oh, no! Committed himself to a slum scheme, just as he did to Foggartism. I hardly see him."

Soames made a sound within himself. Young Jon Forsyte lurked now behind all his thoughts of her. Did she really resent Michael's absorption in public life, or was it pretence—an excuse for having a private life of her own?

"The slums want attending to, no doubt," he said. "He must have something to do."

Fleur shrugged.

"Michael's too good to live."

"I don't know about that," said Soames; "but he's—er —rather trustful."

"That's not your failing, is it, Dad? You don't trust *me* a bit."

"Not trust you!" floundered Soames. "Why not?"

"Exactly!"

Soames sought refuge in the Fragonard. Sharp! She had seen into him!

"I suppose June wants me to buy a picture," he said.

"She wants you to have me painted."

"Does she? What's the name of her lame duck?"

"Blade, I think."

"Never heard of him!"

"Well, I expect you will."

"Yes," muttered Soames; "she's like a limpet. It's in the blood."

"The Forsyte blood? You and I, then, too, dear."

Soames turned from the Fragonard and looked her straight in the eyes.

"Yes; you and I, too."

"Isn't that nice?" said Fleur.

CHAPTER VIII

THE JOLLY ACCIDENT

IN doubting Fleur's show of resentment at Michael's new "stunt," Soames was near the mark. She did not resent it at all. It kept his attention off herself, it kept him from taking up birth control, for which she felt the country was not yet quite prepared, and it had a popular appeal denied to Foggartism. The slums were under one's nose, and what was under the nose could be brought to the attention even of party politics. Being a town proposition, slums would concern six-sevenths of the vote. Foggartism, based on the country life necessary to national stamina and the growth of food within and overseas, concerned the whole population, but only appealed to one-seventh of the vote. And Fleur, nothing if not a realist, had long grasped the fact that the main business of politicians was to be, and to remain, elected. The vote was a magnet of the first order, and unconsciously swayed every political judgment and aspiration; or, if not, it ought to, for was it not the touchstone of democracy? In the committee, too, which Michael was forming, she saw, incidentally, the best social step within her reach.

"If they want a meeting-place," she had said, "why not here?"

"Splendid!" answered Michael. "Handy for the House and clubs. Thank you, old thing!"

Fleur had added honestly:

"Oh, I shall be quite glad. As soon as I take Kit to the sea, you can start. Norah Curfew's letting me her cottage at Loring for three weeks." She did not add: "And it's only five miles from Wansdon."

On the Friday, after lunch, she telephoned to June:

"I'm going to the sea on Monday—I *could* come this afternoon, but I think you said Jon was coming. Is he? Because if so——"

"He's coming at 4.30, but he's got to catch a train back at six-twenty."

"His wife, too?"

"No. He's just coming to see Harold's work."

"Oh!—well—I think I'd better come on Sunday, then."

"Yes, Sunday will be all right; then Harold will see you. He never goes out on Sunday. He hates the look of it so."

Putting down the receiver, Fleur took up the time-table. Yes, there was the train! What a coincidence if she happened to take it to make a preliminary inspection of Norah Curfew's cottage! Not even June, surely, would mention their talk on the 'phone.

At lunch she did not tell Michael she was going—he might want to come, too, or at least to see her off. She knew he would be at 'the House' in the afternoon, she would just leave a note to say that she had gone to make sure the cottage would be in order for Monday. And after lunch she bent over and kissed him between the eyes, without any sense of betrayal. A sight of Jon was due to her after these dreary weeks! Any sight of Jon was always due to her who had been defrauded of him. And, as the afternoon drew on, and she put her night things into her dressing-case, a red spot became fixed in each cheek, and she wandered swiftly, her hands restive, her spirit homeless. Having had tea, and left the note giving her address—an hotel at Nettlefold—she went early to Victoria Station. There, having tipped the guard to secure emptiness, she left her bag in a corner seat and took up her stand by the bookstall, where Jon must pass with his ticket. And, while she stood there, examining the fiction of the day, all her faculties were busy with reality. Among the shows and shadows of existence, an hour and a half of real life lay before her. Who could blame her for filching it back from a filching Providence? And if anybody could, she didn't care! The hands of the station clock moved on, and Fleur gazed at this novel after that, all of them full of young women in awkward situations, and vaguely wondered whether they were more awkward than her own. Three minutes to the time! Wasn't he coming after all? Had that wretched June kept him for the night? At last in despair she caught up a tome called "Violin Obbligato," which at least would be modern, and paid for it. And then, as she was receiving her change, she saw him hastening. Turning, she passed through the wicket, walking quickly, knowing that he was walking more quickly. She let him see her first.

"Fleur!"

"Jon! Where are you going?"

"To Wansdon."

"Oh! And I'm going to Nettlefold, to see a cottage at Loring for my baby. Here's my bag, in here—quick! We're off!"

The door was banged to, and she held out both her hands.

"Isn't this queer, and jolly?"

Jon held the hands, and dropped them rather suddenly.

"I've just been to see June. She's just the same—bless her!"

"Yes, she came round to me the other day; wants me to be painted by her present pet."

"You might do worse. I said he should paint Anne."

"Really? Is he good enough for *her*?"

And she was sorry; she hadn't meant to begin like that! Still—must begin somehow—must employ lips which might otherwise go lighting on his eyes, his hair, *his* lips! And she rushed into words: Kit's measles, Michael's committee, "Violin Obbligato," and the Proustian School; Val's horses,

Jon's poetry, the smell of England—so important to a poet—anything, everything, in a sort of madcap medley.

"You see, Jon, I must talk; I've been in prison for a month." And all the time she felt that she was wasting minutes that might have been spent with lips silent and heart against his, if the heart, as they said, really extended to the centre of the body. And all the time, too, the proboscis of her spirit was scenting, searching for the honey and the saffron of his spirit. Was there any for her, or was it all kept for that wretched American girl he had left behind him, and to whom—alas!—he was returning? But Jon gave her no sign. Unlike the old impulsive Jon, he had learned secrecy. By a whim of memory, whose ways are so inscrutable, she remembered being taken, as a very little girl, to Timothy's on the Bayswater Road to her great-aunt Hester—an old still figure in black Victorian lace and jet, and a Victorian chair, with a stilly languid voice, saying to her father: "Oh, yes, my dear; your Uncle Jolyon, before he married, was very much in love with our great friend Alice Read; but she was consumptive, you know, and of course he felt he couldn't marry her—it wouldn't have been prudent, he felt, because of children. And then she died, and he married Edith Moor." Funny how that had stuck in her ten-year-old mind! And she stared at Jon. Old Jolyon—as they called him in the family—had been his grandfather. She had seen his photograph in Holly's album—a domed head, a white moustache, eyes deep-set under the brows, like Jon's. "It wouldn't have been prudent!" How Victorian! Was Jon, too, Victorian? She felt as if she would never know what Jon was. And she became suddenly cautious. A single step too far, or too soon, and he might be gone from her again for good! He was not—no, he was not modern! For all she knew, there might be something absolute, not relative, in his "make-up," and to Fleur the absolute was strange, almost terrifying.

But she had not spent six years in social servitude without learning to adjust herself swiftly to the playing of a new part. She spoke in a calmer tone, almost a drawl; her eyes became cool and quizzical. What did Jon think about the education of boys—before he knew where he was, of course, he would be having one himself? It hurt her to say that, and, while saying it, she searched his face; but it told her nothing.

"We've put Kit down for Winchester. Do you believe in the Public Schools, Jon? Or do you think they're out of date?"

"Yes; and a good thing, too."

"How?"

"I mean I should send him there."

"I see," said Fleur. "Do you know, Jon, you really have changed. You wouldn't have said that, I believe, six years ago."

"Perhaps not. Being out of England makes you believe in dams. Ideas can't be left to swop around in the blue. In England they're not, and that's the beauty of it."

"I don't care what happens to ideas," said Fleur, "but I don't like stupidity. The Public Schools——"

"Oh, no; not really. Certain things get cut and dried there, of course; but then, they ought to."

Fleur leaned forward, and with faint malice said: "Have you become a moralist, my dear?"

Jon answered glumly:

"Why, no—no more than reason!"

"Do you remember our walk by the river?"

"I told you before—I remember everything."

Fleur restrained her hand from a heart which had given a jump.

"We nearly quarrelled because I said I hated people for their stupid cruelties, and wanted them to stew in their own juice."

"Yes; and I said I pitied them. Well?"

"Repression is stupid, you know, Jon." And, by instinct, added: "That's why I doubt the Public Schools. They teach it."

"They're useful socially, Fleur," and his eyes twinkled.

Fleur pursued her lips. She did not mind. But she would make him sorry for that; because his compunction would be a trump card in her hand.

"I know perfectly well," she said, "that I'm a snob—I was called so publicly."

"What!"

"Oh, yes; there was a case about it."

"Who dared?"

"Oh! my dear, that's ancient history. But of course you knew—Francis Wilmot must have——"

Jon made a horrified gesture.

"Fleur, you never thought I——"

"Oh, but, of course! Why not?" A trump, indeed!

Jon seized her hand.

"Fleur, say you knew I didn't——"

Fleur shrugged her shoulders. "My dear, you have lived too long among the primitives. Over here we stab each other daily, and no harm done."

He dropped her hand, and she looked at him from beneath her lids.

"I was only teasing, Jon. It's good for primitives to have their legs pulled. *Parlons d'autre chose.* Have you found your place, to grow things, yet?"

"Practically."

"Where?"

"About four miles from Wansdon, on the south side of the Downs—Green Hill Farm. Fruit—a lot of glass; and some arable."

"Why, it must be close to where I'm going with Kit. That's on the sea and only five miles from Wansdon. No,

Jon; don't be alarmed. We shall only be there three weeks at most."

"Alarmed! It's very jolly. We shall see you there. Perhaps we shall meet at Goodwood anyway."

"I've been thinking——" Fleur paused, and again she stole a look. "We *can* be steady friends, Jon, can't we?"

Jon answered, without looking up. "I hope so."

If his face had cleared, and his voice had been hearty, how different—how much slower—would have been the beating of her heart!

"Then that's all right," she murmured. "I've been wanting to say that to you ever since Ascot. Here we are, and here we shall be—and anything else would be silly, wouldn't it? This is not the romantic age."

"H'm!"

"What do you mean by that unpleasant noise?"

"I always think it's rot to talk about ages being this or that. Human feelings remain the same."

"Do you really think they do? The sort of life we live affects them. Nothing's worth more than a year or two, Jon. I found that out. But I forgot—you hate cynicism. Tell me about Anne. Is she still liking England?"

"Loving it. You see, she's pure Southern, and the South's old still, too, in a way—or some of it is. What she likes here is the grass, the birds, and the villages. She doesn't feel homesick. And, of course, she loves the riding."

"I suppose she's picking up English fast?"

And to his stare she made her face quite candid.

"I should like you to like her," he said, wistfully.

"Oh! of course I shall, when I know her."

But a fierce little wave of contempt passed up from her heart. What did he think she was made of? Like her! A girl who lay in his arms, who would be the mother of his children. Like her! And she began to talk about the preservation of Box Hill. And all the rest of the way till Jon

got out at Pulborough, she was more wary than a cat—
casual and friendly, with clear candid eyes, and a little
tremble up at him when she said:

"*Au revoir*, then, at Goodwood, if not before! This *has*
been a jolly accident!"

But on the way to her hotel, driving in a station fly
through air that smelled of oysters, she folded her lips between her teeth, and her eyes were damp beneath her
frowning brows.

CHAPTER IX

BUT—JON

BUT Jon, who had over five miles to walk, started with the words of the old English song beating a silent tattoo within him:

> "How happy could I be with either,
> Were t'other dear charmer away!"

To such confusion had he come, contrary to intention, but in accordance with the impulses of a loyal disposition. Fleur had been his first love, Anne his second. But Anne was his wife, and Fleur the wife of another. A man could not be in love with two women at once, so he was tempted to conclude that he was not in love with either. Why, then, the queer sensations of his circulatory system? Was popular belief in error? A French, or Old-English way of looking at his situation, did not occur to him. He had married Anne, he loved Anne—she was a darling! There it ended! Why, then, walking along a grassy strip beside the road, did he think almost exclusively of Fleur? However cynical, or casual, or just friendly she might seem, she no more deceived him than she at heart wished to. He knew she had her old feeling for him, just as he knew he had it, or some of it, for her. But then he had feeling for another, too. Jon was not more of a fool than other men, nor was he more self-deceiving. Like other men before him, he intended to face what was, and to do what he believed to be right; or, rather, not to do what he believed to be wrong. Nor had he any doubt as to what was wrong. His trouble was more simple. It consisted of not having a control of his thoughts and feelings greater than that with which any man has hitherto been endowed. After all, it had not been his fault that he had once been wholly in love with Fleur, nor that she had been wholly in love with him; not his fault that he had met her again, nor that she was still in love with him. Nor again was it his fault that he was in love with his native land and tired of being out of it.

It was not his fault that he had fallen in love a second time or married the object of his affections. Nor, so far as he could see, was it his fault that the sight and the sound and the scent and the touch of Fleur had revived some of his former feelings. He was none the less disgusted at his double-heartedness; and he walked now fast, now slow, while the sun shifted over and struck on a neck always sensitive since his touch of the sun in Granada. Presently, he stopped and leaned over a gate. He had not been long enough back in England to have got over its beauty on a fine day. He was always stopping and leaning over gates, or in other ways, as Val called it, mooning!

Though it was already the first day of the Eton and Harrow Match, which his father had been wont to attend so religiously, hay harvest was barely over, and the scent of stacked hay still in the air. The Downs lay before him to the south, lighted along their northern slopes. Red Sussex cattle were standing under some trees close to the gate, dribbling and slowly swishing their tails. And away over there he could see others lingering along the hill-side. Peace lay thick on the land. The corn in that next field had an unearthly tinge, neither green nor gold, under the slanting sunlight. And in the restful beauty of the evening Jon could well perceive the destructiveness of love—an emotion so sweet, restless, and thrilling, that it drained Nature of its colour and peace, made those who suffered from it bores to their fellows and useless to the life of everyday. To work—and behold Nature in her moods! Why couldn't he get away to that, away from women? Why—like Holly's story of the holiday slum girl, whose family came to see her off by train—why couldn't he just get away and say: "Thank Gawd! I'm shut o' that lot!"

The midges were biting, and he walked on. Should he tell Anne that he had come down with Fleur? Not to tell her was to stress the importance of the incident; but to tell her was somehow disagreeable to him. And then he came on Anne herself, without a hat, sitting on a gate, her hands in the pockets of her jumper. Very lissome and straight she looked.

"Lift me down, Jon!"

He lifted her down in a prolonged manner. And, almost instantly, said:

"Whom do you think I travelled with? Fleur Mont. We ran up against each other at Victoria. She's taking her boy to Loring next week, to convalesce him."

"Oh! I'm sorry."

"Why?"

"Because I'm in love with you, Jon." She tilted her chin, so that her straight and shapely nose looked a little more sudden.

"I don't see—" began Jon.

"You see she's another. I saw that at Ascot. I reckon I'm old-fashioned, Jon."

"That's all right, so am I."

She turned her eyes on him, eyes not quite civilised, nor quite American, and put her arm round his waist.

"Rondavel's off his feed. Greenwater's very upset about it."

" 'Very,' Anne."

"Well, you can't pronounce 'very' as I pronounce it, any more than I can as you do."

"Sorry. But you told me to remind you. It's silly, though: why shouldn't you speak your own lingo?"

"Because I want to speak like you."

"Want, then, not waunt."

"Damn!"

"All right, Darling. But isn't your lingo just as good?" Anne disengaged her arm.

"No, you don't think that. You're awfully glad to be through with the American accent—you *are*, Jon."

"It's natural to like one's own country's best."

"Well, I do want—there!—to speak English. I'm English by law, now, and by descent, all but one French great-grandmother. If we have children, they'll be English, and we're going to live in England. Shall you take Greenhill Farm?"

"Yes. And I'm not going to play at things any more. I've played twice, and this time I'm going all out."

"You weren't playing in North Carolina."

"Not exactly. But this is different. It didn't matter there.—What are peaches, anyway? It does here—it matters a lot. I mean to make it pay."

"Bully!" said Anne: "I mean—er—splendid. But I never believed you'd say that."

"Paying's the only proof. I'm going in for tomatoes, onions, asparagus, and figs; and I mean to work the arable for all it's worth; and if I can get any more land, I will."

"Jon! What energy!" And she caught hold of his chin.

"All right!" said Jon, grimly. "You watch out, and see if I don't mean it."

"And you'll leave the house to me? I'll make it just too lovely!"

"That's a bargain."

"Kiss me, then."

With her lips parted and her eyes looking into his, with just that suspicion of a squint which made them so enticing, Jon thought: 'It's quite simple. The other thing's absurd. Why, of course!' He kissed her forehead and lips, but, even while he did so, he seemed to see Fleur trembling up at him, and to hear her words: "*Au revoir*! It *was* a jolly accident!"

"Let's go and have a look at Rondavel," he said.

In his box, when those two went in, the grey colt stood by the far wall, idly contemplating a carrot in the hand of Greenwater.

"Clean off!" said the latter over his shoulder: "It's goodbye to Goodwood! The colt's sick."

What had Fleur said: "Au revoir at Goodwood, if not before!"

"Perhaps it's just a megrim, Greenwater," said Anne.

"No, Ma'am; the horse has got a temperature. Well, we'll win the Middle Park Plate with him yet!"

Jon passed his hand over the colt's quarter: "Poor old son! Funny! You can tell he's not fit by the feel of his coat!"

"You can that," replied Greenwater: "But where's he got it from? There isn't a sick horse that I know of anywhere about. If there's anything in the world more perverse than horses!— We didn't train him for Ascot, and he goes and wins. We meant him for Goodwood, and he's gone amiss. Mr. Dartie wants me to give him some South African stuff I never heard of."

"They have a lot of horse sickness out there," said Jon.

"See," said the trainer, stretching his hand up to the colt's ears; "no kick in him at all! Looks like blackberry sickness out of season. I'd give a good deal to know how he picked it up."

The two young people left him standing by the colt's dejected head, his dark, hawk-like face thrust forward, as if trying to read the sensations within his favourite.

That night, Jon went up, bemused by Val's opinions on Communism, the Labour Party, the qualities inherent in the off-spring of "Sleeping Dove," with a dissertation on a horse-sickness in South Africa. He entered a dim bedroom. A white figure was standing at the window. It turned when he came near and flung its arms round him.

"Jon, you mustn't stop loving me."

"Why should I?"

"Because men do. Besides, it's not the fashion to be faithful."

"Bosh!" said Jon, gently; "it's just as much the fashion as it ever was."

"I'm glad we shan't be going to Goodwood. I'm afraid of her. She's so clever."

"Fleur?"

"You *were* in love with her, Jon; I feel it in my bones. I wish you'd told me."

Jon leaned beside her in the window.

"Why?" he said, dully.

She did not answer. They stood side by side in the breathless warmth, moths passed their faces, a night-jar churred in the silence, and now and then, from the stables, came the stamp of a sleepless horse. Suddenly Anne stretched out her hand:

"Over there—somewhere—she's awake, and wanting you. I'm not happy, Jon."

"Don't be morbid, darling!"

"But I'm *not* happy, Jon."

Like a great child—slim within his arm, her cheek pressed to his, her dark earlock tickling his neck! And suddenly her lips came round to his, vehement.

"Love me!"

But when she was asleep, Jon lay wakeful. Moonlight had crept in and there was a ghost in the room—a ghost in a Goya dress, twirling, holding out its skirts, beckoning with its eyes, and with its lips seeming to whisper: "Me, too! Me, too!"

And, raising himself on his elbow, he looked resolutely at the dark head beside him. No! There was—there should be nothing but that in the room! Reality—reality!

CHAPTER X

THAT THING AND THIS THING

ON the following Monday at breakfast Val said to Holly: Listen to this!

"DEAR DARTIE,—

"I think I can do you a good turn. I have some information that concerns your 'Sleeping Dove' colt and your stable generally, worth a great deal more than the fifty pounds which I hope you may feel inclined to pay for it. Are you coming up to town this week-end? If so, can I see you at the Brummell? Or I could come to Green Street if you prefer it. It's really rather vital.

"Sincerely yours,
"AUBREY STAINFORD."

"That fellow again!"

"Pay no attention, Val."

"I don't know," said Val, glumly. "Some gang or other are taking altogether too much interest in the colt. Greenwater's very uneasy. I'd better get to the bottom of it, if I can."

"Consult your uncle, then, first. He's still at your mother's."

Val made a wry face.

"Yes," said Holly, "but he'll know what you can do and what you can't. You really mustn't deal single-handed with people like that."

"All right, then. There's hanky-panky in the wind, I'm sure. Somebody knew all about the colt at Ascot."

He took the morning train and arrived at his mother's at lunch time. She and Annette were lunching-out, but

193

Soames, who was lunching-in, crossed a cold hand with his nephew's.

"Have you still got that young man and his wife staying with you?"

"Yes," said Val.

"Isn't he ever going to do anything?"

On being told that Jon was about to do something, Soames grunted.

"Farm—in England? What's he want to do that for? He'll only throw his money away. Much better go back to America, or some other new country. Why doesn't he try South Africa? His half-brother died out there."

"He won't leave England again, Uncle Soames—seems to have developed quite a feeling for the old country."

Soames masticated.

"Amateurs," he said, "all the young Forsytes. How much has he got a year?"

"The same as Holly and her half-sister—only about two thousand, so long as his mother's alive."

Soames looked into his wineglass and took from it an infinitesimal piece of cork. His mother! She was in Paris again, he was told. *She* must have three thousand a year, now, at least. He remembered when she had nothing but a beggarly fifty pounds a year, and that fifty pounds too much, putting the thought of independence into her head. In Paris again! The Bois de Boulogne, that Green Niobe —all drinking water, he remembered it still, and the scene between them, there. . . .

"What have *you* come up for?" he said to Val.

"This, Uncle Soames."

Soames fixed on his nose the glasses he had just begun to need for reading purposes, read the letter, and returned it to his nephew.

"I've known impudence in my time, but this chap——!"

"What do you recommend me to do?"

"Pitch it into the waste-paper basket."

Val shook his head.

"Stainford dropped in on me one day at Wansdon. I told him nothing; but you remember we couldn't get more than fours at Ascot, and it was Rondavel's first outing. And now the colt's sick just before Goodwood; there's a screw loose somewhere."

"What do you think of doing, then?"

"I thought I'd see him, and that perhaps you'd like to be present, to keep me from making a fool of myself."

"There's something in that," said Soames. "This fellow's the coolest ruffian I ever came across."

"He's pedigree stock, Uncle Soames. Blood will tell."

"H'm!" muttered Soames. "Well, have him here, if you must see him, but clear the room first and tell Smither to put away the umbrellas."

Having seen Fleur and his grandson off to the sea that morning, he felt flat, especially as, since her departure, he had gathered from the map of Sussex that she would be quite near to Wansdon and the young man who was always now at the back of his thoughts. The notion of a return match with "this ruffian" Stainford, was, therefore, in the nature of a distraction. And, as soon as the messenger was gone, he took a chair whence he could see the street. On second thoughts he had not spoken about the umbrellas—it was not quite dignified; but he had counted them. The day was warm and rainy, and, through the open window of that ground-floor dining-room, the air of Green Street came in, wetted and a little charged with the scent of servants' dinners.

"Here he is," he said, suddenly, "languid beggar!"

Val crossed from the sideboard and stood behind his Uncle's chair. Soames moved uneasily. This fellow and his nephew had been at College together, and had—goodness knew what other vices in common.

"By Jove!" he heard Val mutter: "He does look ill."

The "languid beggar" wore the same dark suit and hat, and the same slow elegance that Soames had first noted on him; a raised eyebrow and the half-lidded eyes despised as ever the bitter crow's-footed exhaustion on his face. And that indefinable look of a damned soul, lost to all but its contempt for emotion, awakened within Soames, just as it had before, the queerest little quirk of sympathy.

"He'd better have a drink," he said.

Val moved back to the sideboard.

They heard the bell, voices in the hall; then Smither appeared, red, breathless, deprecatory.

"Will you see that gentleman, sir, who took the you know what sir?"

"Show him in, Smither."

Val turned towards the door. Soames remained seated.

The "languid beggar" entered, nodded to Val, and raised his eyebrows at Soames, who said:

"How d'you do, Mr. Stainford?"

"Mr. Forsyte, I think?"

"Whisky or brandy, Stainford?"

"Brandy, thanks."

"Smoke, won't you? You wanted to see me. My uncle here is my solicitor."

Soames saw Stainford smile. It was as if he had said: "Really! How wonderful these people are!" He lighted the proffered cigar, and there was silence.

"Well?" said Val, at last.

"I'm sorry your 'Sleeping Dove' colt's gone amiss, Dartie."

"How did you know that?"

"Exactly! But before I tell you, d'you mind giving me fifty pounds and your word that my name's not mentioned."

Soames and his nephew stared in silence. At last Val said:

"What guarantee have I that your information's worth fifty pounds, or even five?"

"The fact that I knew your colt had gone amiss."

However ignorant of the turf, Soames could see that the fellow had scored.

"You mean you know where the leakage is?"

Stainford nodded.

"We were College pals," said Val. "What would you expect me to do if I knew that about a stable of yours?"

"My dear Dartie, there's no analogy. You're a man of means, I'm not."

Trite expressions were knocking against Soames' palate. He swallowed them. What use in talking to a chap like this!

"Fifty pounds is a lot," said Val. "Is your information of real value?"

"Yes—on my word of honour."

Soames sniffed audibly.

"If I buy this leakage from you," said Val, "can you guarantee that it won't break out in another direction?"

"Highly improbable that two pipes will leak in your stable."

"I find it hard to believe there's one."

"Well, there is."

Soames saw his nephew move up to the table and begin counting over a roll of notes.

"Tell me what you know, first, and I'll give them to you if on the face of it your information's probable. I won't mention your name."

Soames saw the languid eyebrows lift.

"I'm not so distrustful as you, Dartie. Get rid of a boy called Sinnet—that's where your stable leaks."

"Sinnet?" said Val; "My best boy? What proof have you?"

Stainford took out a dirty piece of writing paper and held it up. Val read aloud:

" 'The grey colt's amiss all right—he'll be no good for Goodwood.' All right?" he repeated: "Does that mean he engineered it?"

Stainford shrugged his shoulders.

"Can I have this bit of paper?" said Val.

"If you'll promise not to show it to him."

Val nodded and took the paper.

"Do you know his writing?" asked Soames: "All this is very fishy."

"Not yet," said Val, and to Soames' horror, put the notes into the outstretched hand. The little sigh the fellow gave was distinctly audible. Val said suddenly:

"Did you get at him the day you came down to see me?"

Stainford smiled faintly, shrugged his shoulders again and turned to the door. "Good-bye, Dartie," he said.

Soames' mouth fell open. The return match was over! The fellow had gone!

"Here!" he said. "Don't let him go like that. It's monstrous."

"Dam' funny!" said Val suddenly, and began to laugh. "Oh! dam' funny!"

"Funny!" muttered Soames. "I don't know what the world's coming to."

"Never mind, Uncle Soames. He's taken fifty of the best of me, but it was worth it. Sinnet, my best boy!"

Soames continued to mutter:

"To corrupt one of your men, and get you to pay him for it. It's the limit."

"That's what tickles me, Uncle Soames. Well, I'll go back to Wansdon now, and get rid of that young blackguard."

"I shouldn't have any scruple, if I were you, in telling him exactly how you got the knowledge."

"Well, I don't know. Stainford's on his beam ends. I'm not a moralist, but I think·I'll keep my word to him."

For a moment Soames said nothing; then, with a side-long glance at his nephew:

"Well, perhaps. But he ought to be locked up."

With those words he walked into the hall and counted the umbrellas. Their number was undiminished, and taking one of them, he went out. He felt in need of air. With the exception of that Elderson affair, he had encountered little flagrant dishonesty in his time, and that only in connection with the lower classes. One could forgive a poor devil of a tramp, or even a clerk or domestic servant. They had temptations, and no particular traditions to live up to. But what was coming to the world, if you couldn't rely on gentlemen in a simple matter like honesty! Every day one read cases, and for every one that came into Court one might be sure there were a dozen that didn't! And when you added all the hanky-panky in the City, all the dubious commissions, bribery of the police, sale of honours—though he believed that had been put a stop to—all the dicky-dealing over contracts, it was enough to make one's hair stand on end. They might sneer at the past, and no doubt there was more temptation in the present, but something simple and straightforward seemed to have perished out of life. By hook or by crook people had to get their ends, would no longer wait for their ends to come to them. Everybody was in such a hurry to make good, or rather bad! Get money at all costs—look at the quack remedies they sold and the books they published now-a-days, without caring for truth or decency or anything. And the advertisements! Good Lord!

In the gloom of these reflections he had come to Westminster. He might as well call in at South Square and see if Fleur had telephoned her arrival at the sea! In the hall eight hats of differing shape and colour lay on the coat-sarcophagus. What the deuce was going on? A sound of voices came from the dining-room, then the peculiar drone of somebody making a speech. Some meeting or other of Michael's, and the measles only just out of the house!

"What's going on here?" he said to Coaker.

"Something to do with the slums, sir, I believe; they're converting of them, I heard Mr. Mont say."

"Don't put my hat with those," said Soames; "have you had any message from your mistress?"

"Yes, sir. They had a good journey. The little dog was sick, I believe. He will have his own way."

"Well," said Soames, "I'll go up and wait in the study."

On getting there, he noticed a water-colour drawing on the bureau: a tree with large dark green leaves and globular golden fruit, against a silvery sort of background—peculiar thing, amateurish, but somehow arresting. Underneath, he recognized his daughter's handwriting:

"The Golden Apple: F.M. 1926."

Really he had no idea that she could use water-colour as well as that! She was a clever little thing! And he put the drawing up on end where he could see it better! Apple? Passion-fruit, he would have said, of an exaggerated size. Thoroughly uneatable—they had a glow like lanterns. Forbidden fruit! Eve might have given them to Adam. Was this thing symbolic? Did it fancifully reveal her thoughts? And in front of it he fell into sombre mood, which was broken by the opening of the door. Michael had entered.

"Hallo, Sir!"

"Hallo!" replied Soames: "What's this thing?"

CHAPTER XI

CONVERTING THE SLUMS

IN an Age governed almost exclusively by Committees, Michael knew fairly well what Committees were governed by. A Committee must not meet too soon after food, for then the Committeemen would sleep; nor too soon before food, because then the Committeemen would be excitable. The Committeemen should be allowed to say what they liked, without direction, until each was tired of hearing the others say it. But there must be someone present, preferably the Chairman, who said little, thought more, and could be relied on to be awake when that moment was reached, whereupon a middle policy voiced by him to exhausted receivers, would probably be adopted.

Having secured his bishop, and Sir Godfrey Bedwin, who specialised in chests, and failed with his Uncle Lionel Charwell, who had scented the work destined for Lady Alison his wife, Michael convened the first meeting for three o'clock in South Square on the day of Fleur's departure for the sea. Hilary was present, and a young woman, to take them down. Surprise came early. They all attended, and fell into conversation around the Spanish table. It was plain to Michael that the bishop and Sir Timothy Fanfield had expectations of the Chair; and he kicked his father under the table, fearing that one of them might propose the other in the hope of the other proposing the one. Sir Lawrence then murmured:

"My dear, that's my shin."

"I know," muttered Michael; "shall we get on with it?"

Dropping his eyeglass, Sir Lawrence said:

"Exactly! Gentlemen, I propose that the Squire takes the Chair. Will you second that, Marquess?"

The Marquess nodded.

The blow was well received, and the Squire proceeded to the head of the table. He began as follows:—

"I won't beat about the bush. You all know as much about it as I do, which is precious little. The whole thing is the idea of Mr. Hilary Charwell here, so I'll ask him to explain it to us. The slums are C3 breeders, and verminous into the bargain, and anything we can do to abate this nuisance, I, for one, should be happy to do. Will you give tongue, Mr. Charwell?"

Hilary dropped at once into a warm, witty and thorough exposition of his views, dwelling particularly on the human character of a problem "hitherto," he said, "almost exclusively confined to Borough Councils, Bigotry and Blue Books." That he had made an impression was instantly demonstrated by the buzz of voices. The Squire, who was sitting with his head up and his heels down, his knees apart and his elbows close to his sides, muttered:

"Let it rip! Can we smoke, Mont?" And, refusing the cigars and cigarettes proffered by Michael, he filled a pipe, and smoked in silence for several minutes.

"Then we're all agreed," he said, suddenly, "that what we want to do is to form this Fund."

No one having as yet expressed any such opinion, this was the more readily assented to.

"In that case, we'd better get down to it and draw up our appeal." And, pointing his pipe at Sir Lawrence, he added:

"You've got the gift of the gab with a pen, Mont; suppose you and the bishop and Charwell here go into another room and knock us out a draft. Pitch it strong, but no waterworks."

When the designated three had withdrawn, conversation broke out again. Michael could hear the Squire and Sir

Godfrey Bedwin talking of distemper, and the Marquess discussing with Mr. Montross the electrification of the latter's kitchen. Sir Timothy Fanfield was staring at the Goya. He was a tall, lean man of about seventy, with a thin, hooked nose, brown face, and large white moustaches, who had been in the Household Cavalry and come out of it.

A little afraid of his verdict on the Goya, Michael said hastily:

"Well, Sir Timothy, the coal strike doesn't end."

"No; they ought to be shot. I'm all for the working man; but I'd shoot his leaders to-morrow."

"What about the mine-owners?" queried Michael.

"I'd shoot their leaders, too. We shall never have industrial peace till we shoot somebody. Fact is, we didn't shoot half enough people during the war. Conshies and Communists and Profiteers—I'd have had 'em all against a wall."

"I'm very glad you came on our Committee, sir," Michael murmured; "we want someone with strong views."

"Ah!" said Sir Timothy, and pointing his chin towards the end of the table, he lowered his voice. "Between ourselves—bit too moderate, the Squire. You want to take these scoundrels by the throat. I knew a chap that owned half a slum and had the face to ask me to subscribe to a Missionary Fund in China. I told the fellow he ought to be shot. Impudent beggar—he didn't like it."

"No?" said Michael; and at this moment the young woman pulled his sleeve. Was she to take anything down?

Not at present—Michael thought.

Sir Timothy was again staring at the Goya.

"Family portrait?" he said.

"No," said Michael; "it's a Goya."

"Deuce it is! Goy is Jewish for Christian. Female Christian—what?"

"No, sir. Name of the Spanish painter."

"No idea there were any except Murillo and Velasquez —never see anything like *them* now-a-days. These modern painters, you know, ought to be tortured. I say," and again he lowered his voice, "bishop!—what!—they're always running some hare of their own—Anti-Birth-Control, or Missions of sorts. We want to cut this C3 population off at the root. Stop 'em having babies by hook or crook; and then shoot a slum landlord or two—deal with both ends. But they'll jibe at it, you'll see. D'you know anything about ants?"

"Only that they're busy," said Michael.

"I've made a study of 'em. Come down to my place in Hampshire, and I'll show you my slides—most interestin' insects in the world." He lowered his voice again:

"Who's that talkin' to the old Marquess? What! The rubber man? Jew, isn't he? What axe is *he* grinding? The composition of this Committee's wrong, Mr. Mont. Old Shropshire's a charmin' old man, but—" Sir Timothy touched his forehad—"mad as a March hare about electricity. You've got a doctor, too. They're too mealy-mouthed. What you want is a Committee that'll go for those scoundrels. Tea? Never drink it. Chap who invented tea ought to have been strung up."

At this moment the Sub-Committee re-entering the room, Michael rose, not without relief.

"Hallo!" he heard the Squire say: "you've been pretty slippy."

The look of modest worth which passed over the faces of the Sub-Committee did not altogether deceive Michael, who knew that his Uncle had brought the draft appeal in his coat pocket. It was now handed up, and the Squire, putting on some horn-rimmed spectacles, began reading it aloud, as if it were an entry of hounds, or the rules of a race meeting. Michael could not help feeling that what it lost it gained—the Squire and emphasis were somehow incompatible. When he had finished reading, the Squire said:

"We can discuss it now, clause by clause. But time's getting on, gentlemen. Personally, I think it about fills the bill. What do you say, Marquess?"

The Marquess leaned forward and took his beard in his hand.

"An admirable draft, with one exception. Not sufficient stress is laid on electrification of the kitchens. Sir Godfrey will bear me out. You can't expect these poor people to keep their houses clean unless you can get rid of the smoke and the smells and the flies."

"Well, we can put in something more about that, if you'll give us the wording, Marquess."

The Marquess began to write. Michael saw Sir Timothy twirl his moustaches.

"*I'm* not satisfied," he began abruptly. "I want something that'll make slum landlords sit up. We're here to twist their tails. The appeal's too mild."

"M-m!" said the Squire; "What do you suggest, Fanfield?"

Sir Timothy read from his shirt cuff.

" 'We record our conviction that anyone who owns slum property ought to be shot. These gentlemen——' "

"*That* won't do," said the Squire.

"Why not?"

"All sorts of respectable people own slum property— Widows, Syndicates, Dukes, goodness-knows-who! We can't go calling them gentlemen, and sayin' they ought to be shot. It won't *do.*"

The bishop leaned forward:

"Might we rather word it like this? 'The signatories much regret that those persons who own slum property are not more alive to their responsibilities to the community at large.' "

"Good Lord!" burst from Sir Timothy.

"I think we might pitch it stronger than that, Bishop," said Sir Lawrence: "But we ought to have a lawyer here, to tell us exactly how far we can go."

Michael turned to the Chairman:

"I've got one in the house, sir. My father-in-law—I saw him come in just now. I daresay he'd advise us."

"Old Forsyte!" said Sir Lawrence. "The very man! We ought to have him on the Committee, Squire. He's well up in the law of libel."

"Ah!" said the Marquess: "Mr. Forsyte! By all means —a steady head."

"Let's co-opt him, then." said the Squire; "a lawyer's always useful."

Michael went out.

Having drawn the Fragonard blank, he went up to his study, and was greeted by Soames' "What's this?"

"Pretty good, Sir, don't you think? It's Fleur's—got feeling."

"Yes," muttered Soames; "too much, I shouldn't won-der."

"You saw the hats in the hall, no doubt. My Slum Con-version Committee are just drafting their appeal, and they'd be most frightfully obliged to you, sir, as a lawyer, if you'd come down and cast your eye over one or two of the allusions to slum landlords. They want to go just far enough, you know. In fact, if it wouldn't bore you terri-bly, they'd like to co-opt you on the Committee."

"Would they?" said Soames: "And who are *they*?"

Michael ran over the names.

Soames drew up a nostril. "Lot of titles! Is this a wild-cat thing?"

"Oh! no, Sir. Our wish to have you on is a guarantee against that. Besides, our Chairman, Wilfred Bentworth, has refused a title three times."

"Well," said Soames, "I don't know. I'll come and have a look at them."

"That's very good of you. I think you'll find them thoroughly respectable," and he preceded Soames downstairs.

"This is quite out of my line," said Soames on the threshold. He was greeted with a number of little silent bows and nods. It was his impression that they'd been having a scrap.

"Mr.—Mr. Forsyte," said what he supposed was this Bentworth, "we want you as a lawyer to come on this Committee and keep us—er—straight—check our fire-eaters, like Fanfield there, if you know what I mean;" and he looked over his tortoiseshell spectacles at Sir Timothy. "Just cast your eye over this, will you be so good?" He passed a sheet of paper to Soames, who had sat down on a chair slipped under him by the young woman. Soames began to read:

" 'While we suppose that there may be circumstances which justify the possession of slum property, we nevertheless regret profoundly the apparent indifference of most slum owners to this great national evil. With the hearty co-operation of slum property owners, much might be done which at present cannot be done. We do not wish to hold them up to the execration of anyone, but we want them to realise that they must at least co-operate in getting rid of this blot on our civilisation.' "

He read it twice, holding the end of his nose between his thumb and finger; then said: " 'We don't wish to hold them up to the execration of anyone.' If you don't, you don't; then why say so? The word 'execration'! H'm!"

"Exactly!" said the Chairman: "Most valuable to have you on the Committee, Mr.—Forsyte."

"Not at all," said Soames, staring round him: "I don't know that I'm coming on."

"Look here, sir!" And Soames saw a fellow who looked like a General in a story-book, leaning towards him: "D'you mean to say we can't use a mild word like 'execration,' when we know they ought to be shot?"

Soames gave a pale smile: if there was a thing he couldn't stand, it was militarism.

"You can use it if you like," he said, "but not with me or any other man of judgment on the Committee."

At his words at least four members of the Committee burst into speech. Had he said anything too strong?

"We'll pass that without those words, then," said the Chairman. "Now for your clause about the kitchens, Marquess. That's important."

The Marquess began reading; Soames looked at him almost with benevolence. They had hit it off very well over the Morland. No one objected to the addition, and it was adopted.

"That's that, then. I don't think there's anything more. I want to get off."

"A minute, Mr. Chairman." Soames saw that the words were issuing from behind a walrus-like moustache. "I know more of these people than any of you here. I started life in the slums, and I want to tell you something. Suppose you get some money, suppose you convert some streets, will you convert those people? No, gentlemen; you won't."

"Their children, Mr. Montross, their children," said a man whom Soames recognized as one of those who had married Michael to his daughter.

"I'm not against the appeal, Mr. Charwell, but I'm a self-made man and a realist, and I know what we're up against. I'm going to put some money into this, gentlemen, but I want you to know that I do so with my eyes open."

Soames saw the eyes, melancholy and brown, fixed on himself, and had a longing to say: "You bet!" But, looking at Sir Lawrence, he saw that "old Mont" had the longing, too, and closed his lips firmly.

"Capital!" said the Chairman. "Well, Mr. Forsyte, are you joining us?"

Soames looked round the table.

"I'll go into the matter," he said, "and let you know."

Almost instantly the Committee broke towards their hats, and he was left opposite the Goya with the Marquess.

"A Goya, Mr. Forsyte, I think, and a good one. Am I mistaken, or didn't it once belong to Burlingford?"

"Yes," said Soames, astonished. "I bought it when Lord Burlingford sold his pictures in 1910."

"I thought so. Poor Burlingford! He got very rattled, I remember over the House of Lords. But, you see, they've done nothing since. How English it all was!"

"They're a dilatory lot," murmured Soames, whose political recollections were of the vaguest.

"Fortunately, perhaps," said the Marquess; "there is so much leisure for repentance."

"I can show you another picture or two, here, if you care for them," said Soames.

"Do," said the Marquess; and Soames led him across the hall, now evacuated by the hats.

"Watteau, Fragonard, Pater, Chardin," said Soames.

The Marquess was gazing from picture to picture with his head a little on one side.

"Delightful!" he said. "What a pleasant, and what a worthless age that was! After all, the French are the only people that can make vice attractive, except perhaps the Japanese, before they were spoiled. Tell me, Mr. Forsyte, do you know any Englishman who has done it?"

Soames, who had never studied the question and was hampered by not knowing whether he wanted an Englishman to do it, was hesitating when the Marquess added:

"And yet no such domestic people as the French."

"My wife's French," said Soames, looking round his nose.

"Indeed!" said the Marquess: "How pleasant!"

Soames was again about to answer, when the Marquess continued:

"To see them go out on Sundays—the whole family, with their bread and cheese, their sausage and wine! A truly remarkable people!"

"I prefer ourselves," said Soames, bluntly. "Less ornamental, perhaps, but——" he stopped short of his country's virtues.

"The first of my family, Mr. Forsyte, was undoubtedly a Frenchman—not even a Norman Frenchman. There's a tradition that he was engaged to keep William Rufus's hair red, when it was on the turn. They gave him lands, so he must have been successful. We've had a red streak in the family ever since. My granddaughter—" He regarded Soames with a bird-like eye—"But she and your daughter hardly got on, I remember."

"No," said Soames, grimly, "they hardly got on."

"I'm told they've made it up."

"I don't think so," said Soames; "but that's ancient history."

In the stress of his present uneasiness he could have wished it were modern.

"Well, Mr. Forsyte, I'm delighted to have seen these pictures. Your son-in-law tells me he's going to electrify the kitchen here. Believe me, there's nothing more conducive to a quiet stomach than a cook who never gets heated. Do tell Mrs. Forsyte that!"

"I will," said Soames; "but the French are conservative."

"Lamentably so," replied the Marquess, holding out his hand: "Good-bye to you!"

"Good-bye!" said Soames, and remained at the window, gazing after the old man's short, quick figure in its grey-green tweeds, with a feeling of having been slightly electrified.

CHAPTER XII

DELICIOUS NIGHT

FLEUR sat under a groyne at Loring. There were few things with which she had less patience than the sea. It was not in her blood. The sea, with its reputation for never being in the same mood, blue, wet, unceasing, had for her a distressing sameness. And, though she sat with her face to it she turned to it the back of her mind. She had been there a week without seeing Jon again. They knew where she was, yet only Holly had been over; and her quick instinct apprehended the cause—Anne must have become aware of her. And now, as Holly had told her, there was no longer even Goodwood to look forward to. Everywhere she was baulked and with all her heart she resented it! She was indeed in a wretched state of indecision. If she had known precisely the end she wished to attain, she could have possessed her soul; but she knew it not. Even the care of Kit was no longer important. He was robust again, and employed, all day, with spade and bucket.

'I can't stand it,' she thought; 'I shall go up to town. Michael will be glad of me.'

She went up after an early lunch, reading in the train a book of reminiscences which took away the reputations of various dead persons. Quite in the mode, it distracted her thoughts more than she had hoped from its title; and her spirits rose as the scent of oysters died out of the air. She had letters from her father and Michael in her bag, and got them out to read again.

"DEAR HEART" (ran Michael's—yes, she supposed she *was* still his dear heart)—

"I hope this finds you and Kit as it leaves me 'at the

present time of speaking.' But I miss you horribly as usual, and intend to descend on you before long, unless you descend on me first. I don't know if you saw our appeal in the papers on Monday. People are already beginning to take bonds. The committee weighed in well for a send-off. The walrus put down five thousand of the best, the Marquess sent your father's Morland cheque for six hundred, and your Dad and Bart each gave two-fifty. The Squire gave five hundred; Bedwin and Sir Timothy a hundred apiece, and the Bishop gave us twenty and his blessing. So we opened with six thousand eight hundred and twenty from the committee alone—none so dusty. I believe the thing will go. The appeal has been re-printed, and is going out to everyone who ever gives to anything; and amongst other propaganda, we've got the Polytheum to promise to show a slum film if we can get one made. My Uncle Hilary is very bucked. It was funny to see your Dad—he was a long time making up his mind, and he actually went down to look at the Meads. He came back saying—he didn't know, it was a tumble-down neighbourhood, he didn't think it could be done for five hundred a house. I had my uncle to him that evening, and he knocked under to Hilary's charm. But next morning he was very grumpy —said his name would be in the papers as signing the appeal, and seemed to think it would do him harm. 'They'll think I've taken leave of my senses,' was his way of putting it. However, there he is, on the committee, and he'll get used to it in time. They're a rum team, and but for the bugs I don't think they'd hold together. We had another meeting to-day. Old Blythe's nose is properly out of joint; he says I've gone back on him and Foggartism. I haven't, of course—but, dash it, one must have something real to do!

"All my love to you and Kit.   "MICHAEL."

"I've got your drawing framed and hung above my

bureau, and very jolly it looks. Your Dad was quite struck. M."

Above his bureau—"The golden apple!" How ironical! Poor Michael—if he knew—!

Her father's letter was short—she had never had a long one from him.

"MY DEAR CHILD, .

"Your mother has gone back to 'The Shelter,' but I am staying on at Green Street about this thing of Michael's. I don't know, I'm sure, whether there's anything in it; there's a lot of gammon talked about the slums; still, for a parson, I find his Uncle Hilary an amiable fellow, and there are some goodish names on the committee. We shall see.

"I had no idea you had kept up your water-colours. The drawing has considerable merit, though the subject is not clear to me. The fruit looks too soft and rich for apples. Still, I suppose you know what you were driving at. I am glad the news of Kit is so good, and that you are feeling the better for the sea air.

"Ever your affectionate father,

"S. F."

Knew what she was driving at! If only she did! And if only her father didn't! That was the doubt in her mind when she tore up the letter and scattered it on Surrey through the window. He watched her like a lynx—like a lover; and she did not want to be watched just now.

She had no luggage, and at Victoria took a cab for Chiswick. June would at least know something about those two; whether they were still at Wansdon, or where they were.

How well she remembered the little house from the one visit she had paid to it—in the days when she and Jon——!

June was in the hall, on the point of going out.

"Oh! It's you!" she said. "You didn't come that Sunday!"

"No, I had too much to do before I went away."

"Jon and Anne are staying here now. Harold is painting a beautiful thing of her. It'll be quite unique. She's a nice little thing, I think," (she was several inches taller than June, according to Fleur's recollection) "and pretty. I'm just going out to get him something he specially wants, but I shan't be a quarter of an hour. If you'll wait in the meal room till I come back, I'll take you up, and then he'll see you. He's the only man who's doing real work just now."

"It's so nice that there's one," said Fleur.

"Here's an album of reproductions of his pictures"— and June opened a large book on a small dining-table. "Isn't that lovely? But all his work has such quality. You look through it, and I'll come back." And, with a little squeeze of Fleur's shoulder, she fled.

Fleur did not look through the album, she looked through the window and round the room. How she remembered it, and that round, dim mirror of very old glass wherein she had seen herself while she waited for Jon. And the stormy little scene they had been through together in this room too small for storms, seven years ago! Jon staying here! Her heart beat, and she stared at herself again in that dim mirror. Surely she was no worse to look at than she had been then! Nay! She was better! Her face had a stamp on it now, line on the roundness of youth! Couldn't she let him know that she was here? Couldn't she see him somehow just for a minute alone! That little one-eyed fanatic—for so in her thoughts Fleur looked on June—would be back directly. And quick mind took quick decision. If Jon were in, she would find him! Touching her hair at the sides, the pearls round her neck, and flicking an almost powderless puff over her nose, she went out into the hall and listened. No sound! And slowly she began mounting the stairs. In his bedroom he would be, or in the studio—there was no other covert. On the first landing, bedroom to right of her, bedroom to left of her, bathroom in front of her, the doors open. Blank!—and blank in her heart! The studio was all there was above. And there—as well as Jon, would be the painter and that girl, his wife. Was it worth it? She took two steps down, and then retraced them. Yes! It was. Slowly, very silently, she went. The studio door was open, for she could hear the quick, familiar shuffle of a painter to his canvas and away again. She closed her eyes a moment, and then again went up. On the landing, close to the open door, she stood still. No need to go further. For, in the room directly opposite to her, was a long, broad mirror, and in it—unseen herself—she could see. Jon was sitting on the end of a low divan with an unsmoked pipe in his hand, staring straight before him. On the dais that girl was standing, dressed in white; her hands held a long-stemmed lily whose flower reached to within an inch of her chin. Oh! she was pretty—pretty and brown, with those dark eyes and that dark hair framing her face. But Jon's expression—deepset on the mask of his visage as the eyes in his head! She had seen lion cubs look like that, seeing nothing close to them, seeing—what?—in the distance. That girl's eyes, what was it Holly had called them?—"best type of water-nymph's"—slid round and looked at him, and at once his eyes left the distance and smiled back. Fleur turned then, hurried down the stairs, and out of the house. Wait for June—hear her rhapsodise—be introduced to the painter—have to control her face in front of that girl? No! Mounting to the top of her 'bus, she saw June skimming round a corner, and thought with malicious pleasure of her disappointment—when one had been hurt, one wanted to hurt somebody. The 'bus carried her away down

the King's Road, Hammersmith, sweating in the westering
sunlight, away into the big town with its myriad lives and
interests, untouchable, indifferent as Fate.

At Kensington Gardens she descended. If she could get
her legs to ache, perhaps her heart would not. And she
walked fast between the flowers and the nursemaids, the old
ladies and the old gentlemen. But her legs were strong,
and Hyde Park Corner came too soon for all but one old
gentleman who had tried to keep pace with her because,
at his age, it did him good to be attracted. She crossed to
the Green Park and held on. And she despised herself
while she walked. She despised herself. She—to whom the
heart was such *vieux jeu;* who had learned, as she thought,
to control or outspeed emotions!

She reached home, and it was empty—Michael not in.
She went upstairs, ordered herself some Turkish coffee, got
into a hot bath, and lay there smoking cigarettes. She experienced some alleviation. Among her friends the recipe
had long been recognized. When she could steep herself no
more, she put on a wrapper and went to Michael's study.
There was her "Golden Apple"—very nicely framed. The
fruit looked to her extraordinarily uneatable at that moment. The smile in Jon's eyes, answering that girl's smile!
Another woman's leavings! The fruit was not worth eating. Sour apples—sour apples! Even the white monkey
would refuse fruit like that. And for some minutes she
stood staring instead, at the eyes of the ape in that Chinese
painting—those almost human eyes that yet were not human because their owner had no sense of continuity. A
modern painter could not have painted eyes like that. The
Chinese artist of all those centuries ago had continuity and
tradition in his blood; he had seen the creature's restless-
ness at a sharper angle than people could see it now, and
stamped it there for ever.

And Fleur—charming in her jade-green wrapper—

tucked a corner of her lip behind a tooth, and went back
to her room to finish dressing. She put on her prettiest frock.
If she could not have the wish of her heart—the wish
that she felt would give her calm and continuity—let her
at least have pleasure, speed, distraction, grasp it with both
hands, eat it with full lips. And she sat down before her
glass to make herself as perfect as she could. She mani-
cured her hands, titivated her hair, scented her eyebrows,
smoothed her lips, put on no rouge, and the merest dusting
of powder, save where the seaside sun had stained her
neck.

Michael found her still seated there—a modern masterpiece—almost too perfect to touch.

"Fleur!" he said, and nothing more; but any more
would have spoiled it.

"I thought I deserved a night out. Dress quickly,
Michael, and let's dine somewhere amusing, and do a
theatre and a club afterwards. You needn't go to the House
this evening, need you?"

He had meant to go, but there was in her voice what
would have stopped him from affairs even more serious.

Inhaling her, he said:

"Delicious! I've been in the slums. Shan't be a jiffy,
darling!" and he fled.

During the jiffy she thought of him and how good he
was; and while, she thought, she saw the eyes and the hair
and the smile of Jon.

The "somewhere amusing" was a little restaurant full
of theatrical folk. Fleur and Michael knew many of them,
and they came up, as they passed out of their theatres, and
said:

"How delightful to see you!" and looked as if they
meant it—so strange! But then, theatre folk were like that!
They looked things so easily. And they kept saying: "Have
you seen our show? Oh! You must. It's just too fright-

ful!" or, "It's a marvellous play!" And then, over the
other shoulder they would see somebody else, and call out:
"Ha! How delightful to see you!" There was no boring
continuity about them. Fleur drank a cocktail and two
glasses of champagne. She went out with her cheeks slightly flushed. "Dat Lubly Lady" had been in progress over
half-an-hour before they reached her; but this did not seem
to matter, for what they saw conveyed to them no more
than what they had not seen. The house was very full, and
people were saying that the thing would "run for years."
It had a tune which had taken the town by storm, a male
dancer whose legs could form the most acute angles, and no
continuity whatever. Michael and Fleur went out humming
the tune, and took a taxi to the dancing club to which
they belonged because it was the thing, rather than because
they ever went there. It was a select club, and contained
among its members a Cabinet Minister who had considered
it his duty. They found a Charleston in progress, seven
couples wobbling weak knees at each other in various corners of the room.

"Gawd!" said Michael. "I do think it's the limit of
vacuity! What's its attraction?"

"Vacuity, my dear. This is a vacuous age—didn't you
know?"

"Is there no limit?"

"A limit, said Fleur, "is what you can't go beyond;
one can always become more vacuous."

The words were nothing, for, after all, cynicism was in
fashion, but the tone made Michael shiver; he felt in it a
personal ring. Did she, then, feel her life so vacuous;
and, if so, why?

"They say," said Fleur, "there's another American dance
coming, called 'The White Beam,' that's got even less in
it."

"Not possible," muttered Michael; "for congenital idi-
ocy this'll never be surpassed. Look at those two!"

The two in question were wobbling towards them with their knees flexed as if their souls had slipped down into them; their eyes regarded Fleur and Michael with no more expression than could have been found in four first-class marbles. A strange earnestness radiated from them below the waist, but above that line they seemed to have passed away. The music stopped, and each of the seven couples stopped also and began to clap their hands, holding them low, as though afraid of disturbing the vacuity attained above.

"I refuse to believe it," said Michael, suddenly.

"What?"

"That this represents our Age—no beauty, no joy, no skill, not even devil—just look a fool and wobble your knees."

"You can't do it, you see."

"D'you mean you can?"

"Of course," said Fleur; "one must keep up with things."

"Well, for the land's sake, don't let me see you."

At this moment the seven couples stopped clapping their hands—the band had broken into a tune to which the knee could not be flexed. Michael and Fleur began to dance. They danced together, two fox-trots and a waltz, then left.

"After all," said Fleur, in the taxi, "dancing makes you forget yourself. That was the beauty of the canteen. Find me another job, Michael; I can bring Kit back in about a week."

"How about joint secretaryship with me of our Slum Conversion Fund? You'd be invaluable to get up balls, bazaars, and matinees."

"I wouldn't mind. I suppose they're worth converting."

"Well, *I* think so. You don't know Hilary; I must get him and Aunt May to lunch; after that you can judge for yourself."

He slipped his hand under her bare arm, and added: "Fleur, you're not quite tired of me, are you?"

The tone of his voice, humble and a little anxious, touched her, and she pressed his hand with her arm.

"I should never be tired of you, Michael."

"You mean you'd never have a feeling so definite towards me."

It was exactly what she had meant, and she hastened to deny it.

"No, dear boy; I mean I know a good thing, and even a good person, when I've got it."

Michael sighed, and, taking up her hand, put it to his lips.

"I wish," cried Fleur, "one wasn't so complex. You're lucky to be single-hearted. It's the greatest gift. Only, don't ever become serious, Michael. That'd be a misfortune."

"No; after all, comedy's the real thing."

"Let's hope so," said Fleur, as the taxi stopped. "Delicious night!"

And Michael, having paid the driver, looked at her lighted up in the open doorway. Delicious night! Yes—for him.

CHAPTER XIII

"ALWAYS"

THE announcement by Michael on the following Monday that Fleur would be bringing Kit home the next morning, caused Soames to say:

"I'd like to have a look at that part of the world. I'll take the car down this afternoon and drive them up to-morrow. Don't say anything to Fleur. I'll let her know when I get down to Nettlefold. There's an hotel there, I'm told."

"Quite a good one," said Michael. "But it'll be full for Goodwood."

"I'll telephone. They must find a room for me."

He did, and they found for him a room which somebody else lost. He started about five—Riggs having informed him that it was a two-and-a-half hours' drive. The day had been somewhat English in character, but by the time he reached Dorking had become fine enough to enjoy. He had seen little of the England that lay beyond the straight line between his river home and Westminster, for many years; and this late afternoon, less preoccupied than usual, he was able to give it a somewhat detached consideration. It was certainly a variegated and bumpy land, incorrigibly green and unlike India, Canada and Japan. They said it had been jungle, heath and marsh not fifteen hundred years ago. What would it be fifteen hundred years hence? Jungle, heath and marsh again, or one large suburb—who could say? He had read somewhere that people would live underground, and come up to take the air in their flying machines on Sundays. He thought it was unlikely. The English would still want their windows down and a thor-

ough draught, and so far as he could see, it would always
be stuffy to play with a ball underground, and impossible
to play with a ball up in the air. Those fellows who wrote
prophetic articles and books, were always forgetting that
people had passions. He would make a bet that the passions
of the English in 3400 A.D. would still be: playing golf,
cursing the weather, sitting in draughts, and revising the
prayer-book.

And that reminded him that old Gradman was getting
very old; he must look out for somebody who could take
his place. There was nothing to do in the family trusts
now—the only essential was perfect honesty. And where
was he going to find it? Even if there was some about,
it could only be tested by prolonged experiment. Must be
a youngish man, too, because he himself couldn't last very
much longer. And, moving at forty miles an hour along
the road to Billingshurst, he recalled being fetched by old
Gradman at six miles an hour from Paddington Station to
Park Lane in a growler with wet straw on the floor—
over sixty years ago—when old Gradman himself was only
a boy of twenty, trying to grow side-whiskers and writing
round-hand all day. "Five Oaks" on a signpost; he couldn't
see the oaks! What a pace that chap Riggs was going! One
of these days he would bring the whole thing to grief, and
be sorry for it. But it was somehow *infra dig.* to pull him
up for speed when there wasn't a woman in the car; and
Soames sat the stiller, with a slightly contemptuous expression as a kind of insurance against his own sensations.
Through Pulborough, down a twisting hill, across a little
bridge, a little river, into a different kind of country—
something new to him—flat meadows all along, that would
be marsh in the winter, he would wager, with large, dark
red cattle, and black-and-white, and strawberry roan cattle;
and over away to the south, high rising downs of a singularly cool green, as if they were white inside. Chalk—out-

cropping here and there, and sheep up on those downs, no doubt—his father had always sworn by Southdown mutton. A very pretty light, a silvery look, a nice prospect altogether, that made you feel thinner at once and lighter in the head! So this was the sort of country his nephew had got hold of, and that young fellow Jon Forsyte. Well! It might have been worse—very individual; he didn't remember anything just like it. And a sort of grudging fairness, latent in Soames' nature, applauded slightly. How that chap Riggs was banging the car up this hill—the deuce of a hill, too, past chalk-pits and gravel-pits, and grassy down and dipping spurs of covert, past the lodge of a park, into a great beech-wood. Very pretty—very still—no life but trees, spreading trees, very cool, very green! Past a monstrous great church thing, now, and a lot of high walls and towers—Arundel Castle, he supposed; huge, great place; would look better, no doubt, the further you got from it; then over another river and up another hill, banging along into this Nettlefold and the hotel, and the sea in front of you!

Soames got out.

"What time's dinner?"

"Dinner is on, sir."

"Do they dress?"

"Yes, sir. There's a fancy dress dance, sir, this evening, before Goodwood."

"What a thing to have! Get me a table; I'll be down directly."

He had once read in a Victorian novel that the mark of a gentleman was being able to dress for dinner in ten minutes, tying his own tie. He had never forgotten it. He was down in twelve. Most people had nearly finished, but there was no one in fancy dress. Soames ate leisurely, contemplating a garden with the sea beyond. He had not, like Fleur, an objection to the sea—had he not once lived

at Brighton for seven years, going up and down to his work
in town? That was the epoch when he had been living
down the disgrace of being deserted by his first wife.
Curious how the injured party was always the one in disgrace! People admired immorality, however much they
said they didn't. The deserted husband, the deserted wife,
were looked on as poor things. Was it due to some thing
still wild in human nature, or merely to reaction against
the salaried morality of judges and parsons, and so forth?
Morality you might respect, but salaried morality—no! He
had seen it in people's eyes after his own trouble; he had
seen it in the Marjorie Ferrar case. The fact was, people
took the protection of the law and secretly disliked it because it was protective. The same thing with taxes—you
couldn't do without them, but you avoided paying them
when you could.

Having finished dinner, he sat with his cigar in a somewhat deserted lounge, turning over weekly papers full of
ladies with children or dogs, ladies with clothes in striking
attitudes, ladies with no clothes in still more striking attitudes; men with titles, men in aeroplanes, statesmen in
trouble, racehorses; large houses prefaced with rows of
people with the names printed clearly for each, and other
evidences of the millennium. He supposed his fellow-
guests were "dolling up" (as young Michael would put
it) for this ball—fancy dressing up at their age! But
people *were* weak-minded—no question of that!—Fleur
would be surprised when he dropped in on her to-morrow
early. Soon she would be coming down to him on the river
—its best time of year—and perhaps he could take her for
a motor trip into the west somewhere; it might divert her
thoughts from this part of the country and that young man.
He had often promised himself a visit to where the old
Forsytes came from; only he didn't suppose she would care
to look at anything so rustic as genuine farmland. The

magazine dropped from his fingers, and he sat staring out of the large windows at the flowers about to sleep. He hadn't so many more years before him now, he supposed. They said that people lived longer than they used to, but how he was going to outlive the old Forsytes, he didn't know—the ten of them had averaged eighty-seven years— a monstrous age! And yet he didn't feel it would be natural to die in another sixteen years, with the flowers growing like that out there, and his grandson coming along nicely. With age one suffered from the feeling that one might have enjoyed things more. Cows, for instance, and rooks, and good smells. Curious how the country grew on you as you got older! But he didn't know that it would ever grow on Fleur—she wanted people about her; still she might lose that when she found out once for all that there was so little in them. The light faded on the garden and his reverie. There were lots of people out on the sea front, and a band had begun to play. A band was playing behind him, too, in the hotel somewhere. They must be dancing! He might have a look at that before he went up. On his trip round the world with Fleur he had often put his nose out and watched the dancing on deck—funny business nowadays, shimmying, bunnyhugging, didn't they call it?— dreadful! He remembered the academy of dancing where he had been instructed as a small boy in the polka, the mazurka, deportment and calisthenics. And a pale grin spread over his chaps—that little old Miss Shears, who had taught him and Winifred, what wouldn't she have died of if she had lived to see these modern dances! People despised the old dances, and when he came to think of it, he had despised them himself, but compared with this modern walking about and shaking at the knees, they had been dances, after all. Look at the Highland schottische, where you spun round and howled, and the old galop to the tune "D'ye ken John Peel"—some stingo in them; and you had to

change your collar. No changing collars nowadays—they
just dawdled. For an age that prided itself on enjoying
life, they had a funny idea of it. He remembered once,
before his first marriage, going—by accident—to one of
those old dancing clubs, the Athenians, and seeing George
Forsyte and his cronies waltzing and swinging the girls
round and round clean off their feet. The girls at those
clubs, then, were all professional lights-o'-love. Very different now, he was told; but there it was—people posed
nowadays, they posed as *viveurs*, and all the rest of it, but
they didn't vive; they thought too much about how to.

The music—all jazz—died behind him and rose again,
and he, too, rose. He would just have a squint and go to
bed.

The ball-room was somewhat detached, and Soames went
down a corridor. At its end he came on a twirl of sound
and colour. They were hard at it, "dolled up" to the nines
—Mephistopheleses, ladies of Spain, Italian peasants, Pier-
rots. His bewildered eyes with difficulty took in the strut-
ting, wheeling mass; his bewildered ears decided that the
tune was trying to be a waltz. He remembered that the
waltz was in three-time, remembered the waltz of olden
days—too well—that dance at Roger's, and Irene, his own
wife, waltzing in the arms of young Bosinney; to this day
remembered the look on her face, the rise and fall of her
breast, the scent of the gardenias she was wearing, and that
fellow's face when she raised to his her dark eyes—lost to
all but themselves and their guilty enjoyment; remembered
the balcony on which he had refuged from that sight, and
the policeman down below him on the strip of red carpet
from house to street.

" 'Always'—good tune!" said someone behind his ears.

Not bad, certainly—a sort of sweetness in it. His eyes,
from behind the neck of a large lady who seemed trying
to be a fairy, roved again among the dancers. What! Over

there! Fleur! Fleur in her Goya dress, grape-coloured—
"La Vendimia—the Vintage"—floating out from her knees,
with her face close to the face of a sheik, and his face close
to hers. Fleur! And that sheik, that Moor in a dress all
white and flowing! In Soames a groan was converted to a
cough. *Those two*! So close—so—so lost—it seemed to
him! As Irene with Bosinney, so she with that young
Jon! They passed, not seeing him behind the fairy's com-
petent bulk. Soames' eyes tracked them through the shifting, yawing throng. Round again they came—her eyes so
nearly closed that he hardly knew them; and young Jon's
over her fichued shoulder, deep-set and staring. Where was
the fellow's wife? And just then Soames caught sight of
her, dancing, too, but looking back at them—a nymph all
trailing green, the eyes surprised, and jealous. No wonder, since under her very gaze was Fleur's swinging skirt,
the rise and falling of her breast, the languor in her eyes!
"Always!" Would they never stop that cursed tune, stop
those two, who with every bar seemed to cling closer and
closer! And, fearful lest he should be seen, Soames turned
away and mounted slowly to his room. He had had his
squint. It was enough!

The band had ceased to play on the sea front, people
were deserting, lights going out; by the sound out there, the
tide must be rising. Soames touched himself where he was
sore, beneath his starched shirt, and stood still. "Always!"
Incalculable consequences welled in on his consciousness,
like the murmuring tide of that sea. Daughter exiled,
grandson lost to him; memories deflowered; hopes in the
dust! "Always!" Forsooth! Not if he knew it—not for
Joe! And all that grim power of self-containment which
but twice or three times in his life had failed him, and
always with disastrous consequence, again for a moment
failed him, so that to any living thing present in the dim
and austere hotel bedroom, he would have seemed like one

demented. The paroxysm passed. No use to rave! Worse than no use—far; would only make him ill, and he would want all his strength. For what? For sitting still; for doing nothing; for waiting to see! Venus! Touch not the goddess—the hot, the jealous one with the lost dark eyes! He had touched her in the past, and she had answered with a blow. Touch her not! Possess his sore and anxious heart! Nothing to do but wait and see!

PART III

CHAPTER I

SOAMES GIVES ADVICE

ON her return to Nettlefold from her night in town, Fleur had continued to 'eat her heart out' by 'the sad sea wave.' For still neither Jon nor his wife came to see her. Clearly she was labelled "poison." Twice she had walked over to Green Hill Farm hoping for another "jolly accident." She had seen there an attractive old house with aged farm buildings flanked by a hill and a wide prospect towards the sea. Calm, broad, and homelike, the place roused hostility in her. It could never be *her* home, and so was inimical, part of the forces working against her. Loose ends in Jon's life were all in her favour. In exploitation of those calm acres he would be secured to that girl his wife, out of her reach again, this time for good— the twice-burnt child! And yet, with all her heartache, she was still uncertain what, precisely, she wanted. Not having to grapple with actual decision, things seemed possible which, in her bones, she knew might not be possible. Even to fling her 'cap over the windmill,' did not seem like rank and staring madness. To retrieve Spain with Jon! Her hands clenched and her lips loosened at the thought of it— an Odyssey together, till in the shifting, tolerant, modern world, all was forgotten, if not forgiven! Every form of companionship with him from decorous and platonic friendship to the world well lost; from guilty and secret liaison to orderly and above-board glimpses of him at not too long intervals. According to the tides in her blood, all seemed possible, if not exactly probable, so long as she did not lose him again altogether.

To these feverish veerings of her spirit, a letter from her Aunt Winifred supplied a point of anchorage:

"I hear from Val that they are not going to Goodwood
after all—their nice two-year-old is not in form. Such a
bore. It's the most comfortable meeting of the year. They
seem to be very busy settling about the farm that Jon Forsyte is going to take. It will be pleasant for Val and
Holly to have them so close, though I'm afraid that American child will find it dull. Holly writes that they are going
to an amusing little fancy dress affair at the hotel in Nettlefold. Anne is to go as a water-nymph—she will make quite
a good one with her nice straight legs. Holly is to be Madame Vigée le Brun; and Val says he'll go as a tipster or
not at all. I do hope he won't redden his nose. Young
Jon Forsyte has an Arab dress he brought from Egypt."

'And I,' thought Fleur, 'have the dress I wore the night
I went to his room at Wansdon.' How she wished now
that she had come out of that room his wife; after that
nothing could have divided them. But they had been such
innocents then!

For at once she had made up her mind to go to that
dance herself. She was there first, and with malicious pleasure watched the faces of those two when she met them at
the entrance of the room. Her grape-dress. She could see
that Jon remembered it, and quickly she began to praise
Anne's. A water-nymph to the life! As for Jon—another
wife or two was all he needed to be perfect! She was discretion itself until that waltz; and even then she had tried
to be discreet to all but Jon. For him she kept (or so she
hoped) the closeness, the clinging, and the languor of her
eyes; but in those few minutes she let him know quite
surely that love ran in her veins.

" 'Always,' " was all she said when at last they stopped.

And, after that dance, she stole away; having no heart
to see him dance with his water-nymph. She crept up to
her small bedroom trembling, and on her bed fell into a
passion of silent weeping. And the water-nymph's browned

face and eyes and legs flitted torturingly in the tangled glades of her vision. She quieted down at last. At least, for a few minutes, she had had him to herself, heart against heart. That was something.

She rose late, pale and composed again. At ten o'clock the startling appearance of her father's car completed the masking of her face. She greeted him with an emphatic gratitude quite unfelt.

"Dad! How lovely! Where have you sprung from?"

"Nettlefold. I spent the night there."

"At the hotel?"

"Yes."

"Why! I was there myself last night at a dance!"

"Oh!" said Soames, "that fancy dress affair—they told me of it. Pleasant?"

"Not very; I left early. If I'd known you were there! Why didn't you tell me you were coming down to fetch us home?"

"It just came into my mind that it was better for the boy than the train."

And Fleur could not tell what he had seen, or if, indeed, he had seen anything.

Fortunately, during the journey up, Kit had much to say, and Soames dozed, very tired after a night of anxiety, indecision, and little sleep. The aspect of the South Square house, choice and sophisticated, and the warmth of Michael's greeting, quite beautifully returned by Fleur, restored to him at least a measure of equanimity. Here, at all events, was no unhappy home; that counted much in the equation of a future into which he could no longer see.

After lunch he went up to Michael's study to discuss slum conversion. Confronted, while they were talking, with Fleur's water-colour, Soames rediscovered the truth that individuals are more interesting than the collection of them called the State. Not national welfare, but the painter of those passion fruits, possessed his mind. How prevent her from eating them?

"Yes, sir. That's really quite good, isn't it? I wish Fleur would take seriously to water-colour work."

Soames started.

"I wish she'd take seriously to anything, and keep her mind occupied."

Michael looked at him. 'Rather like a dog,' Soames thought, 'trying to understand.' Suddenly, he saw the young man wet his lips.

"You've got something to tell me, sir, I believe. I remember what you said to me some weeks ago. Is it anything to do with that?"

"Yes," answered Soames, watching his eyes. "Don't take it too much to heart, but I've reason to believe she's never properly got over the feeling she used to have. I don't know how much you've heard about that boy and girl affair."

"Pretty well all, I think." Again he saw Michael moisten his lips.

"Oh! From her?"

"No. Fleur's never said a word. From Miss June Forsyte."

"That woman! *She's* sure to have plumped it all out. But Fleur's fond of you."

"I belong."

It seemed to Soames a queer way of putting it; pathetic, somehow!

"Well," he said, "I've not made a sign. Perhaps you'd like to know how I formed my view."

"No, sir."

Soames glanced quickly at him and away again. This was a bitter moment, no doubt, for young Michael! Was one precipitating a crisis which one felt, deeply yet vaguely, had to be reached and passed? He himself knew how to wait, but did this modern young man, so feather-pated and scattery? Still, he was a gentleman. That at least had become a cardinal belief with Soames. And it was a comfort to him, looking at the "White Monkey," on the wall, who had so slender a claim to such a title.

"The only thing," he muttered, "is to wait——"

"Not 'and see,' sir; anything but that. I can wait and not see, or I can have the whole thing out."

"No," said Soames, with emphasis, "don't have it out! I may be mistaken. There's everything against it; she knows which side her bread is buttered."

"Don't!" said Michael, and got up.

"Now, now," murmured Soames; "I've upset you. Everything depends on keeping your head."

Michael emitted an unhappy little laugh.

"*You* can't go round the world again, sir. Perhaps *I'd* better, this time, and alone."

Soames looked at him. "This won't do," he said. "She's got a strong affection for you; it's just feverishness, if it's anything. Take it like a man, and keep quiet." He was talking to the young man's back now, and found it easier. "She was always a spoiled child, you know; spoiled children get things into their heads, but it doesn't amount to anything. Can't you get her interested in these slums?"

Michael turned round.

"How far has it gone?"

"There you go!" said Soames. "Not any way so far as I know. I only happened to see her dancing with him last night at that hotel, and noticed her——her expression."

The word "eyes" had seemed somehow too extravagant.

"There's always his wife," he added, quickly, "she's an attractive little thing; and he's going to farm down there —they tell me. That'll take him all his time. How would it be if I took Fleur to Scotland for August and September? With this strike on there'll be some places in the market still."

"No, sir. That's only putting off the evil day. It must go to a finish, one way or the other."

Soames did not answer for some time.

"It's never any good to meet trouble half way," he said at last. "You young people are always in a hurry. One can do things, but one can't undo them. It's not," he went on, shyly, "as if this were anything new—an unfortunate old business revived for the moment; it'll die away again as it did before, if it's properly left alone. Plenty of exercise, and keep her mind well occupied."

The young man's expression was peculiar. "And have you found that successful, sir, in your experience?" it seemed to say. That woman June had been blurting out his past, he shouldn't wonder!

"Promise me, anyway, to keep what I've said to yourself, and do nothing rash."

Michael shook his head. "I can't promise anything; it must depend, but I'll remember your advice, sir."

And with this Soames had to be content.

Acting on that instinct, born of love, which guided him in his dealings with Fleur, he bade her an almost casual farewell, and next day returned to Mapledurham. He detailed to Annette everything that was not of importance, for to tell her what was would never do.

His home on these last days of July was pleasurable; and almost at once he went out fishing in the punt. There, in contemplation of his line and the gliding water, green with reflection, he felt rested. Bullrushes, water lilies, dragon flies, and the cows in his own fields, the incessant cooing of the wood pigeons—with their precious "Take *two* cows, David!"—the distant buzz of his gardener's lawn mower, the splash of a water rat, shadows lengthening out from the poplars and the willow-trees, the scent of grass and of elder flowers bright along the banks, and the slow drift of the white river clouds—peaceful—very peaceful;

and something of Nature's calm entered his soul, so that the disappearance of his float recalled him to reality with a jerk.

'It'll be uneatable,' he thought, winding at his line.

CHAPTER II

OCCUPYING THE MIND

COMEDY the real thing? Was it? Michael wondered. In saying to Soames that he could not wait and see, he had expressed a very natural abhorrence. Watch, spy, calculate—impossible! To go to Fleur and ask for a frank exposure of her feelings was what he would have liked to do; but he could not help knowing the depth of his father-in-law's affection and concern, and the length of his head; and he had sufficient feeling to hesitate before imperilling what was as much 'old Forsyte's' happiness as his own. The 'old boy' had behaved so decently in pulling up his roots and going round the world with Fleur, that every considera-tion was due to him. It remained, then, to wait without at-tempting to see—hardest of all courses because least active. "Keep her mind well occupied!" So easy! Recollecting his own prenuptial feelings, he did not see how it was to be done. And Fleur's was a particularly difficult mind to oc-cupy with anything except that on which she had set her heart. The slums? No! She possessed one of those emi-nently sane natures which rejected social problems, as fruitless and incalculable. An immediate job, like the can-teen, in which she could shine a little—she would per-form beautifully; but she would never work for a remote object, without shining! He could see her clear eyes look-ing at the slums as they had looked at Foggartism, and his experiment with the out-of-works. He might take her to see Hilary and Aunt May, but it would be futile in the end.

Night brought the first acute trouble. What were to be his relations with her, if her feelings were really engaged elsewhere? To wait and not see meant continuation of the married state. He suspected Soames of having wished to counsel that. Whipped by longing, stung and half numbed by a jealousy he must not show, and unwishful to wound her, he waited for a sign, feeling as if she must know why he was waiting. He received it, and was glad, but it did not convince him. Still!

He woke much lighter in spirit.

At breakfast he asked her what she would like to do, now that she was back and the season over. Did this slum scheme amuse her at all, because, if so, there was a lot to do in it; she would find Hilary and May great sports.

"Rather! Anything really useful, Michael!"

He took her round to the Meads. The result was better than he had hoped.

For his uncle and aunt were human buildings the like of which Fleur had not yet encountered—positively fashioned, concreted in tradition, but freely exposed to sun and air, tiled with taste, and windowed with humour. Michael, with something of their 'make-up,' had neither their poise, nor active certainty. Fleur recognized at once that those two dwelt in unity unlike any that she knew, as if, in their twenty odd years together, they had welded a single instrument to carry out a new discovery—the unselfconscious day. They were not fools, yet cleverness in their presence seemed jejune, and as if unrelated to reality. They knew —especially Hilary—a vast deal about flowers, printing, architecture, mountains, drains, electricity, the price of living, Italian cities; they knew how to treat the ailments of dogs, play musical instruments, administer first and even second aid, amuse children, and cause the aged to laugh. They could discuss anything from religion to morality with fluency, and the tolerance that came from experience of the trials of others and forgetfulness of their own. With her natural intelligence Fleur admired them. They were good, but they were not dull—very odd! Admiring them, she could not help making up to them. Their attitude in life— she recognised—was superior to her own, and she was prepared to pay at least lip-service. But lip-service 'cut no ice' in the Meads. Hand, foot, intellect and heart were the matter-of-course requirements. To occupy her mind, however, she took the jobs given her. Then trouble began. The jobs were not her own, and there was no career in them, Try as she would, she could not identify herself with Mrs. Corrigan or the little Topmarshes. The girls, who served at Petter and Poplins and kept their clothes in paper bags, bored her when they talked and when they didn't. Each new type amused her for a day, and then just seemed unlovely. She tried hard, however, for her own sake, and in order to deceive Michael. She had been at it more than a week before she had an idea.

"You know, Michael, I feel I should be ever so much more interested if I ran a place of my own in the country —a sort of rest-house that I could make attractive for girls who wanted air and that."

To Michael, remembering the canteen, it seemed "an idea" indeed. To Fleur it seemed more—a "lease and release," as her father might have put it. Her scheming mind had seen the possibilities. She would be able to go there without let or cavil, and none would know what she did with her time. A base of operations with a fool-proof title was essential for a relationship, however innocent, with Jon. She began at once to learn to drive the car; for the "rest-house" must not be so near him as to excite suspicion. She approached her father on the finance of the matter. At first doubtfully, and then almost cordially, Soames approved. If he would pay the rent and rates of the house, she would manage the rest out of her own pocket. She could not have bettered such a policy by way of convincing him that her interest was genuine; for he emphatically distrusted the interest of people in anything that did not cost them money. A careful study of the map suggested to her the neighbourhood of Dorking. Box Hill had a reputation for air and beauty, and was within an hour's fast drive of Wansdon. In the next three weeks she found and furnished a derelict house, rambling and cheap, close to the road on the London side of Box Hill, with a good garden and stables that could be converted easily. She completed her education with the car, and engaged a couple who could be left in charge with impunity. She consulted Michael and the Hilarys freely. In fact, like a mother cat, who carefully misleads the household as to where she is going to 'lay' her kittens, so Fleur, by the nature of her preparations, disguised her roundabout design. The Meads "Rest House," as it was called, was opened at the end of August.

All this time she possessed her soul with only the scantiest news of Jon. A letter from Holly told her that negotiations for Green Hill Farm were 'hanging fire' over the price, though Jon was more and more taken with it; and Anne daily becoming more rural and more English. Rondavel was in great form again, and expected to win at Doncaster. Val had already taken a long shot about him for the Derby next year.

Fleur replied in a letter so worded as to give the impression that she had no other interest in the world just then but her new scheme. They must all drive over and see whether her "Rest House" didn't beat the canteen. The people were "such dears"—it was all "terribly amusing." She wished to convey the feeling that she had no fears of herself, no alarm in the thought of Jon; and that her work in life was serious. Michael, never wholly deserted by the naïveté of a good disposition, was more and more deceived. To him her mind seemed really occupied; and certainly her body, for she ran up from Dorking almost daily and spent the week-ends with him either at "The Shelter," where Kit

was installed with his grandparents, or at Lippinghall,
where they always made a fuss of Fleur. Rowing her on
the river in bland weather, Michael recaptured a feeling of
security. "Old Forsyte" must have let his imagination run
away with him; the old boy *was* rather like a hen where
Fleur was concerned, clucking and turning an inflamed
eye on everything that came near!

Parliament had risen, and slum conversion work was
now all that he was doing. These days on that river, which
he ever associated with his wooing, were the happiest he had
spent since the strike began——the strike that in narrowed
form dragged wearyingly on, so that people ceased to mention it, the weather being warm.

And Soames? By his daughter's tranquil amiability, he,
too, was tranquilised. He would look at Michael and say
nothing, in accordance with the best English traditions, and
his own dignity. It was he who revived the idea of Fleur's
being painted by June's "lame duck." He felt it would oc-
cupy her mind still further. He would like, however, to see
the fellow's work first, though he supposed it would mean a
visit to June's.

"If she were to be out," he said to Fleur, "I shouldn't
mind having a look round her studio."

"Shall I arrange that, then, Dad?"

"Not too pointedly," said Soames; "or she'll get into a
fantod."

Accordingly at the following week-end Fleur said to
him:

"If you'll come up with me on Monday, dear, we'll go
round. The Rafaelite will be in, but June won't. She
doesn't want to see you any more than you want to see her."

"H'm!" said Soames. "She always spoke her mind."

They went up, in his car. After forming his opinion
Soames was to return, and Fleur to go on home. The
Rafaelite met them at the head of the stairs. To Soames

he suggested a bull-fighter (not that he had ever seen one in the flesh), with his short whiskers, and his broad, pale face which wore the expression: "If you suppose yourself capable of appreciating my work, you make a mistake." Soames' face, on the other hand, wore the expression: "If you suppose that I want to see your work, you make a greater." And, leaving him to Fleur, he began to look round. In truth he was not unfavourably impressed. The work had turned its back on modernity. The surfaces were smooth, the drawing in perspective, and the colouring full. He perceived a new note, or rather the definite revival of an old one. The chap had undoubted talent; whether it would go down in these days he did not know, but its texture was more agreeable to live with than any he had seen for some time. When he came to the portrait of June he stood for a minute, with his head on one side, and then said, with a pale smile:

"You've got her to the life." It pleased him to think that June had evidently not seen in it what he saw. But when his eyes fell on the picture of Anne, his face fell, too, and he looked quickly at Fleur, who said:

"Yes, Dad? What do you think of that?"

The thought had flashed through Soames' mind: 'Is it to get in touch with *him* that she's ready to be painted?'

"Finished?" he asked.

The Rafaelite answered:

"Yes. Going down to them to-morrow."

Soames' face rose again. That risk was over then!

"Quite clever!" he murmured. "The lily's excellent." And he passed on to a sketch of the woman who had opened the door to them.

"That's recognisable! Not at all bad."

In these quiet ways he made it clear that, while he approved on the whole, he was not going to pay any extravagant price. He took an opportunity when Fleur was out of hearing, and said:

"So you want to paint my daughter. What's your figure?"

"A hundred and fifty."

"Rather tall for these days—you're a young man. However—so long as you make a good thing of it!"

The Rafaelite bowed ironically.

"Yes," said Soames, "I daresay; you think all your geese are swans—never met a painter who didn't. You won't keep her sitting long, I suppose—she's busy. That's agreed, then. Good-bye! Don't come down!"

As they went out he said to Fleur:

"I've fixed that. You can begin sitting when you like. His work's better than you'd think from the look of him. Forbidding chap, I call him."

"A painter has to be forbidding, Dad; otherwise people would think he was cadging."

"Something in that," said Soames. "I'll get back now, as you won't let me take you home. Good-bye! Take care of yourself, and don't overdo it." And, receiving her kiss, he got into the car.

Fleur began to walk towards her eastward-bound 'bus as his car moved west, nor did he see her stop, give him some law, then retrace her steps to June's.

CHAPTER III

POSSESSING THE SOUL

JUST as in a very old world to find things or people of
pure descent is impossible, so with actions; and the psy-
chologist who traces them to single motives is like Soames,
who believed that his daughter wanted to be painted in order
that she might see herself hanging on a wall. Everybody,
he knew, had themselves hung sooner or later, and generally sooner. Yet Fleur, though certainly not averse to being
hung, had motives that were hardly so single as all that.
In the service of this complexity, she went back to June's.
That little lady, who had been lurking in her bedroom so
as not to meet her kinsman, was in high feather.

"Of course the price is nominal," she said. "Harold
ought really to be getting every bit as much for his por-
traits as Thom or Lippen. Still, it's so important for him to
be making something while he's waiting to take his real
place. What have you come back for?"

"Partly for the pleasure of seeing you," said Fleur,
"and partly because we forgot to arrange for the first sitting. I think my best time would be three o'clock."

"Yes," murmured June, doubtfully, not so much from
doubt as from not having suggested it herself. "I think
Harold could manage that. Isn't his work exquisite?"

"I particularly like the thing he's done of Anne. It's
going down to them to-morrow, I hear."

"Yes; Jon's coming to fetch it."

Fleur looked hastily into the little dim mirror to see that
she was keeping expression off her face.

"What do you think I ought to wear?"

June's gaze swept her from side to side.

"Oh! I expect he'll want an artificial scheme with you."

"Exactly! But what colour? One must come in something."

"We'll go up and ask him."

The Rafaelite was standing before his picture of Anne. He turned and looked at them, without precisely saying: "Good Lord! These women!" and nodded, gloomily, at the suggestion of three o'clock.

"What do you want her in?" asked June.

The Rafaelite stared at Fleur as if determining where her ribs left off and her hip bones began.

"Gold and silver," he said, at last.

June clasped her hands.

"Now, isn't that extraordinary? He's seen through you at once. Your gold and silver room. Harold, how *did* you?"

"I happen to have an old 'Folly' dress," said Fleur, "silver and gold, with bells, that I haven't worn since I was married."

"A 'Folly'!" cried June. "The very thing. If it's pretty. Some are hideous, of course."

"Oh! it's pretty, and makes a charming sound."

"He can't paint that," said June. Then added dreamily: "But you could suggest it, Harold—like Leonardo."

"Leonardo!"

"Oh! Of course! I know, he wasn't——"

The Rafaelite interrupted.

"Don't make your face up," he said to Fleur.

"No," murmured Fleur. "June, I do so like that of Anne. Has it struck you that she's sure to want Jon painted now?"

"Of course, I'll make him promise when he comes to-morrow."

"He's going to begin farming, you know; he'll make that an excuse. Men hate being painted."

"Oh, that's all nonsense," said June. "In old days they loved it. Anyway, Jon must sit before he begins. They'll make a splendid pair."

Behind the Rafaelite's back Fleur bit her lip.

"He must wear a turn-down shirt. Blue, don't you think, Harold—to go with his hair?"

"Pink, with green spots," muttered the Rafaelite.

"Then three o'clock to-morrow?" said Fleur, hastily.

June nodded. "Jon's coming to lunch, so he'll be gone before you come."

"All right, then. *Au revoir!*"

She held her hand out to the Rafaelite, who seemed surprised at the gesture.

"Good-bye, June!"

June came suddenly close and kissed her on the chin. At that moment the little lady's face looked soft and pink, and her eyes soft; her lips were warm, too, as if she were warm all through.

Fleur went away thinking: 'Ought I to have asked her not to tell Jon I was going to be painted?' But surely June, the warm, the single-eyed, would never tell Jon anything that might stop him being useful to her Rafaelite. She stood, noting the geography around "the Poplars." The only approach to this backwater was by a road that dipped into it and came out again. Just here, she would not be seen from the house, and could see Jon leaving after lunch whichever way he went. But then he would have to take a taxi, for the picture. It struck her bitterly that she, who had been his first-adored, should have to scheme to see him. But if she didn't, she would never see him! Ah! what a ninny she had been at Wansdon in those old days when her room was next to his. One little act, and nothing could have kept him from her for all time, not his mother nor the old feud; not her father; nothing; and then there had been no vows of hers or his, no Michael, no Kit, no nymph-eyed girl in barrier between them; nothing but youth and innocence. And it seemed to her that youth and innocence were over-rated.

She lit on no plan by which she could see him without giving away the fact that she had schemed. She would have to possess her soul a little longer. Let him once get his head into the painter's noose, and there would be not one but many chances.

She arrived at three o'clock with her Folly's dress, and was taken into June's bedroom to put it on.

"It's just right," said June; "delightfully artificial. Harold will love it."

"I wonder," said Fleur. The Rafaelite's temperament had not yet struck her as very loving. They went up to the studio without having mentioned Jon.

The portrait of Anne was gone. And when June went to fetch "the exact thing" to cover a bit of background, Fleur said at once:

"Well? Are you going to paint my cousin Jon?"

The Rafaelite nodded.

"He didn't want to be, but *she* made him."

"When do you begin?"

"To-morrow," said the Rafaelite. "He's coming every morning for a week. What's the good of a week?"

"If he's only got a week I should have thought he'd better stay here."

"He won't without his wife, and his wife's got a cold."

"Oh!" said Fleur, and she thought rapidly. "Wouldn't it be more convenient, then, for him to sit early in the afternoons? I could come in the mornings; in fact, I'd rather —one feels fresher. June could give him a trunk call."

The Rafaelite uttered what she judged to be an approving sound. When she left, she said to June: "I want to come at ten every morning, then I get my afternoons free for my 'Rest House' down at Dorking. Couldn't you get

Jon to come in the afternoons instead? It would suit him better. Only don't let him know I'm being painted—my picture won't be recognisable for a week, anyway."

"Oh!" said June, "you're quite wrong, there. Harold always gets an unmistakable likeness at once; but of course he'll put it face to the wall, he always does while he's at work on a picture."

"Good! He's made quite a nice start. Then if you'll telephone to Jon, I'll come to-morrow at ten." And for yet another day she possessed her soul. On the day after, she nodded at a canvas whose face was to the wall, and asked:

"Do you find my cousin a good sitter?"

"No," said the Rafaelite; "he takes no interest. Got something on his mind, I should think."

"He's a poet, you know," said Fleur.

The Rafaelite gave her an epileptic stare. "Poet! His head's the wrong shape—too much jaw, and the eyes too deep in."

"But his hair! Don't you find him an attractive subject?"

"Attractive!" replied the Rafaelite—"I paint anything, whether it's pretty or ugly as sin. Look at Rafael's Pope—did you ever see a better portrait, or an uglier man? Ugliness is not attractive, but it's there."

"That's obvious," said Fleur.

"I state the obvious. The only real novelties now are platitudes. That's why my work is important and seems new. People have got so far away from the obvious that the obvious startles them, and nothing else does. I advise you to think that over."

"I'm sure there's a lot in it," said Fleur.

"Of course," said the Rafaelite, "a platitude has to be stated with force and clarity. If you can't do that, you'd better go on slopping around and playing parlour tricks like the Ga-gaists. They're a bathetic lot, trying to prove that cocktails are a better drink than old brandy. I met a man last night who told me he'd spent four years writing twenty-two lines of poetry that nobody can understand. How's that for bathos? But it'll make him quite a reputation, till somebody writes twenty-three lines in five years still more unintelligible. Hold your head up. . . . Your cousin's a silent beggar."

"Silence is quite a quality," said Fleur.

The Rafaelite grinned. "I suppose you think I haven't got it. But you're wrong, madam. Not long ago I went a fortnight without opening my lips except to eat and say yes or no. *She* got quite worried."

"I don't think you're very nice to her," said Fleur.

"No, I'm not. She's after my soul. That's the worst of women—saving your presence—they're not content with their own."

"Perhaps they haven't any," said Fleur.

"The Mohammedan view—well, there's certainly something in it. A woman's always after the soul of a man, a child, or a dog. Men are content with wanting bodies."

"I'm more interested in your platitudinal theory, Mr. Blade."

"Can't afford to be interested in the other? Eh! Strikes home? Turn your shoulder a bit, will you? No, to the left. . . . Well, it's a platitude that a woman always wants some other soul—only people have forgotten it. Look at the Sistine Madonna! The baby has a soul of its own, and the Madonna's floating on the soul of the baby. That's what makes it a great picture, apart from the line and colour. It states a great platitude; but nobody sees it, now. None of the cognoscenti, anyway—they're too far gone."

"What platitude are you going to state in your picture of me?"

"Don't you worry," said the Rafaelite. "There'll be one

all right when it's finished, though I shan't know what it is while I'm at it. Character will out, you know. Like a rest?"

"Enormously. What platitude did you express in the portrait of my cousin's wife?"

"Coo Lummy!" said the Rafaelite. "Some catechism!"

"You surely didn't fail with that picture? Wasn't it platitudinous?"

"It got her all right. She's not a proper American."

"How?"

"Throws back to something—Irish, perhaps, or Breton. There's nymph in her."

"She was brought up in the backwoods, I believe," said Fleur, acidly.

The Rafaelite eyed her.

"You don't like the lady?"

"Certainly I do, but haven't you noticed that picturesque people are generally tame? And my cousin—what's his platitude to be?"

"Conscience," said the Rafaelite; "that young man will go far on the straight and narrow. He worries."

A sharp movement shook all Fleur's silver bells.

"What a dreadful prophecy! Shall I stand again?"

CHAPTER IV

TALK IN A CAR

FOR yet one more day Fleur possessed her soul; then, at the morning's sitting, accidentally left her vanity bag, behind her, in the studio. She called for it the same afternoon. Jon had not gone. Just out of the sitter's chair, he was stretching himself and yawning.

"Go on, Jon! Every morning I wish I had your mouth. Mr. Blade, I left my bag; it's got my cheque book in it, and I shall want it down at Dorking to-night: By the way, I shall be half an hour late for my sitting to-morrow, I'm afraid. Did you know I was your fellow victim, Jon? We've been playing 'Box and Cox.' How are you? I hear Anne's got a cold. Give her my sympathy. Is the picture going well? Might I have a peep, Mr. Blade, and see how the platitude is coming out? Oh! It's going to be splendid! I can quite see the line."

"Can you?" said the Rafaelite: "I can't."

"Here's my wretched bag! If you've finished, Jon, I could run you out as far as Dorking; you'd catch an earlier train. Do come and cheer me on my way. Haven't seen you for such ages!"

Threading over Hammersmith Bridge, Fleur regained the self-possession she had never seemed to lose. She spoke lightly of light matters, letting Jon grow accustomed to proximity.

"I go down every evening about this time, to see to my chores, and drive up in the morning early. So any afternoon you like I can take you as far as Dorking. Why shouldn't we see a little of each other in a friendly way, Jon?"

"When we do, it doesn't seem to make for happiness, Fleur."

"My dear boy, what is happiness? Surely life should be as harmlessly full as it can be?"

"Harmlessly!"

"The Rafaelite says you have a terrible conscience, Jon."

"The Rafaelite's a bounder."

"Yes; but a clever one. You *have* changed, you usen't to have that line between your eyes, and your jaw's getting too strong. Look, Jon dear, be a friend to me—as they say, and we won't think of anything else. I always like Wimbledon Common—it hasn't been caught up yet. Have you bought that farm?"

"Not quite."

"Let's go by way of Robin Hill, and look at it through the trees? It might inspire you to a poem."

"I shall never write any more verse. It's quite gone."

"Nonsense, Jon. You only want stirring up. Don't I drive well, considering I've only been at it five weeks?"

"You do everything well, Fleur."

"You say that as if you disapproved. Do you know we'd never danced together before that night at Nettlefold? Shall we ever dance together again?"

"Probably not."

"Optimistic Jon! That's right—smile! Look! Is that the church where you were baptized?"

"I wasn't."

"Oh! No. That was the period, of course, when people were serious about those things. I believe I was done twice over—R.C. and Anglican. That's why I'm not so religious as you, Jon."

"Religious? I'm not religious."

"I fancy you *are*. You have moral backbone, anyway."

"Really!"

"Jon, you remind me of American notices outside their

properties—'Stop—look—take care—keep out!' I suppose you think me a frightful butterfly."

"No, Fleur. Far from it. The butterfly has no knowledge of a straight line between two points."

"Now what do you mean by that?"

"That you set your heart on things."

"Did you get that from the Rafaelite?"

"No, but he confirmed it."

"He did—did he? That young man talks too much. Has he expounded to you his theory that a woman must possess the soul of someone else, and that a man is content with bodies?"

"He has."

"Is it true?"

"I hate to agree with him, but I think it is, in a way."

"Well, I can tell you there are plenty of women about now who keep their own souls and are content with other people's bodies."

"Are you one of them, Fleur?"

"Ask me another! There's Robin Hill!"

The fount of Forsyte song and story stood grey and imposing among its trees, with the sinking sun aslant on a front where green sunblinds were still down.

Jon sighed. "I had a lovely time there."

"Till I came and spoiled it."

"No; that's blasphemy."

Fleur touched his arm.

"That's nice of you, dear Jon. You always were nice, and I shall always love you—in a harmless way. The coppice looks jolly. God had a brain-wave when he invented larches."

"Yes, Holly says that the coppice was my grandfather's favourite spot."

"Old Jolyon—who wouldn't marry his beloved, because she was consumptive?"

"I never heard that. But he was a great old fellow, my mother and father adored him."

"I've seen his photographs—don't get a chin like his, Jon! The Forsytes all have such chins. June's frightens me."

"June is one of the best people on earth."

"Oh! Jon, you are horribly loyal."

"Is that an offence?"

"It makes everything terribly earnest in a world that isn't worth it. No, don't quote Longfellow. When you get home, shall you tell Anne you've been driving with me?"

"Why not?"

"She's uneasy about me as it is, isn't she? You needn't answer, Jon. But I think it's unfair of her. I want so little, and you're so safe."

"Safe?" It seemed to Fleur that he closed his teeth on the word, and for a moment she was happy.

"Now you've got your lion-cub look. Do lion-cubs have consciences? It's going to be rather interesting for the Rafaelite. I think your conscience might stop before telling Anne, though. It's a pity to worry her if she has a talent for uneasiness." Then, by the silence at her side, she knew she had made a mistake.

"This is where I put in my clutch," she said, "as they say in the 'bloods!'" And through Epsom and Leatherhead they travelled in silence.

"Do you love England as much as ever, Jon?"

"More."

"It *is* a gorgeous country."

"The last word I should have used—a great and lovely country."

"Michael says its soul is grass."

"Yes, and if I get my farm, I'll break some up, all right."

"I can't see you as a real farmer."

"You can't see me as a real anything—I suppose.—Just an amateur."

"Don't be horrid! I mean you're too sensitive to be a farmer."

"No. I want to get down to the earth, and I will."

"You must be a throw-back, Jon. The primeval Forsytes were farmers. My father wants to take me down and show me where they lived."

"Have you jumped at it?"

"I'm not sentimental; haven't you realised that? I wonder if you've realised anything about me?" And drooping forward over her wheel, she murmured: "Oh! It's a pity we have to talk like this!"

"I said it wouldn't work!"

"No, you've got to let me see you sometimes, Jon. This is harmless enough. I must and will see you now and then. It's owed to me!"

Tears stood in her eyes, and rolled slowly down. She felt Jon touch her arm.

"Oh! Fleur, don't!"

"I'll put you out at North Dorking now, you'll just catch the five forty-six. That's my house. Next time I must show you over it. I'm trying to be good, Jon; and you must help me. . . . Well, here we are! Good-bye, dear Jon; and don't worry Anne about me, I beseech you!"

A hard handgrip, and he was gone. Fleur turned from the station and drove slowly back along the road.

She put away the car, and entered her "Rest House." It was full, late holiday time still, and seven young women were resting limbs, tired out in the service of "Petter, Poplin," and their like.

They were at supper, and a cheery buzz assailed Fleur's ears. These girls had nothing, and she had everything, except—the one thing that she chiefly wanted. For a moment she felt ashamed, listening to their talk and laughter. No! She would not change with them—and yet without that one thing she felt as if she could not live. And, while she went about the house, sifting the flowers, ordering for to-morrow, inspecting the bedrooms, laughter, cheery and uncontrolled, floated up and seemed to mock her.

CHAPTER V

MORE TALK IN A CAR

JON had too little sense of his own importance to be simultaneously loved with comfort to himself by two pretty and attractive young women. He drove home from Pulborough, where now daily he parked Val's car, with a sore heart and a mind distraught. He had seen Fleur six times since his return to England, in a sort of painful crescendo. That dance with her had disclosed to him her state of heart, but still he did not suspect her of consciously pursuing him; and no amount of heart-searching seemed to make his own feelings clearer. Ought he to tell Anne about to-day's meeting? In many small and silent ways she had shown that she was afraid of Fleur. Why add to her fears without real cause? The portrait was not his own doing, and only for the next few days was he likely to be seeing Fleur. After that they would meet, perhaps, two or three times a year. "Don't tell Anne—I beseech you!" Could he tell her after that? Surely he owed Fleur that much consideration. She had never consented to give him up; she had not fallen in love with Michael, as he with Anne. Still undecided, he reached Wansdon. His mother had once said to him: "You must never tell a lie, Jon, your face will always give you away." And so, though he did not tell Anne, her eyes following him about noted that he was keeping something from her. Her cold was in the bronchial stage, so that she was still upstairs, and tense from lack of occupation. Jon came up early again after dinner, and began to read to her. He read from 'The Worst Journey in the World,' and on her side she lay with her face pillowed on her arm and watched him over it. The smoke of a wood fire, the scent of balsamic remedies, the drone of his own voice, retailing that epic of a penguin's egg, drowsed him till the book dropped from his hand.

"Have a snooze Jon, you're tired." Jon lay back, but he did not snooze. He thought instead. In this girl, his wife, he knew well that there was what her brother, Francis Wilmot, called 'sand.' She knew how to be silent when shoes pinched. He had watched her making up her mind that she was in danger; and now it seemed to him that she was biding her time. Anne always knew what she wanted. She had a singleness of purpose not confused like Fleur's by the currents of modernity, and she was resolute. Youth in her South Carolinian home had been simple and self-reliant; and unlike most American girls, she had not had too good a time. It had been a shock to her, he knew, that she was not his first love and that his first love was still in love with him. She had shown her uneasiness at once, but now, he felt, she had closed her guard. And Jon could not help knowing, too, that she was still deeply in love with him for all that they had been married two years. He had often heard that American girls seldom really knew the men they married; but it seemed to him sometimes that Anne knew him better than he knew himself. If so, what did she know? What was he? He wanted to do something useful with his life; he wanted to be loyal and kind. But was it all just wanting? Was he a fraud? Not what she thought him? It was all confused and heavy in his mind, like the air in the room. No use thinking! Better to snooze, as Anne said—better to snooze! He woke and said:

"Hallo! Was I snoring?"

"No. But you were twitching like a dog, Jon."

Jon got up and went to the window.

"I was dreaming. It's a beautiful night. A fine September's the pick of the year."

"Yes; I love the 'fall.' Is your mother coming over soon?"

"Not until we're settled in. I believe she thinks we're better without her."

"Your mother would always feel she was *de trop* before she was."

"That's on the right side, anyway."

"Yes, I wonder if I should."

Jon turned. She was sitting up, staring in front of her, frowning. He went over and kissed her.

"Careful of your chest, darling!" and he pulled up the clothes.

She lay back, gazing up at him; and again he wondered what she saw. . . .

He was met next day by June's: "So Fleur was here yesterday and gave you a lift! I told her what I thought this morning."

"What *did* you think?" said Jon.

"That it mustn't begin again. She's a spoiled child not to be trusted."

His eyes moved angrily.

"You'd better leave Fleur alone."

"I always leave people alone," said June; "but this is my house, and I had to speak my mind."

"I'd better stop sitting then."

"Now, don't be silly, Jon. Of course you can't stop sitting—neither of you. Harold would be frightfully upset."

"Damn Harold!"

June took hold of his lapel.

"That's not what I meant at all. The pictures are going to be splendid. I only meant that you mustn't meet here."

"Did you tell Fleur that?"

"Yes."

Jon laughed, and the sound of the laugh was hard.

"We're not children, June."

"Have you told Anne?"

"No."

"There, you see!"

"What?"

His face had become stubborn and angry.

"You're very like your father and grandfather, Jon—they couldn't bear to be told anything."

"Can *you?*"

"Of course, when it's necessary."

"Then please don't interfere."

Pink rushed into June's cheeks, tears into her eyes; she winked them away, shook herself, and said coldly:

"I never interfere."

"No?"

She went more pink, and suddenly stroked his sleeve. That touched Jon, and he smiled.

He "sat" disturbed all that afternoon, while the Rafael-ite painted, and June hovered, sometimes with a frown, and sometimes with yearning in her face. He wondered what he should do if Fleur called for him again. But Fleur did not call, and he went home alone. The next day was Sunday and he did not go up; but on Monday when he came out of "The Poplars," after "sitting," he saw Fleur's car standing by the curb.

"I do want to show you my house to-day. I suppose June spoke to you, but I'm a reformed character, Jon. Get in!" And Jon got in.

The day was dull, neither lighted nor staged for emotion, and the "reformed character" played her part to perfection. Not a word suggested that they were other than best friends. She talked of America, its language and books. Jon maintained that America was violent in its repressions and in its revolt against repressions.

"In a word," said Fleur, "young."

"Yes; but so far as I can make out, it's getting younger every year."

"I liked America."

"Oh! I liked it all right. I made quite a profit, too, on my orchard when I sold."

"I wonder you came back, Jon. The fact is—you're old-fashioned."

"How?"

"Take sex—I couldn't discuss sex with you."

"Can you with other people?"

"Oh! with nearly anyone. Don't frown like that! You'd be awfully out of it, my dear, in London, or New York, for that matter."

"I hate fluffy talk about sex," said Jon gruffly. "The French are the only people who understand sex. It isn't to be talked about as they do here and in America; it's much too real."

Fleur stole another look.

"Then let us drop that hot potato. I'm not sure whether I could even discuss art with you."

"Did you see that St. Gaudens statue at Washington?"

"Yes; but that's *vieux jeu* nowadays."

"Is it?" growled Jon. "What do they want, then?"

"You know as well as I."

"You mean it must be unintelligible?"

"Put it that way if you like. The point is that art now is just a subject for conversation; and anything that anybody can understand at first sight is not worth talking about and therefore not art."

"I call that silly," said Jon.

"Perhaps. But more amusing."

"If you see through it, how can you be amused?"

"Another hot potato. Let's try again! I bet you don't approve of women's dress, these days?"

"Why not? It's jolly sensible."

"La, la! Are we coming together on that?"

"Naturally, you'd all look better without hats. You can wash your heads easily now, you know."

"Oh! don't cut us off hats, Jon. All our stoicism would go. If we hadn't to find hats that suited us, life would be much too easy."

"But they don't suit you."

"I agree, my dear; but I know the feminine character better than you. One must always give babies something to cut their teeth on."

"Fleur, you're too intelligent to live in London."

"My dear boy, the modern young woman doesn't live anywhere. She floats in an ether of her own."

"She touches earth sometimes, I suppose."

Fleur did not answer for a minute; then, looking at him:

"Yes; she touches earth sometimes, Jon." And in that look she seemed to say again: "Oh! what a pity we have to talk like this!"

She showed him the house in such a way that he might get the impression that she considered to some purpose the comfort of others. Even her momentary encounters with the denizens had that quality. Jon went away with a tingling in his palm, and the thought: 'She likes to make herself out a butterfly, but at heart—!' The memory of her clear eyes smiling at him, the half-comic quiver of her lips when she said: "Good-bye, bless you!" blurred his vision of Sussex all the way home. And who shall say that she had not so intended?

Holly had come to meet him with a hired car.

"I'm sorry, Jon, Val's got the car. He won't be able to drive you up and down to-morrow as he said he would. He's had to go up to-day. And if he can get through his business in town, he'll go on to Newmarket on Wednesday. Something rather beastly's happened. His name's been forged on a cheque for a hundred pounds by an old college friend to whom he'd been particularly decent."

"Very adequate reasons," said Jon. "What's Val going to do?"

"He doesn't know yet; but this is the third time he's played a dirty trick on Val."

"Is it quite certain?"

"The Bank described him unmistakably. He seems to think Val will stand anything; but it can't be allowed to go on."

"I should say not."

"Yes, dear boy; but what would you do? Prosecute an old College friend? Val has a queer feeling that it's only a sort of accident that he himself has kept straight."

Jon stared. *Was* it an accident that one kept straight? Was this fellow in the war?" he asked.

"I doubt it. He seems to be an absolute rotter. I saw his face once—bone slack and bone selfish."

"Beastly for Val!" said Jon.

"He's going to consult his uncle, Fleur's father. By the way, have you seen Fleur lately?"

"Yes. I saw her to-day. She brought me as far as Dorking, and showed me her house there."

The look on Holly's face, the reflective shadow between her eyes, were not lost on him.

"Is there any objection to my seeing her?" he said, abruptly.

"Only you can know that, dear boy."

Jon did not answer, but the moment he saw Anne he told her. She showed him nothing by face or voice, just asked how Fleur was and how he liked the house. That night, after she seemed asleep, he lay awake, gnawed by uncertainty. *Was* it an accident that one kept straight— was it?

CHAPTER VI

SOAMES HAS BRAIN WAVES

THE first question Soames put to his nephew in Green
Street, was: "How did he get hold of the cheque
form? Do you keep your cheque books lying about?"

"I'm afraid I do, rather, in the country, Uncle Soames."

"Um," said Soames, "then you deserve all you get.
What about your signature?"

"He wrote from Brighton asking if he could see me."

"You should have made your wife sign your answer."

Val groaned. "I didn't think he'd run to forgery."

"They run to anything when they're as far gone as that.
I suppose when you said 'No,' he came over from Brighton
all the same?"

"Yes, he did; but I wasn't in."

"Exactly; and he sneaked a form. Well, if you want to
stop him, you'd better prosecute. He'll get three years."

"That'd kill him," said Val, "to judge by his looks."

Soames shook his head. "Improve his health—very
likely. Has he ever been in prison?"

"Not that I know of."

"H'm!"

Silence followed this profound remark.

"I can't prosecute," said Val suddenly. "College pal.
There, but for the grace of God and all that, don't you
know; one might have gone to the dogs oneself."

Soames stared at him.

"Well," he said, "I suppose you might. Your father
was always in some scrape or other."

Val frowned. He had suddenly remembered an evening
at the Pandemonium, when, in company with another College friend, he had seen his own father, drunk.

"But somehow," he said, "I've got to see that he doesn't do it again. If he didn't look such a 'heart' subject, one could give him a hiding."

Soames shook his head. "Personal violence—besides, he's probably out of England by now."

"No; I called at his club on the way here—he's in town all right."

"You didn't see him?"

"No. I wanted to see you first."

Flattered in spite of himself, Soames said sardonically: "Perhaps he's got what they call a better nature?"

"By Jove, Uncle Soames, I believe that's a brain wave!"

Soames shook his head. "Not to judge by his face."

"I don't know," said Val. "After all, he was born a gentleman."

"That means nothing nowadays. And, àpropos, before I forget it. Do you remember a young fellow called Butterfield, in the Elderson affair—no, you wouldn't. Well, I'm going to take him out of his publishing firm, and put him under old Gradman, to learn about your mother's and the other family Trusts. Old Gradman's on his last legs, and this young man can step into his shoes—it's a permanent job, and better pay than he's getting now. I can rely on him, and that's something in these days. I thought I'd tell you."

"Another brain wave, Uncle Soames. But about your first. Could you see Stainford, and follow that up?"

"Why should *I* see him?"

"You carry so much more weight than I do."

"H'm! Seems to me I always have to do the unpleasant thing. However, I expect it's better than your seeing him."

Val grinned. "I shall feel much happier if you do it."

"*I* shan't," said Soames. "That Bank cashier hasn't made a mistake, I suppose?"

"Who could mistake Stainford?"

"Nobody," said Soames. "Well, if you won't prosecute, you'd better leave it to me."

When Val was gone he remained in thought. Here he was, still keeping the family affairs straight; he wondered what they would do without him some day. That young Butterfield might be a brain wave, but who could tell—the fellow was attached to him, though, in a curious sort of way, with his eyes of a dog! He should put that in hand at once, before old Gradman dropped off. Must give old Gradman a bit of plate, too, with his name engraved, while he could still appreciate it. Most people only got them when they were dead or dotty. Young Butterfield knew Michael, too, and that would make him interested in Fleur's affairs. But as to this infernal Stainford? How was he going to set about it? He had better get the fellow here if possible, rather than go to his club. If he'd had the brass to stay in England after committing such a bare-faced forgery, he would have the brass to come here again and see what more he could get. And, smiling sourly, Soames went to the telephone.

"Mr. Stainford in the club? Ask him if he'd be good enough to step over and see Mr. Forsyte at Green Street."

After a look round to see that there were no ornaments within reach, he seated himself in the dining-room and had Smither in.

"I'm expecting that Mr. Stainford, Smither. If I ring, while he's here, pop out and get a policeman."

At the expression on Smither's face he added:

"I don't anticipate it, but one never knows."

"There's no danger, I hope, Mr. Soames?"

"Nothing of the sort, Smither; I may want him arrested—that's all."

"Do you expect him to take something again, sir?"

Soames smiled, and waved his hand at the lack of ornaments. "Very likely he won't come, but if he does, show him in here."

When she had gone, he settled down with the clock—a Dutch piece too heavy to take away; it had been 'picked up' by James, chimed everything, and had a moon and a lot of stars on its face. He did not feel so 'bobbish' before this third encounter with that fellow; the chap had scored twice, and so far as he could see, owing to Val's reluctance to prosecute, was going to score a third time. And yet there was a sort of fascination in dealing with what they called 'the limit,' and a certain quality about the fellow which raised him almost to the level of romance. It was as if the idolised maxim of his own youth 'Show no emotion,' and all the fashionableness that, under the aegis of his mother Emily, had clung about Park Lane, were revisiting him in the shape of this languid beggar. And probably the chap wouldn't come!

"Mr. Stainford, sir."

When Smither—very red—had withdrawn, Soames did not know how to begin, the fellow's face, like old parchment, was as if it had come from some grave or other. At last he said:

"I wanted to see you about a cheque. My nephew's name's been forged."

The eyebrows rose, the eyelids drooped still further.

"Yes. Dartie won't prosecute."

Soames' gorge rose.

"You seem very cocksure," he said; "my nephew has by no means made up his mind."

"We were at college together, Mr. Forsyte."

"You trade on that, do you? There's a limit, Mr. Stainford. That was a very clever forgery, for a first."

There was just a flicker of the face; and Soames drew the forged cheque from his pocket. Inadequately protected, of course, not even automatically crossed! Val's cheques would have to have the words "Not negotiable; Credit payee" stamped on them in future. But how could he give this fellow a thorough scare?

"I have a detective at hand," he said, "only waiting for me to ring. This sort of thing must stop. As you don't seem to understand that——" and he took a step towards the bell.

A faint and bitter smile had come on those pale lips.

"You've never been down and out, I imagine, Mr. Forsyte?"

"No," answered Soames, with a certain disgust.

"I always am. It's very wearing."

"In that case," said Soames, "you'll find prison a rest." But even as he spoke them, the words seemed futile and a little brutal. The fellow wasn't a man at all—he was a shade, a languid bitter shade. It was as if one were bullying a ghost.

"Look here!" he said. "As a gentleman by birth, give me your word not to try it on again with my nephew, or any of my family, and I won't ring."

"Very well, you have my word—such as it is!"

"We'll leave it at that, then," said Soames. "But this is the last time. I shall keep the evidence of this."

"One must live, Mr. Forsyte."

"I don't agree," said Soames.

The "Shade" uttered a peculiar sound—presumably a laugh, and Soames was alone again. He went hastily to the door, and watched the fellow into the street. Live? Must one? Wouldn't a fellow like that be better dead? Wouldn't most people be better dead? And, astonished at so extravagant a thought, he went up to the drawing room. Forty-five years since he had laid its foundations, and there it was, as full of marqueterie as ever. On the mantlepiece was a little old daguerreotype, slightly pinked in the cheeks, of his grandfather—'Superior Dosset' set in a deep, enamelled frame. Soames contemplated it. The chin of the founder of the Forsyte clan was settled comfortably between the widely separated points of an old-fashioned collar. The eyes—with thick under-lids, were light and shrewd and rather japing; the side-whiskers grey; the mouth looked as if it could swallow a lot; the old-time tail-coat was of broadcloth; the hands those of a man of affairs. A stocky old boy, with a certain force, and a deal of character! Well-nigh a hundred years since that was taken of him. Refreshing to look at character, after that languid seedy specimen! He would like to see where that old chap had been born and bred before he emerged at the end of the eighteenth century and built the house of For-syte. He would take Riggs, and go down, and if Fleur wouldn't come—perhaps all the better! Be dull for her! Roots were nothing to young people. Yes, he would go and look at his roots while the weather was still fine. But first to put old Gradman in order. It would do him good to see the old fellow after this experience—he never left the office till half-past five. And, replacing the daguerreotype, Soames took a taxi to the Poultry, reflecting as he went. How diffi-cult it was to keep things secure, with chaps like Elderson and this fellow Stainford always on the look-out. There was the country too,—no sooner was it out of one than it was into another mess; the coal strike would end when people began to feel the winter pinch, but something else would crop up, some war or disturbance or other. And then there was Fleur—she had fifty thousand of her own. Had he been wrong to make her so independent? And yet— the idea of controlling her through money had always been repulsive to him. Whatever she did—she was his only child, one might say his only love. If she couldn't keep straight for love of her infant and himself, to say nothing of her husband—he couldn't do it for her by threat of cutting her off or anything like that! Anyway, things were looking better with her, and perhaps he had been wrong.

The City had just begun to disgorge its daily life. Its denizens were scurrying out like rabbits; they didn't scurry in like that, he would bet—work-shy, nowadays! Ten where it used to be nine; five where it used to be six. Still, with the telephone and one thing and another, they got through as much perhaps; and didn't drink all the beer and sherry and eat all the chops they used to—a skimpier breed altogether, compared with that old boy whose effigy he had just been gazing at, a shadowy, narrow-headed lot, with a nervy, anxious look, as if they'd invested in life and found it a dropping stock. And not a tail-coat or a silk hat to be seen. Settling his own more firmly on his head, he got out at the familiar backwater off the Poultry, and entered the offices of Cuthcott, Kingson and Forsyte.

Old Gradman was still there, his broad, bent back just divested of its workaday coat.

"Ah! Mr. Soames, I was just going. Excuse me while I put on my coat."

A frock-coat made in the year one, to judge by the cut of it!

"I go at half-past five now. There isn't much to do as a rule. I like to get a nap before supper. It's a pleasure to see you; you're quite a stranger."

"Yes," said Soames. "I don't come in much, but I've been thinking. If anything should happen to either or both of us, things would soon be in Queer Street, Gradman."

"Aow! We won't think about tha-at!"

"But we must; we're neither of us young men."

"Well, I'm not a chicken, but you're *no* age, Mr. Soames."

"Seventy-one."

"Dear, dear! It seems only the other day since I took you down to school at Slough. I remember what happened then better than I do what happened yesterday."

"So do I, Gradman; and that's a sign of age. Do you recollect that young chap who came here and told me about Elderson?"

"Aow, yes! Nice young feller. Buttermilk or some such name."

"Butterfield. Well, I'm going to put him under you here, and I want you to get him *au fait* with everything."

The old fellow seemed standing very still; his face, in its surround of grey beard and hair, was quite expressionless. Soames hurried on:

"It's just precautionary. Some day you'll be wanting to retire."

Gradman lifted his hand with a heavy gesture.

"I'll die in 'arness, I 'ope," he said.

"That's as you like, Gradman. You'll remain as you always have been—in full charge; but you'll have someone to rely on if you don't feel well or want a holiday or what not."

"I'd rather not, Mr. Soames. To have a young man about the place——"

"A good young fellow, Gradman. And, for some reason, grateful to me and to my son-in-law. He won't give you any trouble. We none of us live for ever, you know."

The old chap's face had puckered queerly, his voice grated more than usual.

"It seems going to meet trouble. I'm quite up to the work, Mr. Soames."

"Oh! I know how you feel," said Soames. "I feel much the same myself, but Time stands still for no man, and we must look to the future."

A sigh escaped from its grizzled prison.

"Well, Mr. Soames, if you've made up your mind, we'll say no more; but I don't like it."

"Let me give you a lift to your station."

"I'd rather walk, thank you; I like the air. I'll just lock up."

Soames perceived that not only drawers but feeling required locking-up, and went out.

Faithful old chap! One might go round to Polking-ford's and see if one could pick up that bit of plate.

In that emporium, so lined with silver and gold, that a man wondered whether anything had ever been sold there, Soames stood considering. Must be something that a man could swear by——nothing arty or elegant. He supposed the old chap didn't drink punch——a chapel-goer! How about those camels in silvergilt with two humps each and candles coming out of them? "Joseph Gradman, in gratitude from the Forsyte family" engraved between the humps? Grad-man lived somewhere near the Zoo. M'm! Camels? No! A bowl was better. If he didn't drink punch he could put rose-leaves or flowers into it.

"I want a bowl," he said, "a really good one."

"Yes, sir, I think we have the very article."

They always had the very article!

"How about this, sir——massive silver——a very chaste de-sign."

Chaste!" said Soames. "I wouldn't have it at a gift."

"No, sir; it isn't perhaps *exactly* what you require. Now, this is a nice little bowl."

"No, no; something plain and solid that would hold about a gallon."

"Mr. Bankwait——come here a minute. This gentleman wants an old-fashioned bowl."

"Yes, sir; I think we have the very thing."

Soames uttered an indistinguishable sound.

"There isn't much demand for the old-fashioned bowl; but we have a very fine second-hand, that used to be in the Rexborough family."

"With arms on?" said Soames. "That won't do. It must be new, or free from arms, anyway."

"Ah! Then this will be what you want, sir."

"My Lord!" said Soames; and raising his umbrella he pointed in the opposite direction. "What's that thing?"

With a slightly chagrined air the shopman brought the article from its case.

Upon a swelling base, with a waist above, a silver bowl sprang generously forth. Soames flipped it with his finger.

"Pure silver, sir; and, as you see, very delicate edging; not too bacchanalian in design; the best gilt within. I should say the very thing you want."

"It might do. What's the price?"

The shopman examined a cabalistic sign.

"Thirty-five pounds, sir."

"Quite enough," said Soames. Whether it would please old Gradman, he didn't know, but the thing was in good taste, and would not do the family discredit. "I'll have that, then," he said. "Engrave these words on it," and he wrote them down. "Send it to that address, and the account to me; and don't be long about it."

"Very good, sir. You wouldn't like those goblets?— they're perfect in their way."

"Nothing more!" said Soames. "Good evening!" And, handing the shopman his card, with a cold circular glance, he went out. That was off his mind!

September sun sprinkled him, threading his way West along Piccadilly into the Green Park. These gentle autumn days were very pleasant. He didn't get hot, and he didn't feel cold. And the plane-trees looked their best, just making up their minds to turn; nice trees, shapely. And, crossing the grassy spaces, Soames felt almost mellow. A rather more rapid step behind impinged on his consciousness. A voice said:

"Ah! Forsyte! Bound for the meeting at Michael's? Might we go along together?"

Old Mont, perky and talkative as ever! There he went —off at once!

"What's your view of all these London changes, Forsyte? You remember the peg-top trouser, and the crinoline—

Leech in his prime—Old Pam on his horse—September makes one reminiscent."

"It's all on the surface," said Soames.

"On the surface? I sometimes have that feeling. But there is a real change. It's the difference between the Austen and Trollope novels and these modern fellows. There are no parishes left. Classes? Yes, but divided by man, not by God, as in Trollope's day."

Soames sniffed. The chap was always putting things in that sort of way!

"At the rate we're going, they'll soon not be divided at all," he said.

"I think you're wrong there, Forsyte. I should never be surprised to see the horse come back."

"The horse," muttered Soames; "what's he got to do with it?"

"What we must look for," said Sir Lawrence, swinging his cane, "is the millennium. Then we shall soon be developing individuality again. And the millennium's nearly here."

"I don't in the least follow you," said Soames.

"Education's free; women have the vote; even the workman has or soon will have his car; the slums are doomed—thanks to you, Forsyte; amusement and news are in every home; the Liberal Party's up the spout; Free Trade's a moveable feast; sport's cheap and plentiful; dogma's got the knock; so has the General Strike; Boy Scouts are increasing rapidly; dress is comfortable; and hair is short—it's all millennial."

"What's all that got to do with the horse?"

"A symbol, my dear Forsyte. It's impossible to standardize or socialize the horse. We're beginning to react against uniformity. A little more millennium and we shall soon be cultivating our souls and driving tandem again."

"What's that noise?" said Soames. "Sounds like a person in distress."

Sir Lawrence cocked his eyebrow.

"It's a vacuum cleaner, in Buckingham Palace. Very human things those."

Soames grunted—the fellow couldn't be serious! Well! He might *have* to be before long. If Fleur—! But he would not contemplate that "if."

"What I admire about the Englishman," said Sir Lawrence, suddenly, "is his evolutionary character. He flows and ebbs, and flows again. Foreigners may think him a stick-in-the-mud, but he's got continuity—a great quality, Forsyte. What are you going to do with your pictures when you take the ferry? Leave them to the nation?"

"Depends on how they treat me. If they're going to clap on any more Death duties, I shall revoke the bequest."

"The principle of our ancestors, eh? Voluntary service, or none. Great fellows, our ancestors."

"I don't know about yours," said Soames; "mine were just yeomen. I'm going down to have a look at them to-morrow," he added defiantly.

"Splendid! I hope you'll find them at home."

"We're late," said Soames, glancing in at the dining-room window, where the committee were glancing out: "Half-past six! What a funny lot they look!"

"We always look a funny lot," said Sir Lawrence, following him into the house, "except to ourselves. That's the first principle of existence, Forsyte."

CHAPTER VII

TO-MORROW

FLEUR met them in the hall. After dropping Jon at Dorking she had exceeded the limit homewards, that she might appear to have nothing in her thoughts but the welfare of the slums. "The Squire" being among his partridges, the Bishop was in the chair. Fleur went to the sideboard, and, while Michael was reading the minutes, began pouring out the tea. The Bishop, Sir Godfrey Bedwin, Mr. Montross, her father-in-law, and herself drank China tea; Sir Timothy—whisky and soda; Michael nothing; the Marquess, Hilary, and her father Indian tea; and each maintained that the others were destroying their digestions. Her father, indeed, was always telling her that she only drank China tea because it was the fashion—she couldn't possibly like it. While she apportioned their beverages she wondered what they would think if they knew what, besides tea, was going on within her. To-morrow was Jon's last sitting and she was going 'over the top!' All the careful possessing of her soul these two months since she had danced with him at Nettlefold would by this time to-morrow be ended. To-morrow at this hour she would claim her own. The knowledge that there must be two parties to any contact did not trouble her. She had the faith of a pretty woman in love. What she willed would be accomplished, but none should know of it! And, handing her cups, she smiled, pitying the ignorance of these wise old men. They should not know, nor anyone else, least of all the young man who last night had held her in his arms. And, thinking of one not yet so holding her, she sat down by the hearth, with her tea and her tables, while her pulses

277

throbbed and her half-closed eyes saw Jon's face turned round to her from the station door. Fulfilment! She, like Jacob, had served seven years—for the fulfilment of her love—seven long, long years! And—while she sat there listening to the edgeless booming of the Bishop and Sir Godfrey, to the random ejaculations of Sir Timothy, to her father's close and cautious comments—that something clear, precise, unflinching woven into her nature with French blood, silently perfected the machinery of the stolen life, that should begin to-morrow after they had eaten of forbidden fruit. A stolen life was a safe life if there were no chicken-hearted hesitation, no squeamishness, and no remorse! She might have experienced a dozen stolen lives already, from the certainty she felt about that. She alone would arrange—Jon should be spared all. And no one should know!

"Fleur, would you take a note of that?"

"Yes."

And she wrote down on her tablets: "Ask Michael what I was to take a note of."

"Mrs. Mont!"

"Yes, Sir Timothy?"

"Could you get up one of those what d'you call 'ems for us?"

"Matinees?"

"No, no—jumble sales, don't they call 'em?"

"Certainly."

The more she got up for them the more impeccable her reputation, the greater her freedom, and the more she would deserve, and ironically enjoy, her stolen life.

Hilary speaking now. What would *he* think if he knew?

"But I think we *ought* to have a matinee, Fleur. The public are so good, they'll always pay a guinea to go to what most of them would give a guinea any day not to go to. What do you say, Bishop?"

"A matinee—by all means!"

"Matinees—dreadful things!"

"Not if we got a pleasant play, Mr. Forsyte—something a little old-fashioned—one of L.S.D.'s. It would advertise us, you know. What do you think, Marquess?"

"My granddaughter Marjorie would get one up for you. It would do her good."

"H'm. If *she* gets it up, it won't be old-fashioned." And Fleur saw her father's face turning towards her, as he spoke. If only he knew how utterly she was beyond all that; how trivial to her seemed that heart-burning of the past.

"Mr. Montross, have you a theatre in your pocket?"

"I can get you one, Mr. Charwell."

"First rate! Then, will you and the Marquess and my nephew here take that under your wings? Fleur, tell us how your Rest-House is doing?"

"Perfectly, Uncle Hilary. It's quite full. The girls are delightful."

"Wild lot, I should think—aren't they?"

"Oh! no, Sir Timothy; they're quite model."

If only the old gentleman could see over his moustache into the model lady who controlled them!

"Well then, that's that. If there's nothing more, Mr. Chairman, will you excuse me? I've got to meet an American about ants. We aren't properly shaking up these landlords in my opinion. Good-night to you all!"

Motioning to Michael to stay behind, Fleur rose to see Sir Timothy out.

"Which umbrella is yours, Sir Timothy?"

"I don't know; that looks the best. If you get up a jumble sale, Mrs. Mont, I wish you'd sell the Bishop at it. I can't stand a fellow with a plum in his mouth, especially in the Chair."

Fleur smiled, and the "old boy" cocked his hat at her.

They all cocked their hats at her, and that was pleasant!
But would they if they knew! Dusk among the trees of
the Square Garden, the lights just turned up—what luck
to have such weather—dry and warm! She stood in the
doorway, taking long breaths. By this time to-morrow
she meant to be a dishonest wife! Well, not more than
she had always been in secret aspiration.

'I'm glad Kit's down at "The Shelter",' she thought. *He*
should never know, no one should! There would be no
change—no change in anything except in her and Jon. The
Life Force would break bounds in a little secret river,
which would flow—ah, where? Who cared?

"My dear Mont, honesty was never the best policy from
a material point of view. The sentiment is purely Victorian. The Victorians were wonderful fellows for squar-
ing circles."

"I agree, Marquess, I agree; they could think what they
wanted better than anybody. When times are fat, you
can."

Those two in the hall behind her—dried-up and with-
ered! Fleur turned to them with her smile.

"My dear young lady—the evening air! You won't
take cold?"

"No thank you, sir; I'm warm all through."

"How nice that is!"

"May I give you a lift, Marquess?"

"Thank you, Mr. Montross. Wish I could afford a car
myself. Are you coming our way, Mont? Do you know
that song, Mr. Montross: 'We'll all go round to Alice's
house'? It seems to have a fascination for my milk boy.
I often wonder who Alice is? I have a suspicion she may
not be altogether proper. Good-night to you, Mrs. Mont.
How charming your house is!"

"Good-night, sir!"

His hand; "the walrus's"; her father-in-law's.

"Kit all right, Fleur?"

"First rate."

"Good-night, my dear!"

His dear—the mother of his grandson! 'To-morrow and to-morrow and to-morrow!'

The rug wrapped round the cargo of age, the door shut —what a smooth, and silent car! Voices again:

"Will you have a taxi, Uncle Hilary?"

"No, thank you, Michael, the Bishop and I will walk."

"Then I'll come with you as far as the corner. Coming, Sir Godfrey? By-bye, darling. Your Dad's staying to dinner. I'll be back from old Blythe's about ten."

The animals went out four by four!

"Don't stand there; you'll get cold!" Her father's voice! The one person whose eyes she feared. She must keep her mask on now.

"Well, Dad, what have you been doing to-day? Come into the 'parlour'—we'll have dinner quite soon."

"How's your picture? Is this fellow taking care not to exaggerate? I think I'd better have a look at it."

"Not just yet, dear. He's a very touchy gentleman."

"They're all that. I thought of going down West to-morrow to see where the Forsytes sprang from. I suppose you couldn't take a rest and come?"

Fleur heard, without giving a sign of her relief.

"How long will you be away, Dad?"

"Back on the third day. 'Tisn't two hundred miles."

"I'm afraid it would put the gentleman out."

"Well, I didn't think you'd care to. There's no kudos there. But I've meant to for a long time; and the weather's fine."

"I'm sure it will be frightfully interesting, dear; you must tell me all about it. But what with the portrait and my Rest-House, I'm very tired, just now."

"Well, then, I'll look for you at the week-end. Your mother's gone to some friends—they do nothing but play bridge; she'll be away till Monday. I always want you,

you know," he added, simply. And to avoid his eyes she got up.

"I'll just run up now, Dad, and change. Those Slum Committee Meetings always make me feel grubby. I don't know why."

"They're a waste of time," said Soames. "There'll always be slums. Still, it's something for you both to do."

"Yes, Michael's quite happy about it."

"That old fool, Sir Timothy!" And Soames went up to the Fragonard. "I've hung that Morland. The Marquess is an amiable old chap. I suppose you know I'm leaving my pictures to the Nation? You've no use for them. You'll have to live at that place Lippinghall some day. Pictures'd be no good there. Ancestors and stags' horns and horses—that sort of thing. M'ff!"

A secret life and Lippinghall! Long, long might that conjunction be deferred!

"Oh, Bart will live for ever, Dad!"

"M'yes! He's spry enough. Well, you run up!"

While she washed off powder and put it on again Fleur thought: 'Dear Dad! Thank God! He'll be far away!'

Now that her mind was thoroughly made up, it was comparatively easy to bluff, and keep her freshly-powdered face, smiling and serene, above the Chelsea dinner service.

"Where are you going to hang your portrait, when it's done?" resumed Soames.

"Why! It'll be yours, dear."

"Mine? Well, of course; but you'll hang it here; Michael'll want it."

Michael—unknowing! *That* gave her a twinge.

Well, she would be as good to him after, as ever. No old-fashioned squeamishness!

"Thank you, dear. I expect he'll like it in the 'parlour.' The scheme *is* silver and gold—my 'Folly' dress."

"I remember it," said Soames; "a thing with bells."

"I think all that part of the picture's very good."

"What? Hasn't he got your face?"

"Perhaps—but I don't know that I approve of it fright-fully." After this morning's sitting, indeed, she had won-dered. Something avid had come into the face as if the Rafaelite had sensed the hardening of resolve within her.

"If he doesn't do you justice I shan't take it," said Soames.

Fleur smiled. The Rafaelite would have something to say to that.

"Oh! I expect it'll be all right. One never thinks one's own effigies are marvellous, I suppose."

"Don't know," said Soames, "never was painted."

"You ought to be, dear."

"'Waste of time! Has he sent away the picture of that young woman?"

Fleur's eyes did not flinch.

"Jon Forsyte's wife? Oh! yes—long ago."

She expected him to say: "Seen anything of them?" But it did not come. And that disturbed her more than if it had come.

"I had your cousin Val to see me to-day."

Fleur's heart stood still. Had they been talking?

"His name's been forged."

Thank heaven!

"Some people have no moral sense at all," continued Soames. Involuntarily her white shoulder rose; but he wasn't looking. "Common honesty, I don't know where it is."

"I heard the Marquess say to-night that 'Honesty's the best policy' was a mere Victorianism, Dad."

"Well, he's ten years my senior, but I don't know where he got that from. Everything's twisted inside out, now-a-days."

"But if it's the best *policy*, there never was any particular virtue in it, was there?"

Soames took a sharp look at her smiling face.

"Why not?"

"Oh, I don't know. These are Lippinghall partridges, Dad."

Soames sniffed. "Not hung quite long enough. You ought to be able to swear by the leg of a partridge."

"Yes, I've told cook, but she has her own views."

"And the bread sauce should have a touch more onion in it. Victorianism, indeed! I suppose he'd call *me* a Victorian?"

"Well, aren't you, Dad? You had forty-six years of her."

"I've had twenty-five without her, and hope to have a few more."

"Many, many," said Fleur, softly.

"Can't expect that."

"Oh, yes! But I'm glad you don't consider yourself a Victorian; I don't like them. They wore too many clothes."

"Don't you be too sure of that."

"Well, to-morrow you'll be among Georgians, anyway."

"Yes," said Soames. "There's a graveyard there, they say. And that reminds me—I've bought that corner bit in the churchyard down at home. It'll do for me as well as any other. Your mother will want to go to France to be buried, I expect."

"Give Mr. Forsyte some sherry, Coaker."

Soames took a long sniff.

"This is some of your grandfather's. He lived to be ninety."

If she and Jon lived to be ninety—would nobody still know? . . . She left him at ten o'clock, brushing his nose with her lips.

"I'm tired, Dad; and you'll have a long day to-morrow. Good-night, dear!"

Thank God he would be among the Georgians to-morrow!

CHAPTER VIII

FORBIDDEN FRUIT

HALTING the car suddenly in the by-road between Gage's farm and the Robin Hill coppice, Fleur said: "Jon, dear, I've got a whim. Let's get out and go in there. The potentate's in Scotland." He did not move, and she added: "I shan't see you again for a long time, now your picture's finished."

Jon got out, then, and she unlatched the footpath gate. They stood a minute within, listening for sounds of anyone to interrupt their trespass. The fine September afternoon was dying fast. The last "sitting" had been long, and it was late; and in the coppice of larch and birch the dusk was deepening. Fleur slid her hand within his arm.

"Listen! Still, isn't it? I feel as if we were back seven years, Jon. Do you wish we were? Babes in the wood once more?"

Gruffly he answered:

"No good looking back—things happen as they must."

"The birds are going to bed. Used there to be owls?"

"Yes; we shall hear one soon, I expect."

"How good it smells!"

"Trees and the cow-houses!"

"Vanilla and hay, as the poets have it. Are they close?"

"Yes."

"Don't let's go further, then."

"Here's the old log," said Jon. "We might sit down, and listen for an owl."

On the old log seat they sat down, side by side.

"No dew," said Fleur. "The weather will break soon, I expect. I love the scent of drought."

"I love the smell of rain."

"You and I never love the same thing, Jon. And yet—we've loved each other." Against her arm it was as if he shivered.

"There goes the old clock! It's awfully late, Fleur! Listen! The owl!"

Startlingly close through the thin-branched trees the call came. Fleur rose: "Let's see if we can find him."

She moved back from the old log.

"Aren't you coming? Just a little wander, Jon."

Jon got up and went along at her side among the larches.

"Up this way—wasn't it? How quickly it's got dark. Look! The birches are still white. I love birchtrees." She put her hand on a pale stem. "The smoothness, Jon. It's like skin." And, leaning forward, she laid her cheek against the trunk. "There! feel my cheek, and then the bark. Could you tell the difference, except for warmth?"

Jon reached his hand up. She turned her lips and touched it.

"Jon—kiss me just once."

"You know I couldn't kiss you 'just once,' Fleur."

"Then kiss me for ever, Jon."

"No, no! No, no!"

"Things happen as they must—you said so."

"Fleur—don't! I can't stand it."

She laughed—very low, softly.

"I don't want you to. I've waited seven years for this. No! Don't cover your face! Look at me! I take it all on myself. The woman tempted you. But, Jon, you were always mine. There! That's better. I can see your eyes. Poor Jon! Now, kiss me!" In that long kiss her very spirit seemed to leave her; she could not even see whether his eyes were open, or, like hers, closed. And again the owl hooted.

Jon tore his lips away. He stood there in her arms, trembling like a startled horse.

With her lips against his ear, she whispered:
"There's nothing, Jon; there's nothing." She could hear him holding-in his breath, and her warm lips whispered on: "Take me in your arms, Jon; take me!" The light had failed completely now; stars were out between the dark feathering of the trees, and low down, from where the coppice sloped up towards the east, a creeping brightness seemed trembling towards them through the wood from the moon rising. A faint rustle broke the silence, ceased, broke it again. Closer, closer—Fleur pressed against him.

"Not here, Fleur; not here. I can't—I won't——"
"Yes, Jon; here—now! I claim you."

* * * * *

The moon was shining through the tree stems when they sat again side by side on the log seat.

Jon's hands were pressed to his forehead, and she could not see his eyes.

"No one shall ever know, Jon."
He dropped his hands, and faced her.
"I must tell her."
"Jon!"
"I must!"
"You can't unless I let you, and I don't let you."
"What have we done? Oh, Fleur, what *have* we done?"
"It was written. When shall I see you again, Jon?"
He started up.
"Never, unless she knows. Never, Fleur—never! I can't go on in secret!"

As quickly, too, Fleur was on her feet. They stood with their hands on each other's arms, in a sort of struggle. Then Jon wrenched himself free, and, like one demented, rushed back into the coppice.

She stood trembling, not daring to call. Bewildered, she

stood, waiting for him to come back to her, and he did not come.

Suddenly, she moaned, and sank on her knees; and again she moaned. He must hear, and come back! He could not have left her at such a moment—he could not!

"Jon!" No sound. She rose from her knees, and stood peering into the brightened dusk. The owl hooted; and, startled, she saw the moon caught among the tree tops, like a presence watching her. A shivering sob choked in her throat, became a whimper, like a hurt child's. She stood, listening fearfully. No rustling; no footsteps; no hoot of owl—not a sound, save the distant whir of traffic on the London road! Had he gone to the car, or was he hiding from her in that coppice, all creepy now with shadows?

"Jon! Jon!" No answer! She ran towards the gate. There was the car—empty! She got into it, and sat leaning forward over the driving wheel, with a numb feeling in her limbs. What did it mean? Was she beaten in the very hour of victory? He could not—no, he could not mean to leave her thus? Mechanically she turned on the car's lights. A couple on foot, a man on a bicycle, passed. And Fleur still sat there, numbed. This—fulfilment! The fulfilment she had dreamed of? A few moments of hasty and delirious passion—and this! And, to her chagrin, her consternation, were added humiliation that, after such a moment, he could thus have fled from her; and the fear that in winning him she had lost him!

At last she started the engine, and drove miserably on, watching the road, hoping against hope to come on him. Very slowly she drove, and only when she reached the Dorking road did she quite abandon hope. How she guided the car for the rest of the drive, she hardly knew. Life seemed suddenly to have gone out.

CHAPTER IX

AFTERMATH

JON, when he rushed back into the coppice, turned to the left, and, emerging past the pond, ran up through the field towards the house, as if it were still his own. It stood above its terrace and lawns unlighted, ghostly in the spreading moonlight. Behind a clump of rhododendrons, where as a little boy he had played hide and seek, or pursued the staghorn beetle with his bow and arrow, he sank down as if his legs had turned to water, pressing his fists against his cheeks, both burning hot. He had known and he had not known, had dreamed and never dreamed of this! Overwhelming, sudden, relentless! "It was written!" she had said. For her, every excuse, perhaps; but what excuse for him? Among those moonlit rhododendrons he could not find it. Yet the deed was done! Whose was he now? He stood up and looked at the house where he had been born, grown up, and played, as if asking for an answer. Whitened and lightless, it looked the ghost of a house, keeping secrets. "And I don't let you tell! . . . When shall I see you again?" That meant she claimed a secret lover. Impossible! The one thing utterly impossible. He would belong to one or to the other—not to both. Torn in every fibre of his being, he clung to the fixity of that. Behind the rhododendrons stretching along the far end of the lawn he walked, crouching, till he came to the wall of the grounds, the wall he had often scrambled over as a boy; and, pulling himself up, dropped into the top roadway. No one saw him, and he hurried on. He had a dumb and muddled craving to get back to Wansdon, though what he would do when he got there he could not tell. He turned towards Kingston.

All through that two hours' drive in a hired car Jon thought and thought. Whatever he did now, he must be disloyal to one or to the other. And with those passionate moments still rioting within him, he could get no grip on his position; and yet—he must!

He reached Wansdon at eleven, and, dismissing the car in the road, walked up to the house. Everyone had gone to bed, evidently assuming that he was staying the night at June's for a further sitting. There was a light in his and Anne's bedroom; and, at sight of it, the full shame of what he had done smote him. He could not bring himself to attract her attention, and he stole round the house, seeking for some way of breaking in. At last he spied a spare-room window open at the top, and fetching a garden ladder, climbed it and got in. The burglarious act restored some self-possession. He went down into the hall, and out of the house, replaced the ladder, came in again and stole upstairs. But outside their door he halted. No light, now, came from under. She must be in bed. And, suddenly, he could not face going in. He would feel like Judas, kissing her. Taking off his boots and carrying them, he stole down-stairs again to the dining-room. Having had nothing but a cup of tea since lunch, he got himself some biscuits and a drink. They altered his mood—no man could have re-sisted Fleur's kisses in that moonlit coppice—no man! Must he, then, hurt one or the other so terribly? Why not follow Fleur's wish? Why not secrecy? By continuing her lover in secret, he would not hurt Fleur; by not telling Anne, he would not hurt Anne! Like a leopard in a cage, he paced the room. And all that was honest in him refused, and all that was sage. As if one could remain the husband of two women, when one of them knew! As if Fleur would stand that long! And lies, subterfuge! And—Michael Mont!— a decent chap! He had done him enough harm as it was! No! A clean cut one way or the other! He stopped by the hearth, and leaned his arms on the stone mantlepiece. How still! Only that old clock which had belonged to his grandfather, ticking away time—time that cured everything, that made so little of commotions, ticking men and things to their appointed ends. Just in front of him on the mantlepiece was a photograph of his grandfather, old Jolyon, taken in his eighties—the last record of that old face, its broad brow, and white moustache, its sunken cheeks, deep, steady eyes, and strong jaw. Jon looked at it long! "Take a course and stick to it!" the face, gazing back at him so deeply, seemed to say. He went to the bureau and sat down to write.

"I am sorry I rushed away to-night, but it was better, really. I had to think. I have thought. I'm only certain of one thing yet. To go on *in secret* is impossible. I shan't say a word about to-night, of course, until you let me. But, Fleur, unless I can tell everything, it must end. You wouldn't wish it otherwise, would you? Please answer to the Post Office, Nettlefold.

"JON."

He sealed this up, addressed it to her at Dorking, and, pulling on his boots, again stole out and posted it. When he got back he felt so tired, that, wrapped in an old coat, he fell asleep in an armchair. The moonlight played tricks through the half-drawn curtains, the old clock ticked, but Jon slept, dreamless.

He woke at daybreak, stole up to the bathroom, bathed and shaved noiselessly, and went out through a window, so as not to leave the front door unfastened. He walked up through the gap past the old chalk pit, on to the Downs, by the path he had taken with Fleur seven years ago. Till he had heard from her he did not know what to do; and he dreaded Anne's eyes, while his mind was still distraught.

He went towards Chanctonbury Ring. There was a heavy
dew, and the short turf was all spun over with it. All was
infinitely beautiful, remote and stilly in the level sunlight.
The beauty tore at his heart. He had come to love the
Downs—they had a special loveliness, like no other part of
the world that he had seen. Did this mean that he must
now leave them, leave England again—leave everything,
and cleave to Fleur? If she claimed him, if she decided on
declaring their act of union, he supposed it did. And Jon
walked in confusion of heart, such as he had not thought
possible to man. From the Ring he branched away, taking
care to avoid the horses at their early exercise. And this
first subterfuge brought him face to face with immediate
decision. What should he do till he had heard from Fleur?
Her answer could not reach Nettlefold till the evening, or
even next morning. He decided, painfully, to go back to
breakfast, and tell them he had missed his train, and entered in the night burglariously so as not to disturb them.

That day, with its anxiety and its watchfulness of self,
was one of the most wretched he had ever spent; and he
could not free himself from the feeling that Anne was
reading his thoughts. It was as if each passed the day looking at the other unobserved—almost unbearable! In the
afternoon he asked for a horse to ride over to Green Hill
Farm, and said he would be back late. He rode on into
Nettlefold and went to the post-office. There was a telegram: "Must see you. Will be at Green Hill Farm to-
morrow at noon. Don't fail me.—F."

Jon destroyed it, and rode homewards. Wretchedness
and strain for another eighteen hours! Was there anything in the world worse than indecision? He rode slowly
so as to have the less time at home, dreading the night. He
stopped at a wayside inn to eat, and again went by way of
Green Hill Farm to save at least the letter of his tale. It
was nearly ten and full moonlight before he got back.

"It's a wonderful night," he said, when he came into the drawing-room. "The moonlight's simply marvellous." It was Holly who answered; Anne, sitting by the fire, did not even look up. 'She knows,' thought Jon, 'she knows something.' Very soon after, she said she was sleepy, and went up. Jon stayed, talking to Holly. Val had gone on from town to Newmarket, and would not be back till Friday. They sat one on each side of the wood fire. And, looking at his sister's face, charming and pensive, Jon was tempted. She was so wise, and sympathetic. It would be a relief to tell her everything. But Fleur's command held him back—it was not his secret.

"Well, Jon, is it all right about the farm?"

"I've got some new figures; I'm going into them to-night."

"I do wish it were settled, and we knew you were going to be near for certain. I shall be awfully disappointed if you're not."

"Yes; but I must make sure this time."

"Anne's very set on it. She doesn't say much, but she really is. It's such a charming old place."

"I don't want a better, but it must pay its way."

"Is that your real reason, Jon?"

"Why not?"

"I thought perhaps you were secretly afraid of settling again. But you're the head of the family, Jon—you ought to settle."

"Head of the family!"

"Yes, the only son of the only son of the eldest son right back to the primeval Jolyon."

"Nice head!" said Jon, bitterly.

"Yes—a nice head." And, suddenly rising, Holly bent over and kissed the top of it.

"Bless you! Don't sit up too late. Anne's rather in the dumps."

Jon turned out the lamp and stayed, huddled in his chair before the fire. Head of the family! He had done them proud! And if——! Ha! That would, indeed, be illustrious! What would the old fellow whose photograph he had been looking at last night, think, if he knew? Ah, what a coil! For in his inmost heart he knew that Anne was more his mate, more her with whom he could live and work and have his being, than ever Fleur could be. Madness, momentary madness, coming on him from the past— the past, and the potency of her will to have and hold him! He got up, and drew aside the curtains. There, between two elm trees, the moon, mysterious and powerful, shone, and all was moving with its light up to the crest of the Downs. What beauty, what stillness! He threw the window up, and stepped out; like some dark fluid spilled on the whitened grass, the ragged shadow of one elm tree reached almost to his feet. From their window above a light shone. He must go up and face it. He had not been alone with her since——! If only he knew for certain what he was going to do! And he realised now that in obeying that impulse to rush away from Fleur he had been wrong; he ought to have stayed and threshed it out there and then. And yet, who could have behaved reasonably, sanely, feeling as he had felt? He stepped back to the window, and stopped with his heart in his mouth. There between firelight and moonlight stood Anne! Slender, in a light wrapper drawn close, she was gazing towards him. Jon closed the window and drew the curtain.

"Sorry, darling, you'll catch cold—the moonlight got me." She moved to the far side of the hearth, and stood looking at him.

"Jon, I'm going to have a child."

"You——!"

"Yes. I didn't tell you last month because I wanted to be sure."

"Anne!"

She was holding up her hand.

"Wait a minute!"

Jon gripped the back of a chair, he knew what was coming.

"Something's happened between you and Fleur."

Jon held his breath, staring at her eyes; dark, unflinching, startled, they stared back at him.

"Everything's happened, hasn't it?"

Jon bent his head.

"Yesterday? Don't explain, don't excuse yourself or her. Only—what does it mean?"

Without raising his head, Jon answered:

"That depends on you."

"On me?"

"After what you've just told me. Oh! Anne, why didn't you tell me sooner?"

"Yes; I kept it too long!"

He understood what she meant—she had kept it as a weapon of defence. And, seeming to himself unforgiveable, he said:

"Forgive me, Anne—forgive me!"

"Oh! Jon, I don't just know."

"I swear that I will never see her again."

He raised his eyes now, and saw that she had sunk on her knees by the fire, holding a hand out to it, as if cold. He dropped on his knees beside her.

"I think," he said, "love is the cruellest thing in the world."

"Yes."

She had covered her eyes with her hand; and it seemed hours that he knelt there, waiting for a movement, a sign, a word. At last she dropped her hand.

"All right. It's over. But don't kiss me—yet."

CHAPTER X

BITTER APPLE

LIFE revived in Fleur while she went about her business in the morning. Standing in sunshine before the hollyhocks and sunflowers of the "rest-house" garden, she reviewed past and future with feverish vigour. Of course Jon was upset! She had taken him by storm! He was old-fashioned, conscientious; he couldn't take things lightly. But since already he had betrayed his conscience, he would realise that what had happened outweighed what more could happen. It was the first step that counted! They had always belonged to each other. She felt no remorse; then why should he—when his confusion was over? It was for the best, perhaps, that he had run away from her till he could see the inexorability of his position. Her design was quite unshaken by the emotions she had been through. Jon was hers now, he could not betray their secret unless she gave him leave. He must and would conform to the one course possible—secrecy. Infidelity had been achieved—one act or many, what did it matter? Ah! But she would make up to him for the loss of self-respect with her love, and with her wisdom. She would make him a success. In spite of that American chit he should succeed with his farming, become important to his county, to his country, perhaps. She would be circumspection itself—for his sake, for her own, for Michael's, Kit's, her father's.

With a great bunch of autumn flowers to which was clinging one bee, she went back into the house to put them in water. On the table in the hall were a number of little bags of bitter-apple prepared by her caretaker's wife against the moth, which were all over a house that had been derelict for a year. She busied herself with stowing them in drawers. The second post brought her Jon's letter.

She read it, and spots of burning colour became fixed in her cheeks. He had written this before he slept—it was all part of his confusion. But she must see him at once—at once! She got out the car, and, driving to a village where she was not known, sent a telegram to the post-office at Nettlefold. Dreadful to have to wait over the night! But she knew it might be evening or even next morning before he could call for it.

Never did time go so slowly. For now she was shaken again. Was she over-estimating her power, relying too much on her sudden victory in a moment of passion, under-estimating Jon's strength after resolve taken? She remembered how in those old days she had failed to move him from renunciation. And, unable to keep still, she went up lonely on to Box Hill, and wandered among its yew trees and spindleberry bushes, till she was tired out and the sun was nearly down. With the sinking light the loneliness up there repelled her, for she was not a real nature-lover, and for an anxious heart Nature has little comfort. She was glad to be back, listening to the chatter of the supper-eating girls. It had no interest for her, but at least it was not melancholy like the space and shadows of the open. She suddenly remembered that she had missed her "sitting" and had sent no word. The Rafaelite would gnash his teeth; perhaps he had set her "Folly" dress up on a dummy, to paint the sound from its silver bells. Bells! Michael! Poor Michael! But was he to be pitied, who had owned her for years while at heart she belonged to another? She went up to bed early. If only she could sleep till it was time to start! This force that played with hearts, tore them open, left them quivering—made them wait and ache, and ache and wait! Had the Victorian Miss, whom they had taken to praising again, ever to go through what she had gone through since first she saw her fate in front of that grotesque Juno—or was it Venus?—in the gallery off Cork Street? The disciplined Victorian Miss? Admit—oh! freely—that she, Fleur Mont, was undisciplined; still, she hadn't worn her heart upon her sleeve. She hadn't kicked and screamed. Surely she deserved a spell of happiness! Not more than a spell—she wouldn't ask for more than that! Things wore out, hearts wore out! But, to have the heart she wanted against her own, as last night, and then to lose it straightway? It could not be! And so at last she slept, and the moon that had watched over her victory came by, to look in through the curtain chinks, and make her dream.

She woke and lay thinking with the preternatural intensity of early morning thought. People would blame her if they knew; and was there any real possibility that they would not come to know? Suppose Jon remained immovably opposed to secrecy. What then? Was she prepared to give up all and follow him? It would mean more than in the ordinary case. It would mean isolation. For always, in the background, was the old barrier of the family feud; her father and his mother, and their abhorrence of union between her and Jon. And all the worldly sense in Fleur, brought to the edge of hard reality, shivered and recoiled. Money! It was not that they would lack money. But position, approval, appreciation, where in the world could they ever regain all that? And Kit? He would be lost to her. The Monts would claim him. She sat up in bed, seeing with utter clearness in the dark a truth she had never before seen naked—that the condition of conquest is sacrifice. Then she revolted. No! Jon would be reasonable, Jon would come round! In secret they would, they must, be happy, or if not happy, at least not starved. She would have to share him, he to share her; but they would each know that the other only pretended to belong elsewhere. But

would it be pretence with him? Was he at heart all hers?
Was he not, at least, as much his wife's? Horribly clear
she could see that girl's face, its dark, eager eyes, with the
something strange and so attractive in their setting. No!
She would not think of her! It only weakened her power
to win Jon over. Dawn opened a sleepy eye. A bird
cheeped, and daylight crept in. She lay back, resigned again
to the dull ache of waiting. She rose unrested. A fine
morning, dry as ever—save for the dew on the grass! At
ten she would start! It would be easier to wait in motion
even if she had to drive dead slow. She gave her morning
orders, got out the car, and left. She drove by the clock
so as to arrive at noon. The leaves were turning already,
it would be an early fall. Had she put on the right frock?
Would he like this soft russet, the colour of gone-off apples?
The red was prettier; but red caught the eye. And the eye
must not be caught to-day. She drove the last mile at a
foot's pace, and drew up in the wooded lane just where the
garden of Green Hill Farm ended in orchard, and the fields
began. Very earnestly she scrutinized her face in the small
mirror of her vanity bag. Where had she read that one
always looked one's worst in a mirror? If so, it was a
mercy. She remembered that Jon had once said he hated
the look of lip salve; and, not touching her lips, she put
away the mirror and got out. She walked slowly towards
the entrance gate. From there a lane divided the house
from the straw yards and farm buildings sloping up behind
it. In the fine autumn sunlight they ranged imposing, dry
and deserted—no stock, not so much as a hen. Even Fleur's
unlearned mind realised the stiff job before anyone who
took this farm. Had she not often heard Michael say that
farming was more of a man's job than any other in the
England of to-day! She would let him take it, then that
wretched conscience of his would be at rest on one score
at least. She passed the gate and stood before the old house,

gabled and red with Virginia creeper. Twelve had struck
down in the village as she passed through. Surely he had
not failed her! Five minutes she waited that seemed like
five hours. Then, with her heart beating fast, she went up
and rang the bell. It sounded far away in the empty house.
Footsteps—a woman's!

"Yes, ma'am?"

"I was to meet Mr. Forsyte here at noon about the farm."

"Oh, yes, ma'am; Mr. Forsyte came early. He was very
sorry he had to go away. He left this note for you."

"He's not coming back?"

"No, ma'am, he was very sorry, but he couldn't come
back to-day."

"Thank you."

Fleur went back to the gate. She stood there, turning the
note over and over. Suddenly she broke the seal and read:

"Last night Anne told me of her own accord that she
knew what had happened. She told me, too, that she is to
have a child. I have promised her not to see you again.
Forgive me and forget me, as I must forget you.

"JON."

Slowly, as if not knowing, she tore the sheet of paper
and the envelope into tiny fragments and buried them in
the hedge. Then she walked slowly, as if not seeing, to
her car, and got in. She sat there stonily, alongside the
orchard with the sunlight on her neck and scent from wind-
fallen rotting apples in her nostrils. For four months, since
in the canteen she saw Jon's tired smile, he had been one
long thought in her mind. And this was the end! Oh!
Let her get away—away from here!

She started the car, and, once out of the lane, drove at
a great pace. If she broke her neck, all the better! But
Providence, which attends the drunk and desperate, was

about her—spying out her ways; and she did not break
her neck. For more than two hours she drove, hardly knowing where. At three in the afternoon she had her first sane
impulse—a craving to smoke, a longing for tea. She got
some at an inn, and turned her car towards Dorking.
Driving more slowly now, she arrived between four and
five. She had been at the wheel for nearly six hours. And
the first thing she saw outside the "rest-house" was her
father's car. He! What had *he* come for? Why did people pester her? On the point of starting the engine again,
she saw him come out of the front door, and stand looking
up and down the road. Something groping in that look of
his touched her, and, leaving the car, she walked towards
him.

CHAPTER XI

"GREAT FORSYTE"

ON the morning after the Slum Conversion Committee meeting Soames had started early. It was his intention to spend the night somewhere "down there," look at his roots the following morning, and motor part of the way home. On the day after, he would return to town and see if he couldn't carry Fleur back with him to Mapledurham for a long week-end. He reached a seaside hostel ten miles from his origin about six o'clock, ate a damp dinner, smoked his own cigar, and went to a bed in which, for insurance sake, he placed a camel's hair shawl.

He had thought things out, and was provided with an ordinance map on an inordinate scale. He meant to begin his investigation by seeing the church. For he had little to go by except a memory that his father James had once been down, and had returned speaking of a church by the sea, and supposing that there might be "parish entries and that, but it was a long time back and he didn't know."

After an early breakfast he directed Riggs towards the church. As James had said, it was close to the sea, and it was open. Soames went in. A little old grey church with funny pews, and a damp smell. There wouldn't be any tablets to his name, he supposed. There were not, and he went out again, to wander among the gravestones, overcome by a sense of unreality—everything underground, and each gravestone, older than the last century, undecipherable. He was about to turn away when he stumbled. Looking down in disapproval at a flat stone, he saw on the worn and lichened surface a capital F. He stood for a minute, scrutinizing, then went down on his knees with a sort of thrill. Two names—the first had an undoubted capital *J*, a *y*, and an *n*; the second name began with that capital F, and had what looked like an *s* in the middle, and the remains of a tall letter last but one! The date? By George—the date was legible! 1777. Scraping gingerly at the first name, he disinterred an *o*. Four letters out of the six in Jolyon; three letters out of Forsyte. There could hardly be a doubt that he had stumbled over his great-great-grandfather! Supposing the old chap had lived to the ordinary age of a Forsyte, his birth would be near the beginning of the eighteenth century! His eyes gimletted the stone with a hard grey glance as though to pierce to the bones beneath—clean as a whistle long since, no doubt! Then he rose from his knees and dusted them. He had a date now. And, singularly fortified, he emerged from the graveyard, and cast a suspicious look at Riggs. Had he been seen on his knees? But the fellow was seated, as usual, with his back to everything, smoking his eternal cigarette. Soames got into the car.

"I want the vicarage now, or whatever it is."

"Yes, sir."

He was always saying "Yes, sir," without having an idea of where places were.

"You'd better ask," he said, as the car moved up the rutted lane. Sooner than ask, the fellow would go back to London! Not that there was anyone to ask. Soames was impressed, indeed, by the extreme emptiness of this parish where his roots lay. It seemed terribly hilly, and full of space, with large fields, some woods in the coombe to the left, and a soil that you couldn't swear by—not red and not white and not brown exactly; the sea was blue, however, and the cliffs, so far as he could judge, streaky. The lane bent to the right, past a blacksmith's forge.

"Hi!" said Soames, "pull up!" He himself got out to ask. That fellow never made head or tail of what he was told.

The blacksmith was hammering at a wheel, and Soames waited till his presence was observed.

"Where's the vicarage?"

"Up the lane, third 'ouse on the right."

"Thank you," said Soames, and, looking at the man suspiciously, added:

"Is the name Forsyte known hereabouts nowadays?"

"What's that?"

"Have you ever heard the name Forsyte?"

"Farsyt? Noa."

Soames heard him with a disappointed relief, and resumed his seat. What if he'd said: "Yes, it's mine!"

A blacksmith's was a respectable occupation, but he felt that he could do without it in the family. The car moved on.

The vicarage was smothered in creeper. Probably the Vicar would be, too! He rang a rusty bell and waited. The door was opened by a red-cheeked girl. It was all very rustic.

"I want the Vicar," said Soames. "Is he in?"

"Yes, sir. What name?"

But at this moment a thin man in a thin suit and a thin beard came out from a doorway, saying:

"Am I wanted, Mary?"

"Yes," said Soames; "here's my card."

There ought—he felt—to be a way of enquiring about one's origin that would be distinguished; but, not finding it, he added simply:

"My family came from hereabouts some generations back; I just wanted to have a look at the place, and ask you a question or two."

"Forsyte?" said the Vicar, gazing at the card; "I don't know the name, but I daresay we shall find something."

His clothes were extremely well worn, and Soames had the impression that his eyes would have been glad if they could. 'Smells a fee,' he thought; 'poor devil!'

"Will you come in?" said the Vicar. "I've got some records and an old tythe map. We might have a look at them. The registers go back to 1580. I could make a search for you."

"I don't know if that's worth while," said Soames, following him into a room that impressed him as dismal beyond words.

"Do sit down," said the Vicar. "I'll get that map. Forsyte? I seem to remember the name now."

The fellow was agreeable, and looked as if he could do with an honest penny!

"I've been up to the church," said Soames; "it seems very close to the sea."

"Yes; they used to use the pulpit, I'm afraid, to hide their smuggled brandy."

"I got a date in the graveyard—1777; the stones are very much let down."

"Yes," said the Vicar, who was groping in a cupboard; "one's difficulty is the sea air. Here's the map I spoke of"; and, unrolling a large and dingy map, he laid it on the table, weighting down the corners with a tin of tobacco, an inkstand, a book of sermons, and a dog whip. The latter was not heavy enough, and the map curled slowly away from Soames.

"Sometimes," said the Vicar, restoring the corner, and looking round for something to secure it, "we get very useful information from these old maps."

"I'll keep it down," said Soames, bending over the map. "I suppose you get a lot of Americans, fishing for ancestors?"

"Not a lot," said the Vicar, with a sideway glance that Soames did not quite like. "I can remember two. Ah! here," and his finger came down on the map, "I *thought* I remembered the name—it's unusual. Look! This field close to the sea is marked 'Great Forsyte!'"

Again Soames felt a thrill.

"What size is that field?"

"Twenty-four acres. There was the ruin of an old house, I remember, just there; they took the stones away in the war to make our shooting range. 'Great Forsyte'—isn't that interesting?"

"More interesting to me," said Soames, "if they'd left the stones."

"The spot is still marked with an old cross—the cattle use it for a rubbing stone. It's close to the hedge on the right hand side of the coombe."

"Could I get to it with the car?"

"Oh, yes; by going round the head of the coombe. Would you like me to come?"

"No, thanks," said Soames. The idea of being over-looked while inspecting his roots was unpleasant to him. "But if you'd kindly make a search in the register while I'm gone, I could call back after lunch and see the result. My great-grandfather, Jolyon Forsyte, died at Studmouth. The stone I found was Jolyon Forsyte, buried in 1777—he'd be my great-great-grandfather, no doubt. I daresay you could pick up his birth, and perhaps *his* father's—I fancy they were a long-lived lot. The name Jolyon seems to have been a weakness with them."

"I could make a search at once. It would take some hours. What would you think reasonable?"

"Five guineas?" hazarded Soames.

"Oh! That would be generous. I'll make a very thorough search. Now, let me come and tell you how to get to it." With a slight pang Soames followed him—a gentleman in trousers shiny behind.

"You go up this road to the fork, take the left-hand branch past the post-office, and right on round the head of the coombe, always bearing to the left, till you pass a farm called 'Uphays.' Then on till the lane begins to drop;

there's a gate on the right, and if you go through it you'll find yourself at the top of that field with the sea before you. I'm so pleased to have found something. Won't you have a little lunch with us when you come back?"

"Thank you," said Soames, "very good of you, but I've got my lunch with me," and was instantly ashamed of his thought. 'Does he think I'm going to make off without paying?' Raising his hat slightly, he got into the car, with his umbrella in his hand, so as to poke Riggs in the back when the fellow took his wrong turnings.

He sat, contented, using the umbrella gingerly now and then. So! To get baptized and buried, they used to cross the coombe. Twenty-four acres was quite a field. "Great Forsyte"; there must have been "Little Forsytes," too.

The farm the Vicar had spoken of appeared to be a rambling place of old buildings, pigs and poultry.

"Keep on," he said to Riggs, "until the lane drops, and go slow, I want a gate on the right."

The fellow was rushing along as usual, and the lane already dropping downhill.

"Hold hard! There it is!" The car came to a standstill at a rather awkward bend.

"You've overshot it!" said Soames, and got out. "Wait here! I may be some time."

Taking off his overcoat and carrying it on his arm, he went back to the gate, and passed through into a field of grass. He walked downwards to the hedge on the left, followed it round, and presently came in view of the sea, bright, peaceful, hazy, with a trail of smoke in the distance. The air beat in from the sea, fresh air, strong and salt. Ancestral! Soames took some deep breaths, savouring it, as one might an old wine. Its freshness went a little to his head, so impregnated with ozone or iodine, or whatever it was nowadays. And then, below him, perhaps a hundred yards away, above a hollow near the hedge he saw the stone, and again felt that thrill. He looked back. Yes! He was out of sight of the lane, and had his feelings to himself! And going up to the stone, he gazed down at the hollow between him and the hedge. Below it the field sloped to the beach, and what looked like the ghost of a lane ran up towards the hollow from the coombe. In that hollow then, the house had been; and there they'd lived, the old Forsytes, for generations, pickled in this air, without another house in sight—nothing but this expanse of grass in view and the sea beyond, and the gulls on that rock, and the waves beating over it. There they'd lived, tilling the land, and growing rheumatic, and crossing the coombe to church, and getting their brandy free, perhaps. He went up and examined the stone—upright, with another bit across the top—lintel of a barn, perhaps—nothing on it. Descending into the hollow, he poked about with his umbrella. During the war—the parson had said—they had removed the ruins. Only twelve years ago, but not a sign! Grassed over utterly, not even the shape visible. He explored up to the hedge. They'd made a clean sweep all right—nothing but grass now and a scrubble of fern and young gorse, such as would seize on a hollow for their growing. And, sitting on his overcoat with his back against the stone, Soames pondered. Had his forbears themselves built the house there in this lonely place—been the first to seat themselves on this bit of wind-swept soil? And something moved in him, as if the salty independence of that lonely spot were still in his bones. Old Jolyon and his own father and the rest of his uncles—no wonder they'd been independent, with this air and loneliness in their blood; and crabbed with the pickling of it—unable to give up, to let go, to die. For a moment he seemed to understand even himself. Southern spot, south aspect, not any of your northern roughness, but free, and salt, and solitary from sunrise to sunset, year in, year out, like that lonely rock with

the gulls on it, for ever and for ever. And drawing the
air deep into his lungs, he thought: 'I'm not surprised old
Timothy lived to be a hundred!' A long time he sat there,
nostalgically bemused, strangely unwilling to move. Never
had he breathed anything quite like that air; or so, at least,
it seemed to him. It had been the old England, when they
lived down here——the England of pack-horses and very
little smoke, of peat and wood fires, and wives who never
left you, because they couldn't, probably. A static England,
that dug and wove, where your parish was your world,
and you were a churchwarden if you didn't take care. His
own grandfather——begotten and born one hundred and
fifty-six years ago, in the best bed, not two dozen paces
from where he was sitting. What a change since then! For
the better? Who could say? But here was this grass, and
rock and sea, and the air and the gulls, and the old church
over there beyond the coombe, precisely as they had been,
only more so. If this field were in the market, he wouldn't
mind buying it as a curiosity. Only, if he did, nobody
would come and sit here! They'd want to play golf over
it or something. And, uneasy at having verged on the sentimental, Soames put his hand down and felt the grass. But
it wasn't damp, and he couldn't conscientiously feel that
he was catching rheumatism; and still he sat there, with the
sunlight warming his cheeks, and his eyes fixed on the sea.
The ships went up and down, far out——steamers; no smug-
glers nowadays, and you paid the deuce of a price for
brandy! In the old time here, without newspapers, with
nothing from the outer world, you'd grow up without any
sense of the State or that sort of thing. There'd be the
church and your Bible, he supposed, and the market some
miles away, and you'd work and eat and sleep and breathe
the air and drink your cider and embrace your wife and
watch your children, from June to June; and a good thing,
too! What more did you do now that brought you any sat-

isfaction? 'Change, it's all on the surface,' thought Soames; 'the roots are the same. You can't get beyond them—try as you will!' Progress, civilization, what were they for? Un-less—unless, indeed, to foster hobbies—collecting pictures, or what not? He didn't see how the old chaps down here could have had hobbies—except for bees, perhaps. Hobbies? Just for that—just to give people a chance to have hobbies? He'd had a lot of amusement out of his own; and but for progress would never have had it. No! He'd have been down here still, perhaps, shearing his sheep or following a plough, and his daughter would be a girl with sturdy ankles and one new hat. Perhaps it was just as well that you couldn't stop the clock! Ah! and it was time he was getting back to the lane before that chap came to look for him. And, getting up, Soames descended once more into the hol-low. This time, close to the hedge, an object caught his eye, a very old boot—a boot so old that you could hardly swear by it. His lips became contorted in a faint smile. He seemed to hear his dead cousin George with his wry For-sytean humour cackling: "The ancestral boot! What ho, my wild ones! Let the portcullis fall!" Yes! They would laugh at him in the family if they knew he'd been looking at their roots. He shouldn't say anything about it. And suddenly he went up to the boot, and, hooking the point of his umbrella under what was left of the toecap, flung it pettishly over the hedge. It defiled the loneliness—the feel-ing he had known, drinking-in that air. And very slowly he went back to the lane, so as not to get hot, and have to sit all damp in the car. But at the gate he stood, transfixed. What was all this? Two large, hairy horses were attached tandem to the back of his car with ropes, and beside them were three men, one of whom was Riggs, and two dogs, one of whom was lame. Soames perceived at once that it was all "that fellow!" In trying to back up the hill, which he ought never to have gone down, he had jammed the car so that it couldn't move. He was always doing something! At this moment, however, "the fellow" mounted the car and moved the wheel; while one of the men cracked a whip. "Haup!" The hairy horses moved. Something in that slow, strong movement affected Soames. Progress! They had been obliged to fetch horses to drag Progress up the hill!

"That's a good horse!" he said, pointing to the biggest.

"Ah! We call 'im Lion—'e can pull, Haup!"

The car passed on to the level ground, and the horses were detached. Soames went up to the man who had said "Haup!"

"Are you from the farm back there?"

"Yes."

"Do you own this field?"

"I farm it."

"What do you call it?"

"Call it? The big field."

"It's marked 'Great Forsyte' on the tithe map. D'you know that name?"

"Farsyt? There's none of the name now. My grand-mother was called Farsyt."

"Was she?" said Soames, and again felt the thrill.

"Ah!" said the farmer.

Soames controlled himself.

"And what's *your* name, if I may ask?"

"Beer."

Soames looked at him rather long, and took out his note case.

"You must allow me," he said, "for your horses and your trouble." And he offered a pound note. The farmer shook his head.

"That's naught," he said; "you're welcome. We're always haulin' cars off this 'ill."

"I really can't take something for nothing," said Soames. "You'll oblige me!"

"Well," said the farmer, "I thank yeou," and he took the note. "Haup!"

The released horses moved forward and the men and dogs followed after them. Soames got into the car, and, opening his packet of sandwiches, began to eat.

"Drive back to the vicarage—slowly." And, while he ate, he wondered why he had felt a thrill on discovering that some of his own blood ran in a hard-bitten looking chap called Beer—if, indeed, that *was* his name.

It was two o'clock when he reached the vicarage, and the Vicar came to him with his mouth full.

"I find a great many entries, Mr. Forsyte; the name goes back to the beginning of the register. I shall have to take my time to give you the complete list. That Jolyon seems to have been born in 1710, son of Jolyon and Mary; he didn't pay his tithes in 1757. There was another Jolyon born in 1680, evidently the father—he was church-warden from 1715 on; described as 'Yeoman of Hays—' he married a Bere."

Soames gazed at him, and took out his note case. "How do you spell it?" he said.

"B-e-r-e."

"Oh! The farmer up there said that was his name, too. I thought he was gammoning me. It seems his grandmother was called Forsyte, and she was the last of them here. Perhaps you could send me the Bere entries, too, for an inclusive seven guineas?"

"Oh! Six will be ample."

"No. We'll make it seven. You've got my card. I saw the stone. A healthy spot, right away from everything." He laid the seven guineas on the table, and again had an impression, as of glad eyes. "I must be getting back to London now. Good-bye!"

"Good-bye, Mr. Forsyte. Anything I can find out I shall make a point of sending you."

Soames shook his hand and went out to the car with the feeling that his roots would be conscientiously pulled up. After all, it was something to be dealing with a parson.

"Go on," he said to Riggs; "we'll get the best part of the way home."

And, lying back in the car, thoroughly tired, he mused. Great Forsyte! Well! He was glad he had come down.

CHAPTER XII

DRIVING ON

SOAMES spent the night at Winchester, a place he had often heard of but never seen. The Monts had been at school there, and Kit's name had been put down automatically. He himself would prefer his own Marlborough, or Harrow, perhaps—some school that played at Lords—but not Eton, where young Jolyon had been. But then one wouldn't be alive to see Kit play; so perhaps it didn't matter.

The town seemed an old place. There was something in a cathedral, too; and after breakfast he went to it. The chancel was in activity—some choir practice or other. He entered noiselessly, for his boots were rubbered against damp, and sat down at the point of balance. With chin uplifted, he contemplated the arches and the glass. The place was rather dark, but very rich—like a Christmas pudding! These old buildings certainly gave one a feeling. He had always had it with St. Paul's. One must admit at least a continuity of purpose somewhere. Up to a point—after that he wasn't sure. You had a great thing, like this, almost perfect; and then an earthquake or an air-raid, and down it went! Nothing permanent about anything, so far as he could see, not even about the best examples of ingenuity and beauty. The same with landscape! You had a perfect garden of a country, and then an ice-age came along. There was continuity, but it was always changing. That was why it seemed to him extremely unlikely that he would live after he was dead. He had read somewhere—though not in *The Times*—that life was just animated shape, and that when shape was broken it was no longer animated.

Death broke your shape and there you were, he supposed. The fact was, people couldn't bear their own ends; they tried to dodge them with soft sawder. They were weak-minded. And Soames lowered his chin. They had lighted some candles up there in the chancel, insignificant in the daylight. Presently they would blow them out. There you were again, everything was blown out sooner or later. And it was no good pretending it wasn't. He had read the other day, again not in *The Times*, that the world was coming to an end in 1928, when the earth got between the moon and the sun—it had been predicted in the Pyramids—some such scientific humbug! Well, if it did, he, for one, wouldn't much mind. The thing had never been a great success, and if it were wiped out at one stroke there would be nothing left behind anyway; what was objectionable about death was leaving things that you were fond of behind. The moment, too, that the world came to an end, it would begin again in some other shape, anyway—that, no doubt, was why they called it "world without end, Amen." Ah! They were singing now. Sometimes he wished he had an ear. In spite of the lack, he could tell that this was good singing. Boys' voices! Psalms, too, and he knew the words. Funny! Fifty years since his church-going days, yet he remembered them as if it were yesterday! "He sendeth the springs into the rivers; which run among the hills." "All beasts of the fields drink thereof; and the wild asses quench their thirst." "Beside them shall the fowls of the air have their habitation; and sing among the branches." They were flinging the verses at each other across the aisle, like a ball. It was lively, and good, vigorous English, too. "So is the great and wide sea also, wherein are things creeping innumerable, both small and great beasts." "There go the ships, and there is that Leviathan, whom Thou hast made to take his pastime therein." Leviathan! That word used to please him. "Man goeth forth to his work, and to his labour, until the evening." He certainly went forth, but whether he did any work, any labour, was the question, nowadays. "I will sing unto the Lord as long as I live; I will praise my God while I have my being." Would he? He wondered. "Praise thou the Lord, O my soul, praise the Lord." The singing ceased, and Soames again lifted up his chin. He sat very still—not thinking now; lost, as it were, among the arches, and the twilight of the roof. He was experiencing a peculiar sensation, not unpleasant. To be in here was like being within a jewelled and somewhat scented box. The world might roar and stink and buzz outside, strident and vulgar, childish and sensational, cheap and nasty—all jazz and cockney accent, but here—not a trace of it heard or felt or seen. This great box—God-box the Americans would call it—had been made centuries before the world became industrialised; it didn't belong to the modern world at all. In here everyone spoke and sang the King's English; it smelt faintly of age and incense; and nothing was unbeautiful. He sat with a sense of escape.

A verger passed, glancing at him curiously, as if unaccustomed to a raised chin; halting just behind, he made a little noise with his keys. Soames sneezed; and, reaching for his hat, got up. He had no intention of being taken round by that chap, and shown everything he didn't want to see, for half-a-crown. And with a "No, thank you; not to-day," he passed the verger, and went out to the car.

"You ought to have gone in," he said to Riggs; "they used to crown the kings of England there. To London now."

The opened car travelled fast under a bright sun, and not until he was in the new cut, leading to Chiswick, did Soames have the idea which caused him to say: "Stop at that house, 'The Poplars,' where you took us the other day."

It was not yet lunch time, and in all probability Fleur would still be "sitting"; so why not pick her up and take her straight away with him for the week-end? She had clothes down at "The Shelter." It would save some hours of fresh air for her. The foreign woman, however, who opened the door, informed him that the lady had not been to "sit" to-day or yesterday.

"Oh!" said Soames. "How's that?"

"Nobody did know, sir. She 'ave not sent any message. Mr. Blade is very decomposed."

Soames chewed his thoughts a moment.

"Is your mistress in?"

"Yes, sir."

"Then ask her if she'll see me, please. Mr. Soames Forsyte."

"Will you in the meal room wait, sir."

Soames waited uneasily in that very little room. Fleur had said she could not come with him because of her "sittings"; and she had not "sat." Was she ill, then?

He was roused from disquiet contemplation of the poplar trees outside by the words:

"Oh! It's you. I'm not sorry you came."

The cordiality of this greeting increased his uneasiness, and stretching out his hand, he said:

"How are you, June? I called for Fleur. When did she come last?"

"Tuesday morning. I saw her late on Tuesday afternoon, too, in her car, outside——" Soames could see her eyes moving from side to side, and knew that she was about to say something unpleasant. It came. "She picked up Jon."

Feeling as if he had received a punch in his wind, Soames exclaimed:

"What! Your young brother? What was he doing here?"

" 'Sitting,' of course."

" 'Sitting'? What business——!" and, checking the words,

"had he to 'sit,' " he stared at his cousin, who, flushing a deep pink, said:

"I told her she was not to see him here. I told Jon the same."

"Then she'd done it before?"

"Yes, twice. She's so spoiled, you see."

"Ah!" The reality of the danger had disarmed him. Antagonism seemed to him, thus faced with a sort of ruin, too luxurious.

"Where is she?"

"On Tuesday morning she said she was going down to Dorking."

"And she picked him up?" repeated Soames.

June nodded. "Yes, after his 'sitting.' His picture's finished. If you think that I want them to—any more than you——"

"No one in their senses could want them to——" said Soames, coldly. "But why did you make him 'sit,' while she was coming here?"

June flushed a deeper pink.

"*You* don't know how hard it is for real artists. I *had* to think of Harold. If I hadn't got Jon before he began his farming——"

"Farming!" said Soames. "For all we know they may ——" but again he checked his words. "I've been expecting something of this sort ever since I heard he was back. Well! I'd better get on to Dorking. D'you know where his mother is?"

"In Paris."

Ah! But not this time would he have to beg that woman to let her son belong to his daughter! No! It would be to beg her to stop his belonging—if at all.

"Good-bye!" he said.

"Soames," said June, suddenly, "don't let Fleur—it's she who——"

"I'll hear nothing against her," said Soames.

June pressed her clenched hands to her flat breast.

"I like you for that," she said; "and I'm sorry if——"

"That's all right," muttered Soames.

"Good-bye!" said June. "Shake hands!"

Soames put his hand in one which gave it a convulsive squeeze, then dropped it like a cold potato.

"Down to Dorking," he said to Riggs, on regaining his car. The memory of Fleur's face that night at Nettlefold, so close to the young man's, so full of what he had never seen on her face before, haunted him the length of Hammersmith Bridge. Ah! What a wilful creature! Suppose—suppose she had flung her cap over the windmill! Suppose the worst! Good God! What should—what *could* he do, then? The calculating tenacity of her passion for this young man—the way she had kept it from him, from everyone, or tried to! Something deadly about it, and something that almost touched him, rousing the memory of his own pursuit of that boy's mother—memory of a passion that would not, could not let go; that had won its ends, and destroyed in winning. He had often thought she had no continuity, that, like all these "fizz-gig" young moderns, she was just fluttering without basic purpose or direction. And it was the irony of this moment that he perceived how she—when she knew what she wanted—had as much tenacity of will as himself and his generation.

It didn't do, it seemed, to judge by appearances! Beneath the surface passions remained what they had been, and in the draughty corridors and spaces there was the old hot stillness when they woke and breathed. . . .

That fellow was taking the Kingston road! Soon they would be passing Robin Hill. How all this part had changed since the day he went down with Bosinney to choose the site. Forty years—not more—but what a change! "*Plus ça change—*" Annette would say—"*plus c'est la même*

chose!" Love and hate—no end to that, anyway! The beat
of life went on beneath the wheels and whirr of traffic and
the jazzy music of the band. Fate on its drum, or just the
human heart? God knew! God? Convenient word. What
did one mean by it? He didn't know, and never would!
In the cathedral that morning he had thought—and then—
that verger! There were the poplars, and the stable clock-
tower, just visible, of the house he had built and never in-
habited. If he could have foreseen a stream of cars like this
passing day after day, not a quarter of a mile off, he would
not have built it, and that tragedy might never—— And
yet—did it matter what you did?—some way, somehow life
took you up and put you where it would. He leaned forward and touched his chauffeur's back.

"Which way are you going?"

"Through Esher, sir, and off to the left."

"Well," said Soames, "it's all the same to me."

It was past lunch time, but he wasn't hungry. He
wouldn't be hungry till he knew the worst. But that chap
would be, he supposed.

"Better stop somewhere," he said, "and have a snack,
and a cigarette."

"Yes, sir."

He wasn't long in stopping. Soames sat on in the car,
gazing idly at the sign—"Red Lions, Angels and White
Horses"—nothing killed them off. One of these days they'd
try and bring in Prohibition, he shouldn't wonder; but that
cock wouldn't fight in England—too extravagant! Treat-
ing people like children wasn't the way to make them grow
up; as if they weren't childish enough as it was. Look at
this coal strike, that went on and on—perfectly childish,
hurting everybody and doing good to none! Weak-minded!
To reflect on the weak-mindedness of his fellow-citizens
was restful to Soames, faced with a future that might
prove disastrous. For, in view of her infatuation, what

could taking that young man about in her car mean—except disaster? What a time Riggs was! He got out, and walked up and down. Not that there was anything he could do—he supposed—when he did get there. No matter how much you loved a person, how anxious you were about her, you had no power—perhaps less power in proportion to your love. But he must speak his mind at last, if he had the chance. Couldn't let her go over the edge without putting out a hand! The sun struck on his face, and he lifted it a little blindly, as if grateful for the warmth. All humbug about the world coming to an end, of course, but he'd be glad enough for it to come before he was brought down in sorrow to the grave. He saw with hideous clearness how complete disaster must be. If Fleur ran off, there'd be nothing left to him that he really cared about, for the Monts would take Kit. He'd be stranded among his pictures and his cows, without heart for either, till he died. 'I won't have it,' he thought. 'If it hasn't happened, I won't have it.' Yes! But how prevent it? And with the futility of his own resolution staring him in the face, he went back to the car. There was the fellow, at last, smoking his cigarette.

"Let's start!" he said. "Push along!"

He arrived at three o'clock to hear that Fleur had gone out with the car at ten. It was an immense relief to learn that at least she had been there overnight. And at once he began to make trunk calls. They renewed his anxiety. She was not at home; nor at June's. Where, then, if not with that young man? But at least she had taken no things with her—this he ascertained, and it gave him strength to drink some tea, and wait. He had gone out into the road for the fourth time to peer up and down when at last he saw her coming towards him.

The expression on her face—hungry and hard and fever-ish—had the most peculiar effect on Soames; his heart ached, and leaped with relief at the same time. That was not the face of victorious passion! It was tragically unhappy, arid, wrenched. Every feature seemed to have sharpened since he saw her last. And, instinctively, he remained silent, poking his face forward for a kiss. She gave it—hard and parched.

"So you're back," she said.

"Yes; and when you've had your tea, I want you to come straight on with me to 'The Shelter'—Riggs'll put your car away."

She shrugged her shoulders and passed him into the house. It seemed to him that she did not care what he saw in her, or what he thought of her. And this was so strange in Fleur that he was confounded. Had she tried and failed? Could it mean anything so good? He searched his memory to recall how she had looked when he brought her back the news of failure six years ago. Yes! Only then she was so young, her face so round—not like this hardened, sharpened, burnt-up face, that frightened him. Get her away to Kit! Get her away, and quickly! And with that saving instinct of his where Fleur only was concerned, he summoned Riggs, told him to close the car and bring it round.

She had gone up to her room. He sent up a message presently that the car was ready. Soon she came down. She had coated her face with powder and put salve on her lips; and again Soames was shocked by that white mask with compressed red line of mouth, and the live and tortured eyes. And again he said nothing, and got out a map.

"That fellow will go wrong unless I sit beside him. It's cross country;" and he mounted the front of the car. He knew she couldn't talk, and that he couldn't bear to see her face. So they started. An immense time they travelled thus, it seemed to him. Once or twice only he looked round to see her sitting like something dead, so white and motionless. And, within him, the two feelings—relief and pity, continued to struggle. Surely it was the end—she had played her hand and lost! How, where, when—he felt would always be unknown to him; but she had lost! Poor little thing! Not her fault that she had loved this boy, that she couldn't get him out of her head—no more her fault than it had been his own for loving that boy's mother! Only everyone's misfortune! It was as if that passion, born of an ill-starred meeting in a Bournemouth drawing-room forty-six years before, and transmitted with his blood into her being, were singing its swan song of death, through the silent crimsoned lips of that white-faced girl behind him in the cushioned car. "Praise thou the Lord, O my soul! Praise the Lord!" Um! How could one! They were crossing the river at Staines—from now on that fellow knew his road. When they got home, how should he bring some life into her face again! Thank goodness her mother was away! Surely Kit would be some use! And her old dog, perhaps. And yet, tired though he was after his three long days, Soames dreaded the moment when the car should stop. To drive on and on, perhaps, was the thing for her. Perhaps, for all the world, now. To get away from something that couldn't be got away from—ever since the war —driving on! When you couldn't have what you wanted, and yet couldn't let go; and drove, on and on, to dull the aching. Resignation—like painting—was a lost art; or so it seemed to Soames, as they passed the graveyard where he expected to be buried someday.

Close home now, and what was he going to say to her when they got out? Words were so futile. He put his head out of the window and took some deep breaths. It smelled better down here by the river than elsewhere, he always thought—more sap in the trees, more savour in the grass. Not the equal of the air on "Great Forsyte," but more of the earth, more cosy. The gables and the poplars, the scent of a wood fire, the last flight of the doves—here they were! And with a long sigh, he got out.

"You've been doing too much," he said, opening the door. "Would you like to go straight up to bed, when you've seen Kit? I'll send up your dinner."

"Thanks, Dad. Some soup is all I shall want. I've got a chill, I think."

Soames looked at her deeply for a moment, and shook his head; then, touching her whitened cheek with a finger, he turned away.

He went round to the stables and released her old dog. It might want a run before being let into the house; and he took it down towards the river. A thin daylight lingered though the sun had set some time, and while the dog freshened himself among the bushes, Soames stood looking at the water. The swans passed over to their islet while he gazed. The young ones were growing up—were almost white. Rather ghostly in the dusk, the flotilla passed—graceful things and silent. He had often thought of going in for a peacock or two, they put a finish on a garden, but they were noisy; he had never forgotten an early morning in Montpellier Square, hearing their cry, as of lost passion, from Hyde Park. No! The swan was better; just as graceful, and didn't sing. That dog was ruining his dwarf arbutus.

"Come along to your mistress!" he said, and turned back towards the lighted house. He went up into the picture gallery. On the bureau were laid a number of letters and things to be attended to. For half an hour he laboured at them. He had never torn up things with greater satisfaction. Then the bell rang, and he went down to be lonely, as he supposed.

CHAPTER XIII

FIRES

BUT Fleur came down again. And there began for Soames the most confused evening he had ever spent. For in his heart were great gladness and great pity, and he must not show a sign of either. He wished now that he had stopped to look at Fleur's portrait; it would have given him something to talk of. He fell back feebly on her Dorking house.

"It seems a useful place," he said; "the girls——"

"I always feel they hate me. And why not? They have nothing, and I have everything."

Her laugh cut Soames to the quick.

She was only pretending to eat, too. But he was afraid to ask if she had taken her temperature. She would only laugh again. He began, instead, an account of how he had found a field by the sea where the Forsytes came from, and how he had visited Winchester Cathedral; and, while he went on and on, he thought: 'She hasn't heard a word.'

The idea that she would go up to bed consumed by this smouldering fire at which he could not get, distressed and alarmed him greatly. She looked as if—as if she might do something to herself! She had no veronal, or anything of that sort, he hoped. And all the time he was wondering what had happened. If the issue were still doubtful—if she were still waiting, she might be restless, feverish, but surely she would not look like this! No! It was defeat. But how? And was it final, and he freed for ever from the carking anxiety of these last months? His eyes kept questioning her face, where her fevered mood had crept through the coating of powder, so that she looked theatrical and unlike herself. Its expression, hard and hopeless, went to his heart. If only she would cry, and blurt everything out! But he recognised that in coming down at all, and facing him, she was practically saying, "*Nothing* has happened!" And he compressed his lips. A dumb thing, affection—one couldn't put it into words! The more deeply he felt the more dumb he had always been. Those glib people who poured themselves out and got rid of the feelings they had in their chests, he didn't know how they could do it!

Dinner dragged to its end, with little bursts of talk from Fleur, and more of that laughter which hurt him, and afterwards they went to the drawing-room.

"It's hot to-night," she said, and opened the French window. The moon was just rising, low and far behind the river bushes; and a waft of light was already floating down the water.

"Yes, it's warm," said Soames, "but you oughtn't to be in the air if you've got a chill."

And, taking her arm, he led her within. He had a dread of her wandering outside to-night, so near the water.

She went over to the piano.

"Do you mind if I strum, Dad?"

"Not at all. Your mother's got some French songs there." He didn't mind what she did, if only she could get that look off her face. But music was emotional stuff, and French songs always about love! It was to be hoped she wouldn't light on the one Annette was for ever singing:

"*Auprès de ma blonde, il fait bon—fait bon—fait bon,*
Auprès de ma blonde, il fait bon dormir."

That young man's hair! In the old days, beside his mother! What hair *she'd* had! What bright hair and what dark eyes! And for a moment it was as if, not Fleur, but Irene sat there at the piano. Music! Mysterious how it could mean to anyone what it had meant to her. Yes! More than men and more than money—music! A thing

that had never moved him, that he didn't understand!
What a mischance! There she was, above the piano, as he
used to see her in the little drawing-room in Montpellier
Square; there, as he had seen her last in that Washington
hotel. There she would sit until she died, he supposed,
beautiful, he shouldn't wonder, even then. Music!

He came to himself.

Fleur's thin, staccato voice tickled his ears, where he
sat in the fume of his cigar. Painful! She was making a
brave fight. He wanted her to break down, and he didn't
want her to. For if she broke down he didn't know what
he would do!

She stopped in the middle of a song and closed the piano.
She looked almost old—so she would look, perhaps, when
she was forty. Then she came and sat down on the other
side of the hearth. She was in red, and he wished she wasn't
—the colour increased his feeling that she was on fire
beneath that mask of powder on her face and neck. She
sat there very still, pretending to read. And he who had
The Times in his hand, tried not to notice her. Was there
nothing he could do to divert her attention? What about
his pictures? Which—he asked—was her favourite? The
Constable, the Stevens, the Corot, or the Daumier?

"I'm leaving the lot to the Nation," he said. "But I
shall want you to take your pick of four or so; and, of
course, that copy of Goya's 'Vendimia' belongs to you."
Then, remembering she had worn the 'Vendimia' dress at
the dance in the Nettlefold hotel, he hurried on:

"With all this modern taste the Nation mayn't want
them; in that case I don't know. Dumetrius might take
them off your hands! he's had a good deal out of most of
them already. If you chose the right moment, clear of
strikes and things, they ought to fetch money in a good sale.
They stand me in at well over seventy thousand pounds—
they ought to make a hundred thousand at least."

She seemed to be listening, but he couldn't tell.

"In my belief," he went on, desperately, "there'll be none of this modern painting in ten years' time—they can't go on for ever juggling in the air. They'll be sick of experiments by then, unless we have another war."

"It wasn't the war."

"How d'you mean—not the war? The war brought in ugliness, and put everyone into a hurry. You don't remember before the war."

She shrugged her shoulders.

"I won't say," continued Soames, "that it hadn't begun before. I remember the first shows in London of those post-impressionists and early Cubist chaps. But they ran riot with the war, catching at things they couldn't get."

He stopped. It was exactly what she——!

"I think I'll go to bed, Dad."

"Ah!" said Soames. "And take some aspirin. Don't you play about with a chill."

A chill! If only it were! He himself went again to the open window, and stood watching the moonlight. From the staff's quarters came the strains of a gramophone. How they loved to turn on that caterwauling, or the loud speaker! He didn't know which he disliked most.

Moving to the edge of the verandah, he held out his palm. No dew! Dry as ever—remarkable weather! A dog began howling from over the river. Some people would take that for a banshee, he shouldn't wonder! The more he saw of people the more weak-minded they seemed; for ever looking for the sensational, or covering up their eyes and ears. The garden was looking pretty in the moonlight—pretty and unreal. That border of sunflowers and Michaelmas daisies and the late roses in the little round beds, and the low wall of very old brick—he'd had a lot of trouble to get that brick!—even the grass—the moonlight gave them all a stage-like quality. Only the poplars queered the dream-like values, dark and sharply outlined by the moon behind them. Soames moved out on to the lawn. The face of the house, white and creepered, with a light in her bedroom, looked unreal, too, and as if powdered. Thirty-two years he'd been here. One had got attached to the place, especially since he'd bought the land over the river, so that no one could ever build and overlook him. To be overlooked, body or soul—on the whole he'd avoided that in life—at least, he hoped so.

He finished his cigar out there and threw the butt away. He would have liked to see her light go out before he went to bed—to feel that she was sleeping as when, a little thing, she went to bed with toothache. But he was very tired. Motoring was hard on the liver. Well! He'd go in and shut up. After all, he couldn't do any good by staying down, couldn't do any good in any way. The old couldn't help the young—nobody could help anyone, if it came to that, at least where the heart was concerned. Queer arrangement—the heart! And to think that everybody had one. There ought to be some comfort in that, and yet there wasn't. No comfort to him, when he'd suffered, night in, day out, over that boy's mother, that she had suffered, too! No satisfaction to Fleur now, that the young man and his wife, too, very likely, were suffering as well! And, closing the window, Soames went up. He listened at her door, but could hear nothing; and, having undressed, took up Vasari's "Lives of the Painters," and, propped against his pillows, began to read. Two pages of that book always sent him to sleep, and generally the same two, for he knew them so well that he never remembered where he had left off.

He was awakened presently by he couldn't tell what, and lay listening. It seemed that there was movement in the house. But if he got up to see he would certainly begin to worry again, and he didn't want to. Besides, in seeing to whether Fleur was asleep he might wake her up. Turning

over, he dozed off, but again he woke, and lay drowsily
thinking: 'I'm not sleeping well—I want exercise.' Moonlight was coming through the curtains not quite drawn.
And, suddenly, his nostrils twitched. Surely a smell of
burning! He sat up, sniffing. It *was*! Had there been a
short circuit, or was the thatch of the pigeon-house on fire?
Getting out of bed, he put on his dressing-gown and slip-
pers, and went to the window.

A reddish, fitful light was coming from a window above.
Great God! His picture gallery! He ran to the foot of
the stairs that led up to it. A stealthy sound, a scent of
burning much more emphatic, staggered him. He hurried
up the stairs and pulled open the door. Heavens! The far
end of the gallery, at the extreme left corner of the house,
was on fire. Little red flames were licking round the woodwork; the curtains of the far window were already a
blackened mass, and the waste paper basket, between them
and his writing bureau, was a charred wreck! On the
parquet floor he saw some cigarette ash. Someone had been
up here smoking! The flames crackled as he stood there
aghast. He rushed downstairs, and threw open the door of
Fleur's room. She was lying on her bed asleep, but fully
dressed! Fully dressed! Was it——? Had she——? She
opened her eyes, staring up at him.

"Get up!" he said, "there's a fire in the picture gallery.
Get Kit and the servants out at once—at once! Send for
Riggs! Telephone to Reading for the engines—quick! Get
everyone out of the house!" Only waiting to see her on
her feet, he ran back to the foot of the gallery stairs and
seized a fire extinguisher. He carried it up, a heavy, great
thing. He knew vaguely that you dashed the knob on the
floor and sprayed the flames. Through the open doorway
he could see that they had spread considerably. Good God!
They were licking at his Fred Walker, and the two David
Coxes. They had caught the beam, too, that ran round the

gallery, dividing the upper from the lower tier of pictures;
yes, and the upper beam was on fire, also. The Constable!
For a moment he hesitated. Should he rush at that, and save
it, anyway? The extinguisher mightn't work! He dropped
it, and, running the length of the gallery, seized the Constable just as the flames reached the woodwork above it. The
hot breath of them scorched his face as he wrenched the
picture from the wall, and, running back, flung open the
window opposite the door, and placed it on the sill. Then,
seizing the extinguisher again, he dashed it, knob down,
against the floor. A stream of stuff came out, and, picking
the thing up, he directed that stream against the flames.
The room was full of smoke now, and he felt rather giddy.
The stuff was good, and he saw with relief that the flames
didn't like it. He was making a distinct impression on them.
But the Walker was ruined—ah! and the Coxes! He had
beaten the fire back to the window-wall, when the stream
ceased, and he saw that the beams had broken into flame
beyond where he had started spraying. The writing bureau,
too, was on fire now—its papers had caught! Should he
run down and get another of these things, all the way to
the hall! Where was that fellow Riggs? The "Alfred
Stevens"! By heaven! He was not going to lose his
"Stevens" nor his "Gauguins," nor his "Corots"!

And a sort of demon entered into Soames. His taste,
his trouble, his money, and his pride—all consumed? By the
Lord, no! And through the smoke he dashed again up to
the far wall. Flame licked at his sleeve as he tore away
the "Stevens"; he could smell the singed stuff when he
propped the picture in the window beside the Constable.

A lick of flame crossed the Daubigny, and down came
its glass with a clatter—there was the picture exposed and
fire creeping and flaring over it! He rushed back and
grasped at a "Gauguin"— a South Sea girl with nothing
on. She wouldn't come away from the wall; he caught

hold of the wire, but dropped it—red hot; seizing the frame
he gave a great wrench. Away it came, and over he went,
backwards. But he'd got it, his favourite Gauguin! He
stacked that against the others, and ran back to the Corot
nearest the flames. The silvery, cool picture was hot to his
touch, but he got that, too! Now for the Monet! The
engines would be twenty minutes at least. If that fellow
Riggs didn't come soon——! They must spread a blanket
down there, and he would throw the pictures out. And
then he uttered a groan. The flames had got the other
Corot! The poor thing! Wrenching off the Monet, he ran
to the head of the stairs. Two frightened maids in coats
over their nightgowns, and their necks showing, were half
way up.

"Here!" he cried. "Take this picture, and keep your
heads. Miss Fleur and the boy out?"

"Yes, sir."

"Have you telephoned?"

"Yes, sir."

"Get me an extinguisher; and all of you hold a blanket
spread beneath the window down there, to catch the pictures as I throw them out. Don't be foolish—there's no
danger! Where's Riggs?"

He went back into the gallery. Oh——h! There went
his precious little Degas! And with rage in his heart
Soames ran again at the wall, and snatched at his other
Gauguin. If ever he had beaten Dumetrius, it was over
that highly-coloured affair. As if grateful to him, the picture came away neatly in his scorched and trembling hands.
He stacked it, and stood for a moment choked and breathless. So long as he could breathe up here in the draught
between the opened door and window, he must go on getting them off the wall.

It wouldn't take long to throw them out. The Bonning-
ton and the Turner—that fellow Turner wouldn't have

been so fond of sunsets if he'd known what fire was like.
Each time now that he went to the wall his lungs felt as
if they couldn't stand another journey. But they must!

"Dad!"

Fleur with an extinguisher!

"Go down! Go out!" he cried. "D'you hear! Go out
of the house! Get that blanket spread, and make them
hold it tight."

"Dad! Let me! I must!"

"Go down!" cried Soames again, and pushed her to the
stairs. He watched her to the bottom, then dashed the knob
of the extinguisher on the floor and again sprayed the
fire. He put out the bureau, and attacked the flames on the
far wall. He could hardly hold the heavy thing, and when
it dropped empty, he could barely see. But again he had
gained on the fire. If only he could hold on!

And then he saw that his Harpignies was gone—such a
beauty! That wanton loss gave him strength. And rushing up to the wall—the long wall now—he detached picture after picture. But the flames were creeping back again,
persistent as hell itself. He couldn't reach the Sisley and
the Picasso, high in the corner there, couldn't face the flames
so close, for if he slipped against the wall he would be done.
They must go! But he'd have the Daumier! His favourite
—perhaps his very favourite. Safe! Gasping, and avidly
drinking the fresher air, he could see from the window
that they had the blanket down there now stretched between
four maids, holding each a corner.

"Hold tight!" he cried; and tipped the Daumier out. He
watched it falling. What a thing to do to a picture! The
blanket dipped with the weight, but held.

"Hold it tighter!" he shouted. "Look out!" And over
went the Gauguin South Sea girl. Picture after picture he
tipped from the sill; and picture after picture, they took
them from the blanket, and laid them on the grass. When

he had tipped them all, he turned to take the situation in. The flames had caught the floor now, in the corner, and were spreading fast along the beams.

The engines would be in time to save the right hand wall. The left hand wall was hopeless, but most of the pictures there he'd saved. It was the long wall where the flames were beginning to get hold; he must go for that now. He ran as near to the corner as he dared, and seized the Morland. It was hot to his touch, but he got it—six hundred pounds' worth of white pony. He had promised it a good home! He tipped it from the window and saw it pitch headlong into the blanket.

"My word!"

Behind him, in the doorway, that fellow Riggs at last, in shirt and trousers, with two extinguishers, and an open mouth!

"Shut your mouth!" he gasped, "and spray that wall!"

He watched the stream and the flames recoiling from it. How he hated those inexorable red tongues. Ah! That was giving them pause!

"Now the other! Save the Courbet! Sharp!"

Again the stream spurted and the flames recoiled. Soames dashed for the Courbet. The glass had gone, but the picture was not harmed yet; he wrenched it away.

"That's the last of the bloomin' extinguishers, sir," he heard Riggs mutter.

"Here, then!" he called. "Pull the pictures off that wall and tip them out of the window one by one. Mind you hit the blanket. Stir your stumps!"

He, too, stirred his stumps, watching the discouraged flames regaining their lost ground. The two of them ran breathless to the wall, wrenched, ran back to the window, and back again—and the flames gained all the time.

"That top one," said Soames; "I must have that! Get on that chair. Quick! No, I'll do it. Lift me!—I can't reach!"

Uplifted in the grip of that fellow, Soames detached his James Maris, bought the very day the whole world broke into flames. "Murder of the Archduke!" he could hear them at it now. A fine day; the sunlight coming in at the window of his cab, and he lighthearted, with that bargain on his knee. And there it went, pitching down! Ah! What a way to treat pictures!

"Come on!" he gasped.

"Better go down, sir! It's gettin' too thick now."

"No!" said Soames. "Come on!"

Three more pictures salved.

"If you don't go down, sir, I'll have to carry you—you been up 'ere too long."

"Nonsense!" gasped Soames. "Come on!"

" 'Ooray! The engines!"

Soames stood still; besides the pumping of his heart and lungs he could hear another sound. Riggs seized his arm.

"Come along, sir; when they begin to play there'll be a proper smother."

Soames pointed through the smoke.

"I must have that one," he gasped. "Help me. It's heavy."

The "Vendimia" copy stood on an easel. Soames staggered up to it. Half carrying and half dragging, he bore that Spanish effigy of Fleur towards the window.

"Now lift!" They lifted till it balanced on the sill.

"Come away there!" called a voice from the doorway.

"Tip!" gasped Soames, but arms seized him, he was carried to the door, down the stairs, into the air half-conscious. He came to himself in a chair on the verandah. He could see the helmets of firemen and hear a hissing sound. His lungs hurt him, his eyes smarted terribly, and his hands were scorched, but he felt drugged and drowsy and triumphant in spite of his aches and smarting.

The grass, the trees, the cool river under the moon! What a nightmare it had been up there among his pictures—his poor pictures! But he had saved them! The cigarette ash! The waste paper basket! Fleur! No doubt about the cause! What on earth had induced him to put his pictures into her head that evening of all others, when she didn't know what she was doing? What awful luck! Mustn't let her know—unless—unless she did know? The shock—however! The shock might do her good! His Degas! The Harpignies! He closed his eyes to listen to the hissing of the water. Good! A good noise! They'd save the rest! It might have been worse! Something cold was thrust against his drooped hand. A dog's nose. They shouldn't have let him out. And, suddenly, it seemed to Soames that he must see to things again. They'd go the wrong way to work with all that water! He staggered to his feet. He could see better now. Fleur? Ah! There she was, standing by herself—too near the house! And what a mess on the lawn—firemen—engines—maids, that fellow Riggs—the hose laid to the river—plenty of water, anyway! They mustn't hurt the pictures with that water! Fools! He knew it! Why! They were squirting the untouched wall. Squirting through both windows. There was no need of that? The right hand window only—only! He stumbled up to the fireman.

"Not that wall! Not that! That wall's all right. You'll spoil my pictures! Shoot at the centre!" The fireman shifted the angle of his arm, and Soames saw the jet strike the right hand corner of the sill. The Vendimia! There went its precious——! Dislodged by the stream of water, it was tilting forward! And Fleur! Good God! Standing right under, looking up. She must see it, and she wasn't moving! It flashed through Soames that she wanted to be killed.

"It's falling!" he cried. "Look out! Look out!" And, just as if he had seen her about to throw herself under a car, he darted forward, pushed her with his outstretched arms, and fell.

The thing had struck him to the earth.

CHAPTER XIV

HUSH

OLD Gradman, off the Poultry, eating his daily chop, took up the early edition of the evening paper, brought to him with that collation:

"FIRE IN A PICTURE GALLERY."
"WELL-KNOWN CONNOISSEUR SEVERELY INJURED."

"A fire, the cause of which is unknown, broke out last night in the picture gallery of Mr. Soames Forsyte's house at Mapledurham. It was extinguished by fire engines from Reading, and most of the valuable pictures were saved. Mr. Forsyte, who was in residence, fought the fire before the firemen were on the spot, and, single-handed, rescued many of the pictures, throwing them out of the window of the gallery into a blanket which was held stretched out on the lawn below. Unfortunately, after the engines had arrived, he was struck on the head by the frame of a picture falling from the window of the gallery, which is on the second floor, and rendered unconscious. In view of his age and his exertions during the fire, very little hope is entertained of his recovery. Nobody else was injured, and no other part of the mansion was reached by the flames."

Laying down his fork, old Gradman took his napkin, and passed it over a brow which had grown damp. Replacing it on the table, he pushed away his chop, and took up the paper again. You never knew what to believe, nowadays, but the paragraph was uncommonly sober; and he dropped it with a gesture singularly like the wringing of hands.

'Mr. Soames,' he thought. 'Mr. Soames!' His two wives,

his daughter, his grandson, the Forsyte family, himself!
He stood up, grasping the table. An accidental thing like
that! Mr. Soames! Why—he was a young man, comparatively! But perhaps they'd got hold of the wrong stick!
Mechanically he went to the telephone. He found the
number with difficulty, his eyes being misty.

"Is that Mrs. Dartie's—Gradman speaking. Is it true,
ma'am. . . . Not 'opeless, I do trust? Aow! Saving Miss
Fleur's life? You don't say! You're goin' down? I think
I'd better, too. Everything's in order, but he might want
something, if he comes to. . . . Dear, dear! . . . Ah! I'm
sure. . . . Dreadful shock—dreadful!" He hung up the
receiver, and stood quite still. Who would look after things
now? There wasn't one of the family with any sense of
business, compared with Mr. Soames, not one who remembered the old days, and could handle house property as they
used to, then. No, he couldn't relish any more chop—that
was flat! Miss Fleur! Saving her life? Well, what a
thing! She'd always been first with him. What must she be
feelin'! He remembered her as a little girl; yes, and at
her wedding. To think of it. She'd be a rich woman now.
He took his hat. Must go home first and get some things
—might have to wait there days! But for a full three
minutes he still stood, as if stunned—a thick-set figure with
a puggy face, in a round grey beard—confirming his uneasy
grief. If the Bank of England had gone he couldn't have
felt it more. That he couldn't.

When he reached "The Shelter" in a station fly, with a
bag full of night things and papers, it was getting on for
six o'clock. He was met in the hall by that young man,
Mr. Michael Mont, whom he remembered as making jokes
about serious things—it was to be hoped he wouldn't do it
now!

"Ah! Mr. Gradman; so good of you to come! No!
They hardly expect him to recover consciousness; it was

a terrible knock. But if he does, he's sure to want to see
you, even if he can't speak. We've got your room ready.
Will you have some tea?"

Yes, he could relish a cup of tea—he could indeed!
"Miss Fleur?"

The young man shook his head, his eyes looked distressed.

"He saved her life."

Gradman nodded. "So they say. Tt, tt! To think that
he—! His father lived to be ninety, and Mr. Soames was
always careful. Dear, dear!"

He had drunk a nice hot cup of tea when he saw a figure
in the doorway—Miss Fleur herself. Why! What a face!
She came forward and took his hand. And, almost unconsciously, old Gradman lifted his other hand and im-
prisoned hers between his two.

"My dear," he said, "I feel for you. I remember you as
a little girl."

She only answered: "Yes, Mr. Gradman," and it seemed
to him funny. She took him to his room, and left him
there. He had never been in such a pleasant bedroom, with
flowers and a nice smell, and a bathroom all to himself—
really quite unnecessary. And to think that two doors off
Mr. Soames was lying as good as gone!

"Just breathing," she had said, passing the door. "They
daren't operate. My mother's there."

What a face she had on her—so white, so hurt-looking
—poor young thing! He stood at the open window, gazing
out. It was warm—very warm for the end of September.
A pleasant air—a smell of grass. It must be the river
down there. Peaceful—and to think—! Moisture blurred
the river out; he winked it away. Only the other day they'd
been talking about something happening; and now it hadn't
happened to him, but to Mr. Soames himself. The ways
of Providence! For Jesus Christ's sake—Our Lord! Dear,

dear! To think of it! He would cut up a very warm man.
Richer than his father. There were some birds out there
on the water—geese or swans or something—ye-es! Swans!
What a lot! In a row, floating along. He hadn't seen a
swan since he took Mrs. G. to Golder's Hill Park the year
after the war. And they said—hopeless! A dreadful thing
—sudden like that, with no time to say your prayers. Lucky
the Will was quite straightforward. Annuity to Mrs. F.,
and the rest to his daughter for life, remainder to her children in equal shares. Only one child at present, but there'd
be others, no doubt, with all that money. Dear! What a
sight of money there was in the family altogether, and yet,
of the present generation, Mr. Soames was the only warm
man. It was all divided up now, and none of the young
ones seemed to make any. He would have to keep a tight
hand on the estates, or they'd be wanting their capital out,
and Mr. Soames wouldn't approve of that! To think of
outliving Mr. Soames! And something incorruptibly faithful within that puggy face and thick figure, something that
for two generations had served and never expected more
than it had got, so moved old Gradman that he subsided on
the window seat with the words: "I'm quite upset!"

He was still sitting there with his head on his hand, and
darkness thickening outside, when, with a knock on the door,
that young man said:

"Mr. Gradman, will you come down for dinner, or
would you like it up here?"

"Up here, if it's all the same to you. Cold beef and
pickles or anything there is, and a glass of stout, if it's quite
convenient."

The young man drew nearer.

"You must feel it awfully, Mr. Gradman, having known
him so long. Not an easy man to know, but one felt——"

Something gave way in Gradman and he spoke:

"Ah! I knew him from a little boy—took him to his

first school—taught him how to draw a lease—never knew him to do a shady thing; very reserved man, Mr. Soames, but no better judge of an investment, except his uncle Nicholas. He had his troubles, but he never said anything of them; good son to his father—good brother to his sisters —good father to his child, as you know, young man."

"Yes, indeed! And very good to me."

"Not much of a church-goer, I'm afraid, but straight as a die. Never one to wear his 'eart on his sleeve; a little uncomfortable sometimes, maybe, but you could depend on him. I'm sorry for your young wife, young man—I am that! 'Ow did it 'appen?"

"She was standing below the window when the picture fell, and didn't seem to realise. He pushed her out of the way, and it hit him instead."

"Why! What a thing!"

"Yes. She can't get over it."

Gradman looked up at the young man's face in the twilight.

"You mustn't be down-'earted," he said. "She'll come round. Misfortunes will happen. The family's been told, I suppose. There's just one thing, Mr. Michael—his first wife, Mrs. Irene, that married Mr. Jolyon after; she's still living, they say; she might like to send a message that byegones were byegones, in case he came round."

"I don't know, Mr. Gradman, I don't know."

"Forgive us our trespasses, as we forgive them that trespass—'e was greatly attached to 'er at one time."

"So I believe, but there are things that——. Still, Mrs. Dartie knows her address, if you like to ask her. She's here, you know."

"I'll turn it over. I remember Mrs. Irene's wedding— very pale she was; a beautiful young woman, too."

"I believe so."

"The present one—being French, I suppose, she shows

her feelings. However—if he's unconscious——" It seemed to him that the young man's face looked funny, and he added: "I've never heard much of her. Not very happy with his wives, I'm afraid, he hasn't been."

"Some men aren't, you know, Mr. Gradman. It's being too near, I suppose."

"Ah!" said Gradman: "It's one thing or the other, and that's a fact. Mrs. G. and I have never had a difference —not to speak of, in fifty-two years, and that's going back, as the saying is. Well, I mustn't keep you from Miss Fleur. She'll need cossetting. Just cold beef and a pickle. You'll let me know if I'm wanted—any time, day or night. And if Mrs. Dartie'd like to see me I'm at her service."

The talk had done him good. That young man was a nicer young fellow than he'd thought. He felt that he could almost relish a pickle. After he had done so a message came: Would he go to Mrs. Dartie in the drawing room?

"Wait for me, my dear," he said to the maid; "I'm strange here."

Having washed his hands and passed a towel over his face, he followed her down the stairs of the hushed house. What a room to be sure! Rather empty, but in apple-pie order, with its cream-coloured panels, and its china, and its grand piano. Winifred Dartie was sitting on a sofa before a wood fire. She rose and took his hand.

"Such a comfort to see you, Gradman," she said. "You're the oldest friend we have."

Her face looked strange, as if she wanted to cry and had forgotten how. He had known her as a child, as a fashionable young woman, had helped to draw her marriage settlement, and shaken his head over her husband many a time—the trouble he'd had in finding out exactly what that gentleman owed, after he fell down the staircase in Paris and broke his neck! And every year still he prepared her income tax return.

"A good cry," he said, "would do you good, and I shouldn't blame you. But we mustn't say 'die'; Mr. Soames has a good constitution, and it's not as if he drank; perhaps he'll pull round after all."

She shook her head. Her face had a square grim look that reminded him of her old Aunt Ann. Underneath all her fashionableness she'd borne a lot—she had, when you came to think of it.

"It struck him here," she said; "a slanting blow on the right of the head. I shall miss him terribly; he's the only ——" Gradman patted her hand.

"Ye-es, ye-es! But we must look on the bright side. If he comes round, I shall be there." What exact comfort he thought this was, he could not have made clear. "I did wonder whether he would like Mrs. Irene told. I don't like the idea of his going with a grudge on his mind. It's an old story, of course, but at the Judgment Day——"

A faint smile was lost in the square lines round Winifred's mouth.

"We needn't bother him with that, Gradman; it's out of fashion."

Gradman emitted a sound, as though, within him, faith and respect for the family he had served for sixty years had bumped against each other.

"Well, you know best," he said, "I shouldn't like him to go with anything on his conscience."

"On *her* conscience, Gradman."

Gradman stared at a Dresden shepherdess.

"In a case of forgivin', you never know. I wanted to speak to him too, about his steel shares; they're not all they might be. But we must just take our chance, I suppose. I'm glad your father was spared, Mr. James *would* have taken on. It won't be like the same world again, if Mr. Soames——"

She had put her hand up to her mouth and turned away.

Fashion had dropped from her thickened figure. Much affected, Gradman turned to the door.

"Shan't leave my clothes off, in case I'm wanted. I've got everything here. *Good*-night!"

He went upstairs again, tiptoeing past the door, and, entering his room, switched on the light. They had taken away the pickles; turned his bed down, laid his flannel nightgown out. They took a lot of trouble! And, sinking on his knees, he prayed in a muffled murmur, varying the usual words, and ending: "And for Mr. Soames, O Lord, I specially commend him body and soul. Forgive him his trespasses, and deliver him from all 'ardness of 'eart and impurities, before he goes 'ence, and make him as a little lamb again, that he may find favour in Thy sight. Thy faithful servant. Amen." And, for some time after he had finished, he remained kneeling on the very soft carpet, breathing-in the familiar reek of flannel and old times. He rose easier in his mind. Removing his boots, laced and square-toed, and his old frock coat, he put on his Jaeger gown, and shut the window, to keep out the night air. Then taking the eiderdown, he placed a large handkerchief over his bald head, and, switching off the light, sat down in the armchair, with the eiderdown over his knees.

What an 'ush after London, to be sure, so quiet you could hear yourself think! For some reason he thought of Queen Victoria's first Jubilee, when he was a youngster of forty, and Mr. James had given him and Mrs. G. two seats. They had seen the whole thing—first chop!—the Guards and the procession, the carriages, the horses, the Queen and the Royal family. A beautiful summer day—a real summer that; not like the summers lately. And everything going on, as if it'd go on for ever, with three per cents at nearly par if he remembered, and all going to church regular. And only that same year, a bit later, Mr. Soames had had his first upset. And another memory came. Queer he

should remember that to-night, with Mr. Soames lying there
—must have been quite soon after the Jubilee, too! Going
with a lease that wouldn't bear to wait to Mr. Soames' private house, Montpellier Square, and being shown into the
dining room, and hearing someone singing and playing on
the "pianner." He had opened the door to listen. Why—
he could remember the words now! About "laying on the
grass," "I die, I faint, I fail," "the champaign odours,"
something "on your cheek" and something "pale." Fancy
that! And, suddenly, the door had opened and out she'd
come—Mrs. Irene—in a frock—ah!

"Are you waiting for Mr. Forsyte? Won't you come in
and have some tea?" And he'd gone in and had tea, sitting
on the edge of a chair that didn't look too firm, all gilt and
spindley. And she on the sofa in that frock, pouring it out,
and saying:

"Are you fond of music, then, Mr. Gradman?" Soft, a
soft look, with her dark eyes and her hair—not red and not
what you'd call gold—but like a turned leaf—um?—a
beautiful young woman, sad and sort of sympathetic in the
face. He'd often thought of her—he could see her now!
And then Mr. Soames coming in, and her face all closing
up like—like a book. Queer to remember that to-night!
... Dear me! ... How dark and quiet it was! That poor
young daughter, that it was all about! It was to be 'oped
she'd sleep! Ye-es! And what would Mrs. G. say if she
could see *him* sitting in a chair like this, with his teeth in,
too. Ah! Well—she'd never seen Mr. Soames, never seen
the family—Maria hadn't! But what an 'ush! And slowly
but surely old Gradman's mouth fell open, and he broke
the hush.

Beyond the closed window the moon rode up, a full and
brilliant moon, so that the stilly darkened country dissolved
into shape and shadow, and the owls hooted, and, far off, a
dog bayed; and flowers in the garden became each a little

presence in a night-time carnival graven into stillness; and on the gleaming river every fallen leaf that drifted down carried a moonbeam; while, above, the trees stayed, quiet, measured and illumined, quiet as the very sky, for the wind stirred not.

CHAPTER XV

SOAMES TAKES THE FERRY

THERE was only just life in Soames. Two nights and two days they had waited, watching the unmoving bandaged head. Specialists had come, given their verdict: "Nothing to be done by way of operation"; and gone again. The doctor who had presided over Fleur's birth was in charge. Though never quite forgiven by Soames for the anxiety he had caused on that occasion, "the fellow" had hung on, attending the family. By his instructions they watched the patient's eyes; at any sign, they were to send for him at once.

Michael, from whom Fleur seemed inconsolably caught away, gave himself up to Kit, walking and talking and trying to keep the child unaware. He did not visit the still figure, not from indifference, but because he felt an intruder there. He had removed all the pictures left in the gallery, and, storing them with those which Soames had thrown from the window, had listed them carefully. The fire had destroyed eleven out of the eighty-four.

Annette had cried, and was feeling better. The thought of life without Soames was for her strange and—possible; precisely, in fact, like the thought of life with him. She wished him to recover, but if he didn't she would live in France.

Winifred, who shared the watches, lived much and sadly in the past. Soames had been her mainstay throughout thirty-four years chequered by Montague Dartie, had continued her mainstay in the thirteen unchequered years since. She did not see how things could ever be cosy again. She had a heart, and could not look at that still figure without

trying to remember how to cry. Letters came to her from
the family worded with a sort of anxious astonishment that
Soames should have had such a thing happen to him.

Gradman, who had taken a bath, and changed his trousers
to black, was deep in calculations and correspondence with
the Insurance firm. He walked, too, in the kitchen garden,
out of sight of the house; for he could not get over the
fact that Mr. James had lived to be ninety, and Mr. Timothy a hundred, to say nothing of the others. And, stopping
mournfully before the seakail or the Brussels sprouts he
would shake his head.

Smither had come down to be with Winifred, but was of
little use, except to say: "Poor Mr. Soames! Poor dear
Mr. Soames! To think of it! And he so careful of himself, and everybody!"

For that was it! Ignorant of the long and stealthy march
of passion, and of the state to which it had reduced Fleur;
ignorant of how Soames had watched her, seen that beloved
young part of his very self fail, reach the edge of things and
stand there balancing; ignorant of Fleur's reckless despera-
tion beneath that falling picture, and her father's knowledge thereof—ignorant of all this everybody felt aggrieved.
It seemed to them that a mere bolt from the blue, rather
than the inexorable secret culmination of an old, old story,
had stricken one who of all men seemed the least liable to
accident. How should they tell that it was not so accidental
as all that!

But Fleur knew well enough that her desperate mood had
destroyed her father, just as surely as if she had flung herself into the river and he had been drowned in saving her.
Only too well she knew that on that night she had been
capable of slipping down into the river, of standing before
a rushing car, of anything not too deliberate and active,
that would have put her out of her aching misery. She knew
well enough that she had recklessly stood rooted when the

picture toppled above her. And now, sobered to the very
marrow by the shock, she could not forgive herself.

With her mother, her aunt and the two trained nurses
she divided the watches, so that there were never less than
two, of whom she was nearly always one, in Annette's bedroom where Soames lay. She would sit hour after hour,
almost as still as her father, with her eyes wistful and dark-
circled, fixed on his face. Passion and fever had quite died
out of her. It was as if, with his infallible instinct where
she was concerned, Soames had taken the one step that could
rid her of the fire which had been consuming her. Jon was
remote from her in that room darkened by sun blinds and
her remorse.

Yes! She had meant to be killed by that picture, ironically that of the Goya girl whose dress she had worn when
she visited Jon's room at Wansdon, and when she danced
with him at Nettlefold! Distraught that desperate night,
she did not even now realise that she had caused the fire, by
a cigarette flung down still lighted, not even perhaps that
she had smoked up there. But only too well she realised
that because she had wanted to die, had stood welcoming
sudden extinction, her father was now lying there so nearly
dead. How good he had always been to her! Incredible
that he should die and take that goodness away, that she
should never hear his flat-toned voice again, or feel the
touch of his moustache on her cheeks or forehead. Incredible that he should never give her a chance to show that
she had really loved him—yes really, beneath all the fret
and self-importance of her life. While watching him now,
the little rather than the great things came back to her.
How he would pitch a new doll down in the nursery and
say: "Well, I don't know if you'll care for this one; I just
picked her up." How once, after her mother had whipped
her, he had come in, taken her hand and said: "There, there.
Let's go and see if there are some raspberries!" How he

had stood on the stairs at Green Street after her wedding, watching, pale and unobtrusive, above the guests clustered in the hall, for a turn of her head and her last look back. Unobtrusive! That was the word—unobtrusive, always! Why, if he went, there would be no portrait—hardly even a photograph, to remember him by! Just one of him as a baby, in his mother's arms; one as a little boy, looking sceptically at his velvet knickers; one in '76 as a young man in a full-tailed coat and short whiskers; and a snapshot or two taken unawares. Had any man ever been less photographed? He had never seemed to wish to be appreciated, or even remembered, by anyone. To Fleur, so avid of appreciation, it seemed marvellously strange. What secret force within that spare form, lying there inert, had made him thus self-sufficing? He had been brought up as luxuriously as herself, had never known want or the real need for effort, but somehow had preserved a sort of stoic independence of others, and what they thought of him. And yet, as none knew better than herself, he had longed to be loved. This hurt her most, watching him. He had longed for her affection, and she had not shown him enough. But she had felt it—really felt it all the time. Something in him had repelled feeling, dried up its manifestation. There had been no magnet in his "make-up." And stealing to the bed—her mother's bed where she herself had been conceived and born—she would stand beside that almost deserted body and drawn dun face, feeling so hollow and miserable that she could hardly restrain herself.

So the days and nights passed. On the third day about three o'clock, while she stood there beside him, she saw the eyes open—a falling apart of the lids, indeed, rather than an opening, and no speculation in the gaps; but her heart beat fast. The nurse, summoned by her finger, came, looked, and went quickly out to the telephone. And Fleur stood there with her soul in her eyes, trying to summon his.

It did not come, the lids drooped again. She drew up a chair and sat down, not taking her eyes off his face. The nurse came back to say that the doctor was on his rounds; as soon as he came in he would be sent to them post-haste. As her father would have said; "Of course, 'the fellow' wasn't in when he was wanted!" But it would make no difference. They knew what to do. It was nearly four when again the lids were raised, and this time something looked forth. Fleur could not be sure that he saw anything particular, recognised her or any other object, but there was something there, some flickering light, trying for focus. Slowly it strengthened, then went out again between the lids. They gave him stimulant. And again she sat down to watch. In half an hour his eyes re-opened. This time he *saw!* And for torturing minutes Fleur watched a being trying to *be*, a mind striving to obey the mandate of instinctive will power. Bending so that those eyes, which she now knew recognised her, should have the least possible effort, she waited with her lips trembling, as if in a kiss. The extraordinary tenacity of that struggle to come back terrified her. He *meant* to be a mind, he *meant* to know and hear and speak. It was as if he must die from the sheer effort of it. She murmured to him. She put her hand under his cold hand, so that if he made the faintest pressure she would feel it. She watched his lips desperately. At last that struggle for coherence ceased, the half-blank, half-angry look yielded to something deeper, the lips moved. They said nothing, but they moved, and the faintest tremor passed from his finger into hers.

"You know me, darling?"

His eyes said: "Yes."

"You remember?"

Again his eyes said: "Yes."

His lips were twitching all the time, as if rehearsing for speech, and the look in his eyes deepening. She saw his brows frown faintly, as if her face were too close; drew back a little and the frown relaxed.

"Darling, you are going to be all right."

His eyes said: "No"; and his lips moved, but she could not distinguish the sound. For a moment she lost control, and said with a sob:

"Dad, forgive me!"

His eyes softened; and this time she caught what sounded like:

"Forgive? Nonsense!"

"I love you so."

He seemed to abandon the effort to speak then, and centred all the life of him in his eyes. Deeper and deeper grew the colour and the form and the meaning in them, as if to compel something from her. And suddenly, like a little girl, she said:

"Yes, Dad; I will be good!"

A tremor from his finger passed into her palm; his lips seemed trying to smile, his head moved as if he had meant to nod, and always that look deepened in his eyes.

"Gradman is here, darling, and Mother, and Aunt Wini-'fred, and Kit and Michael. Is there anyone you would like to see?"

His lips shaped: "No—you!"

"I am here all the time." Again she felt the tremor from his fingers, saw his lips whispering:

"That's all."

And suddenly, his eyes went out. There was nothing there! For some time longer he breathed, but before "that fellow" came, he had lost hold—was gone.

CHAPTER XVI

FULL CLOSE

IN accordance with all that was implicit in Soames there was no fuss over his funeral. For a long time now, indeed, he had been the only one of the family at all interested in obsequies.

It was then, a very quiet affair, only men attending.

Sir Lawrence had come down, graver than Michael had ever known him.

"I respected old Forsyte," he said to his son, while they returned on foot from the churchyard, where, in the corner selected by himself, Soames now lay, under a crab-apple tree: "He dated, and he couldn't express himself; but there was no humbug about him—an honest man. How is Fleur bearing up?"

Michael shook his head. "It's terrible for her to think that he——"

"My dear boy, there's no better death than dying to save the one you're fondest of. As soon as you can, let us have Fleur at Lippinghall—where her father and her family never were. I'll get Hilary and his wife down for a holiday—she likes *them*."

"I'm very worried about her, Dad—something's broken."

"That happens to most of us, before we're thirty. Some spring or other goes; but presently we get our second winds. It's what happened to the Age—something broke and it hasn't yet got its second wind. But it's getting it, and so will she. What sort of a stone are you going to put up?"

"A cross, I suppose."

"I think he'd prefer a flat stone with that crab-apple at the head and yew trees round, so that he's not overlooked.

354

No 'Beloved' or 'Regretted.' Has he got the freehold of
that corner? He'd like to belong to his descendants in per-
petuity. We're all more Chinese than you'd think, only
with them it's the ancestors who do the owning. Who was
the old chap who cried into his hat?"

"Old Mr. Gradman—sort of business nurse to the
family."

"Faithful old dog! Well! I certainly never thought
Forsyte would take the ferry before me. He looked permanent, but it's an ironical world. Can I do anything for you
and Fleur? Talk to the Nation about the pictures? The
Marquess and I could fix that for you. He had quite a
weakness for old Forsyte, and his Morland's saved. By the
way, that must have been a considerable contest between
him and the fire up there all alone. It's the sort of thing
one would never have suspected him of."

"Yes," said Michael: "I've been talking to Riggs. He's
full of it."

"He saw it, then?"

Michael nodded. "Here he comes!"

They slackened their pace, and the chauffeur, touching
his hat, came alongside.

"Ah! Riggs," said Sir Lawrence, "you were up there at
the fire, I'm told."

"Yes, Sir Lawrence. Mr. Forsyte was a proper wonder
—went at it like a two-year old, we fair had to carry him
away. So particular as a rule about not getting his coat wet
or sitting in a draught, but the way he stuck it—at his age.
. . . 'Come on!' he kept saying to me all through that
smoke—a proper champion! Never so surprised in all my
life, Sir Lawrence—nervous gentleman like him. And
what a bit o' luck! If he hadn't insisted on saving that last
picture, it'd never have fallen and got 'im."

"How did the fire begin?"

"Nobody knows, Sir Lawrence, unless Mr. Forsyte did,
and he never said nothing. Wish I'd got there sooner, but

I was puttin' the petrol out of action. What that old gentleman did by 'imself up there; and after the day we'd had! Why! We came from Winchester that morning to London, on to Dorking, picked up Mrs. Mont, and on here. And now he'll never tell me I've gone wrong again."

A grimace passed over his thin face, seamed and shadowed by traffic and the insides of his car; and, touching his hat, he left them at the gate.

" 'A proper champion,' " Sir Lawrence repeated, softly: "You might almost put that on the stone. Yes, it's an ironical world!"

In the hall they parted, for Sir Lawrence was going back to Town by car. He took Gradman with him, the provisions of the will having been quietly disclosed. Michael found Smither crying and drawing up the blinds, and in the library Winifred and Val, who had come, with Holly, for the funeral, dealing with condolences, such as they were. Annette was with Kit in the nursery. Michael went up to Fleur in the room she used to have as a little girl—a single room, so that he had been sleeping elsewhere.

She was lying on her bed, graceful, and as if without life.

The eyes she turned on Michael seemed to make of him no less, but no more, than they were making of the ceiling. It was not so much that the spirit behind them was away somewhere, as that there was nowhere for it to go. He went up to the bed, and put his hand on hers.

"Dear Heart!"

Fleur turned her eyes on him again, but of the look in them he could make nothing.

"The moment you wish, darling, we'll take Kit home."

"Any time, Michael."

"I know exactly how you feel," said Michael, knowing well that he did not: "Riggs has been telling us how splendid your father was, up there with the fire."

"Don't!"

There was that in her face which baffled him completely
—something not natural, however much she might be
mourning for her father. Suddenly she said:

"Give me time, Michael. Nothing matters, I suppose,
in the long run. And don't worry about me—I'm not
worth it."

More conscious than he had ever been in his life that
words were of no use, Michael put his lips to her forehead
and left her lying there.

He went out and down to the river and stood watching
it flow, tranquil and bright in this golden autumn weather,
which had lasted so long. Soames' cows were feeding opposite. They would come under the hammer, now; all
that had belonged to him would come under the hammer,
he supposed. Annette was going to her mother in France,
and Fleur did not wish to keep it on. He looked back at the
house, still marked and dishevelled by fire and water. And
melancholy brooded in his heart, as if the dry grey spirit of
its late owner were standing beside him looking at the passing away of his possessions, of all that on which he had lav-
ished so much time and trouble. 'Change,' thought Michael,
'there's nothing but change. It's the one constant. Well!
Who wouldn't have a river rather than a pond!' He went
towards the flower border under the kitchen garden wall.
The hollyhocks and sunflowers were in bloom there, and
he turned to them as if for warmth. In the little summer-
house at the corner he saw someone sitting. Mrs. Val Dartie! Holly—a nice woman! And, suddenly, in Michael,
out of the bafflement he had felt in Fleur's presence, the
need to ask a question shaped itself timidly, ashamedly at
first, then boldly, insistently. He went up to her. She had
a book, but was not reading.

"How is Fleur?" she said.

Michael shook his head and sat down.

"I want to ask you a question. Don't answer if you don't

want; but I feel I've got to ask. Can you—will you tell me: How are things between your young brother and her? I know what there was in the past. Is there anything in the present? I'm asking for her sake—not my own. Whatever you say shan't hurt her."

She looked straight at him, and Michael searched her face. There was that in it from which he knew that whatever she did say, if indeed she said anything, would be the truth.

"Whatever there has been between them," she said, at last, "and there *has* been something since he came back, is over for good. I know that for certain. It ended the day before the fire."

"I see," said Michael, very still: "Why do you say it is over *for good?*"

"Because I know my young brother. He has given his wife his word never to see Fleur again. He must have blundered into something, I know there has been a crisis; but once Jon gives his word—nothing—*nothing* will make him go back on it. Whatever it was is over for good, and Fleur knows it."

And again Michael said: "I see." And then, as if to himself: "Whatever it was."

She put out her hand and laid it on his.

"All right," he said: "I shall get my second wind in a minute. You needn't be afraid that I shall go back on my word, either. I know I've always played second fiddle. It shan't hurt her."

The pressure on his hand increased; and, looking up, he saw tears in her eyes.

"Thank you very much," he said; "I understand now. It's when you don't understand that you feel such a dud. Thank you very much."

He withdrew his hand gently and got up. Looking down at her still sitting there with tears in her eyes, he smiled.

"It's pretty hard sometimes to remember that it's all comedy; but one gets there, you know."

"Good luck!" said Holly. And Michael answered: "Good luck to all of us!" . . .

That evening when the house was shuttered, he lit his pipe and stole out again. He had got his second wind. Whether he would have, but for Soames' death, he did not know. It was as if, by lying in that shadowy corner under a crab-apple tree, 'old Forsyte' were still protecting his beloved. For her, Michael felt nothing but compassion. The bird had been shot with both barrels, and still lived; no one with any sporting instinct could hurt it further. Nothing for it but to pick her up and mend the wings as best he could. Something strong in Michael, so strong that he hadn't known of its existence, had rallied to his aid. Sportsmanship—chivalry? No! It was nameless; it was an instinct, a feeling that there was something beyond self to be considered, even when self was bruised and cast down. All his life he had detested the ebullient egoism of the *crime passionel*, the wronged spouse, honour, vengeance, "all that tommy-rot and naked savagery." To be excused from being a decent man! One was never excused from that. Otherwise life was just where it was in the reindeer age, the pure tragedy of the primeval hunters, before civilisation and comedy began.

Whatever had been between those two—and he felt it had been all—it was over, and she, 'down and out.' He must stand by her and keep his mouth shut. If he couldn't do that now, he ought never to have married her, lukewarm as he had known her to be. And, drawing deeply at his pipe, he went down the dark garden to the river.

The sky was starry, and with the first touch of cold, a slight mist was rising, filming the black water so that it scarcely seemed to move. Now and then in the stillness he could hear the drone of a distant car, and somewhere a little beast squeaking. Starlight, and the odour of bushes and the earth, the hoot of an owl, bats flitting, and those tall poplar shapes, darker than the darkness—what better setting for his mood just then!

An ironical world, his father had said! Yes, queerly ironical, with shape melting into shape, mood into mood, sound into sound, and nothing fixed anywhere, unless it were that starlight, and the instinct within all living things which said: "Go on!"

A drift of music came down the river. There would be a party at some house. They were dancing probably, as he had seen the gnats dancing that afternoon! And then something out of the night seemed to catch him by the throat. God! It was beautiful, amazing! Breathing, in this darkness, as many billion shapes as there were stars above, all living, and all different! What a world! The Eternal Mood at work! And if you died, like that old boy, and lay for ever beneath a crab-apple tree—well, it was the Mood resting a moment in your still shape—no! not even resting, moving on in the mysterious rhythm that one called Life. Who could arrest the moving Mood—who wanted to? And if some pale possessor like that poor old chap, tried and succeeded for a moment, the stars twinkled just a little more when he was gone. To have and to hold! As though you could!

And Michael drew-in his breath. A sound of singing came down the water to him, trailing, distant, high and sweet. It was as if a swan had sung!